Keith DeLacy
A Philosophical Journey

Connor Court Publishing

Published in 2021 by Connor Court Publishing Pty Ltd.

Copyright © Keith DeLacy

Not to be reproduced without the permission of the Copyright holders.

Connor Court Publishing Pty Ltd.
PO Box 7257
Redland Bay QLD 4165
sales@connorcourt.com
www.connorcourt.com

ISBN: 9281922449597

Cover Design by Maria Giordano

Printed in Australia.

Contents

1. **CHARACTER SHAPING** — 1
   - Life's many paths – none of them paved! — 14
   - Papua New Guinea — 23
2. **THE POLITICAL INCARNATION** — 26
   - Keith DeLacy MLA – the sunlit plains ahead — 47
   - The Fitzgerald Inquiry — 51
   - Allan Bond came calling — 62
   - Learning from adversity — 69
   - Sir Leo Hielscher — 72
   - Spiralling Queensland debt — 78
   - Wayne Goss, Premier — 81
   - Dawson Petie — 84
   - The reform of non-bank financial institutions (NBFIs) — 86
   - Government Owned Corporations — 88
   - Intellectual horsepower — 92
   - Casinos – breaking down the barriers — 96
   - Poker machines – coming of age — 99
   - The Gabba's grand transformation — 102
   - The member for Cairns — 108
   - The sun sets on a political career — 115
3. **THE CORPORATE ADVENTURE** — 126
   - Macarthur Coal – Is coal a stranded asset? — 127
   - Cubbie – the trail blazer — 143
   - Queensland Sugar – and its chequered history — 148
   - Lazy balance sheets in an era of asset inflation — 154
   - BioFutures – a blueprint for the future — 156
   - Australian Institute of Company Directors (AICD) — 160

4. PHILOSOPHICAL HOT SPOTS   172
    The over-reach society   173
    Identity politics   175
    White privilege   177
    Racism – stamping it out makes it worse   179
    Sexism - the default setting   188

5. DIVERGING FROM THE FAITH   197
    Labor and its existential threat   214
    Socialisn – utopian promise, dystopian record   226
    Productivity – everyone benefits   235
    Unemployment – most solutions make it worse   236
    Big government – the modern scourge   237
    High taxes – trickle down theory   238
    The welfare prison – the end of opportunity   239
    Energy prices – the abysmal failure   241
    Education – the Snow Flake factory   243
    Freedom of speech – the Left changes sides   247
    Climate change – the great delusion   251
    The Great Barrier Reef – it's not going anywhere it hasn't been before   263
    Renewables – humanity's great folly   266

6. CREATING A MORE PROSPEROUS NATION   278
    Regulating society – we've overcooked it   281
    The free market revolution – not before time   282
    Horizontal Fiscal Equalisation   291
    The nanny state   293
    Own the language and you own the debate   295

7. THE BEST TIME AND THE BEST PLACE IN HISTORY — 299

   Count your blessings (Keith DeLacy 2014) — 300

   Creating a better world — 306

   Our modern lifestyle — 313

   The end of history — 317

   The best country – Let's keep it that way — 321

   Contentious areas – from Patriotism to population, immigration, and jobs for the future — 322

8. THE STRUGGLE FOR THE NATIONAL SOUL — 330

   Judeo-Christian heritage — 331

   Happiness is a life well lived — 334

Foreword

Nick Cater

The concept of male white privilege is one of the many recent fads that Keith DeLacy instinctively rejects in this engaging autobiography. In his view, race, gender and sexuality are irrelevant to a person's worth. Destiny is not determined by one's identity, he says, but one's willingness to have a go.

DeLacy's upbringing on a farm near Dimbulah, 100 km inland from Cairns, may have been white, but it was anything but privileged. His father Ernie was a cane cutter whose character and politics, like many in his time, was forged in the experience of the Great Depression. His strenuous occupation was cut short by the Australian Workers Union who blackballed him for his Communist links. Not to be deterred, DeLacy senior colonised a block of land and took up tobacco farming, enlisting Keith and his siblings as labourers before and after school.

DeLacy's character-shaping early life as a farmer and then a miner offer clues to his later success in politics and business. The unwritten rules of the workplace, which he learned wielding a five-foot steel drill 400 feet below ground, embrace the spirit of egalitarianism that was once universal in Australia: 'Never bludge on your mate, don't suck up to the boss, a good day's work for a good day's pay, take no notice of the shiny arses on the surface, you wouldn't know if you were up them'.

He is probably right to describe his decision to join the Labor Party as a natural consequence of his upbringing, time and place. Locating oneself on the political spectrum by social and economic class was far more common in the 1950s when Labor was unmistakably the party of industrial and agricultural workers. Yet, in reality, Australia was predominately a middle-class society and becoming more so under the prime ministership of Robert Menzies. For Menzies, class politics was an affliction, 'the disease of thinking that the community is divided into the relatively rich and the relatively idle, and the laborious poor, and that every social and political controversy can be resolved into the question: What side are you on?'

The author is entitled to disagree with me, but the evidence strongly suggests that from an early age DeLacy was a liberal trapped inside a socialist's body, if not yet ready to transition.

To my mind, DeLacy, and indeed his Communist father, were lifters not leaners. They ranked among Menzies' forgotten people, members the sober and dynamic middle-class, who strived to better the lot of themselves and their families. DeLacy's account of his formative years evinces signs of the false consciousness one would expect from a man whose politics are out of whack with his everyday experiences and philosophy. The collectivist principles he claims to have espoused are at odds with his distinctly individualist approach to life. DeLacy seized opportunities, without seeking preferment, driven by his father's dictum that the world was his oyster.

Perhaps that explains why DeLacy as a Labor candidate never felt comfortable at door-knocking: 'I felt like a fraud, like a religious evangelist who didn't believe in God.' His inner doubts do not appear to have harmed his political career, however. Six years after being elected for the state seat of Cairns, he became Treasurer and Minister for Regional Development under Premier Wayne Goss.

The conduct of the Goss Government in general, and its rigid fiscal discipline in particular, is a reminder that the Australian Labor Party is not congenitally destined to govern badly and, at its best, governs very well. The 1980s and 1990s was a golden period for sensible centre-left government in New Zealand and Australia, led pragmatically by intelligent men like David Lange, Bob Hawke and Goss, each of whom placed government finances in capable hands. DeLacy, like Lange's bone-dry finance minister, Roger Douglas, Hawke's finance minister, Peter Walsh, imbibed from the same economically rational cup as Britain's Margaret Thatcher and shared her belief that pennies don't come from heaven, they must be earned here on earth.

DeLacy's work may be a ripper of a read, but it serves a deeper purpose in the library of political memoirs. It ranks alongside Walsh's

FOREWORD

Confessions of a Failed Finance Minister and Bill Hayden's *An Autobiography* as a record of Labor as it should aspire to be, a party that discharges its commitment to social policies through prudent spending and efficient service delivery with well-ordered priorities and a strong balance sheet. It should be a party with a firm idea of whom it represents, the working people of outer suburban and regional Australia, whom Julia Gillard once succinctly described as 'the people who set their alarm clocks to get up each morning.'

DeLacy rails against the socialist objective, the commitment enshrined in the ALP's Constitution since 1921 to 'the democratic socialisation of industry, production, distribution and exchange, to the extent necessary to eliminate exploitation and other anti-social features.' Socialism was clearly never part of DeLacy's Labor faith. As Freidrich Hayek said, 'if socialists understood economics they wouldn't be socialists.'

After politics, DeLacy graduated to the boardroom, notably as chairman of the phenomenally successful Macarthur Coal, where the obligation he had previously felt to act in the interests of taxpayers was applied to shareholders. Investors at the time of Macarthur's public offering in July 2001 enjoyed a 1,141 per cent return by the time the company was acquired by Peabody Energy in late 2011.

DeLacy's mental separation from the ALP was hastened by the election of Kevin Rudd, a prime minister who, in DeLacy's judgement, 'was not about fixing things, he was about announcing things'. He was troubled by the growing budget deficit, believing that 'debt doesn't give you more money to spend, it just brings the spending forward'. Treasurer Wayne Swan's repeated invocation of the class war and the politics of envy disturbed Delacy: 'He saw business as the enemy and made no secret of the fact.'

Readers will arrive at different answers to the burning question arising from this captivating political travelogue and foreshadowed in its title: Did DeLacy leave the Labor Party or did the Labor Party leave him? Some of his former comrades suspect his move to the right may have been a delayed reaction to being drenched with DDT from a crop-spraying aircraft at an early age, an incident he recounts in the book.

Yet Labor is a very different party from the one DeLacy joined in the late 1960s and he is entitled to take a rain check. The party no longer represents the people who would stop for a newspaper at 6 am on their way to work when DeLacy was running the Railway Newsagency in Cairns, nor the men in singlets and flannelette shirts with whom he shared a beer at the Railway Hotel. Indeed, Labor today is more often their enemy, which Delacy finds unconscionable. He was appalled at the Rudd Government's extreme policies on climate change and the damage it was causing to the economy and jobs. The effects of the mindless pursuit of renewables were felt most strongly by the poor and those in blue-collar jobs, once Labor's rusted-on constituents. As DeLacy shrewdly points out, there is no place for Hi-Vis shirts in a clean green economyacy.

DeLacy derives wry humour from seeing Labor people throwing in their lot with the educated elites when its reason for existence was fighting the elites. The so-called progressives, he says, 'have nothing more than a patronising, sneering contempt for working class people and their culture.'

DeLacy's merciless destruction of modern left shibboleths in later chapters, climate change, identity politics, cancel culture and the rest, is worth the price of admission alone. While he is not the first author to refute these progressive articles of faith, DeLacy brings a store of grounded wisdom, a lifetime of experience, laconic humour and that rare quality in politics, authenticity. Like the regulars at the Railway Hotel, you will enjoy spending time in his company.

May 2021

1

Character Shaping

My father was a member of the Communist Party. Gee a Commo! I grew up with it. I remember the regular get-togethers (perhaps I should call them ideological affirmation sessions) in the sandy bed of the Walsh River, half-way between Mareeba and Dimbulah to facilitate attendance by the comrades from both centres. I vaguely remember the men addressing each other as 'comrade', various references to Uncle Joe (Stalin) and some funny handshakes. And, looking back, it wasn't just a motley group of dropouts and delinquents. No, quite the opposite, all well dressed, well spoken, and generally well regarded in their communities. Ralph Leinster for instance was the General Manager of the Tobacco Growers Co-operative, the commercial epicentre of the tobacco province – quietly spoken, erudite, and ideologically pure.

Dimbulah was a small town, population circa 600, about 100 kms west of Cairns in Far North Queensland. There wasn't a lot of other social life in the town, except Friday afternoons when all the farmers went to town for ritual meetings with their bank managers and to do the shopping. Then the men adjourned to the pub to compare notes and do their politicking, and the women to the CWA hall to complain about them. We kids ran around town having the times of our lives.

Then there was the occasional 'pictures' on Saturday night, on canvass benches in Vince Blakeney's 'Star Theatre'. We would eat peanuts (what we didn't throw at each other), stand up for *God Save the King* (yes it was King in those days, in the 1940s, King George VI), marvel at the Movietone News (the only big news in this insular town) squeezed between the cartoons and the weekly Western, and heckle the actors … Mickey Hay bellowing out when the leading lady planted a kiss on the cheek of Jimmy Durante: 'What, kiss that baldy-headed old bastard!'

I can also remember the bubbling furore around town when my mother refused to stand for *God Save the King* – a gesture of solidarity with all those who opposed colonialism and imperialism and, incongruously, America!

A member of the Communist Party! Yet my father, Ernie, was one of the most conservative and gentle men you could ever wish to meet, no sign of the rebel, either in dress, in language, in attitude – he didn't drink, didn't smoke (though for a while he tried in order to demonstrate solidarity with that tobacco growing community), never got angry, never beat the wife 'n kids, excessively frugal, and studiously read, and read in the small amount of free time he had – carefully selected ideological material confirming the bias – diseased eyes peering through a magnifying glass in the soft glow of the kerosene lamp, brushing away the flying insects attracted to the flame.

And he was a farmer, a tobacco farmer, but considered himself a member of the proletariat because it was a peasant farm – house fashioned from ant-hill (termite mounds) bricks with a dirt floor, no electricity, no fridge, no hot water, no car, no tractor, no money, no hope … just a horse and mouldboard plough, and a strong back.

Our life was one of waste not, want not. Nothing was thrown away. Socks darned. Pants patched. Sparse wardrobes consisted of hand-me-downs. Clothes washed in a boiler and hung out to dry on a length of 10 gauge wire stretched between two fence posts. And the old treadle Singer sewing machine, what a favourite it was, and what a workout it got. Wanton consumerism, what is that?

It was ecologically pure though, with a carbon footprint the size of a pea. We were saving the planet before we knew it needed saving – so much wasted virtue! As an aside I am amused these days when young people accuse us oldies of jeopardising life on the planet, when their emissions are a thousand times what ours were at the same age!

Ernie was a product of the great depression:

Nothing can ever be as bad again as it has been before!
More dinner times than dinners!

And therein lie the exegesis. Many men, for whom life and the economy had been insufferably unkind – the little man defenceless in the face of insuperable odds, collectivism the only answer – unions for the working man, statutory marketing schemes, and grower co-operatives, for the small farmer, levelling the playing field in an unfair world. The words of Marx were inspiring, and soothing. I can remember Dad explaining, his bobbing index finger punctuating the message: '*From each according to his ability, to each according to his needs.*' – straight out of the Communist Manifesto, but growing in fertile, post depression soil in small town Australia.

Ernie was a cane cutter for many years along the tropical coast, Childers, Tully, Innisfail … he got caught up in the cane cutters' 'burnt cane' strike in 1934, with more induced poverty, and more grist for the revolutionary mill, inspired by the fact that the sporadic strikes in different cane growing centres were organised by communists and opposed by the Australian Workers Union (AWU) which had official industrial coverage. The AWU saw the non-sanctioned industrial activity as a threat to its hegemony. The Queensland Labor Government (which was strongly under the influence of the AWU) and CSR (Colonial Sugar Refining Co) the monopoly miller, also vigorously opposed the strikes.

Cane cutting was one of the toughest games in the Australian work legend. Earlier it was thought that white men weren't up to the task so they imported Kanakas from the Pacific Islands. Most of these South Sea Islanders (Kanaka became a pejorative term) were repatriated in the early 1900s under the *Pacific Island Labourers Act*, prompted not by an act of contrition but by industrial pressure and the White Australia Policy.

Cane cutting was piecework, with men organising themselves into gangs of half a dozen and contracted to the farmer to cut the whole crop. The cutting season only lasted for about six months and alternative work was hard to find. In the early thirties, during the off-season, Ernie colonised a block of land on the Walsh River near

Dimbulah and, along with a motley band of equally delusional pioneers, started the tobacco industry.

After 1934 tobacco farming became Ernie's only option as he was black-banned in the sugar industry by the AWU for siding with the Communists. He married Irene Henson, a cook at the Queens Hotel in Cairns, that same year. His lifetime ban from cane cutting probably closed the door on any forlorn dreams she may have entertained about living a comfortable life, though cane cutting was hardly the road to riches.

Apart from all-consuming subsistence, life in the tobacco industry was politics. At a local level Ernie was an elected Director and Deputy Chairman of the grower-owned North Queensland Tobacco Growers Co-operative Association (NQTGA) for more than twenty years. It was referred to locally as *The Association*, or the *Co-op*, and it provided the organisational, social and commercial infrastructure for the whole Mareeba-Dimbulah district, dominating the retail sector, selling groceries, hardware and chemicals to farmers on credit, 12 months credit, repaid with proceeds from the annual tobacco sales – a nice little touch of incipient socialism.

He was also a Mareeba Shire Councillor representing Dimbulah for fifteen years. How he enjoyed such success in the hotly contested local political world (almost always topping the poll) while carrying the stain (albeit a muted stain in that time and place) of Communism bore testimony to his resolute politicking and impeccable reputation. That he did it without drinking was little short of remarkable because virtually all of the politicking was done in the pub.

Ernie's legacy to the kids, four of us, three boys and a girl, me being the second oldest, was a collectivist mind-set and sound education. Few kids in those days ventured past scholarship (grade 7). Secondary school wasn't available in small centres like Dimbulah, and it never helped you swing an axe anyway. But all DeLacys, funded by Government scholarships and great privation at home, went on to secondary school. Ian and Terry completed university, Denise a teaching diploma, while I did a Diploma of Agriculture at Gatton College.

It is true, and not well understood in those days, that education provided choice in life, as my father incessantly claimed. Generally Dimbulah in the forties and fifties was a no-choice society, you just did what you had to do.

Despite his philosophical if introverted ways, my father was not the driving force in the family. This fell to his wife Irene, my mother. Irene was born in Yorkshire, England, in 1909. She lost her father in the chaos and carnage of the Great War.

Spare a thought for her mother, my grandmother – four feet eight inches in height, three daughters and pregnant with a fourth, husband sacrificed to a watery grave in the English Channel, no social security underpinnings, a country ravaged by war. She was easy prey for an Australian serviceman stationed in England who promised her the good life in Australia. They all set sail for the promised land in 1919, ending up in the tiny isolated mining village of Kidston, about two hundred miles south-west of Cairns on the southern reaches of Cape York Peninsula, about as far from civilisation as it was possible to be. She had another five children in Kidston.

The trauma of the seismic change of address wasn't helped when its agent, my mother's step-father, old Schoey (his surname was Schofield) a charcoal burner, became the town drunk, later to be airbrushed from the family memoirs. There are some people of whom you never speak!

What we didn't comprehend of course was the psychological trauma he endured on the battlefield, the fear and the death and the suffering and the loneliness, a young man 10,000 miles from home fighting someone else's war. With the benefit of modern understandings the family may have been a little more tolerant in their assessment of old Schoey. As they say, don't judge a man till you've walked in his shoes!

My mother was a feisty woman, and a formidable one, unshakeable in her convictions and fierce in her loyalties. Her politics were uncompromising. And for one minute consider the perception these days of women, before being liberated by feminism, as docile and submissive, and playing roles predetermined by the dominant patriarchy. Well if that was the case, my mother didn't know about it. She was the dominant character in our household, and never seemed to regret the destiny of her birth.

It was she who administered the discipline (often co-opting the aid of a wooden coat hanger) and provided the philosophical aphorisms presumably designed to guide us kids through the challenge of life – *Life wasn't meant to be easy*; *Do your job, nobody owes you anything*; *Life isn't fair, get used to it*; *Come here and I will give you something to whinge about*; *Count your blessings*; and its sister maxim, *Thank your lucky stars*.

My Dad was much more reserved. He used to say: *The world is your oyster*, but that was too metaphorical for me at the time. But its essence did ultimately have a real influence on me growing up.

As I reflected later in life, much later in life, those little sayings did provide a philosophical platform for life, and lifelong immunity from the victim and entitlement mentalities that came to infect 21st century Australia. I didn't know what she meant, count your blessings, I didn't think I had any blessings to count. But I realised I did, very much later – few material blessings of course, but a good family with strong values; and a good community which imposed its own values and limits on behaviour. And taught you right from wrong, and to take responsibility for your own actions – confirming that old maxim: *It takes a village to rear a child!*

I compared that, again much later in life, to kids growing up these days in a welfare family, albeit in a much more affluent society with a comprehensive safety net, but a society full of toxic temptations, few guiding values and no role model in the workforce.

But Dimbulah was a tough life nevertheless. I can remember my mother sorting government coupons, to buy butter for instance. There was much government imposed rationing as individual existence was subordinated to the war effort.

We kids had to work on the farm before and after school, planting, chipping, pruning, picking, stringing, grading…. Then four or five miles to school with an old bike on a dirt track through the bush, after rowing a small, dilapidated wooden boat across the Walsh Riv-

Keith, Four years old – a long and interesting journey ahead!

er, water backed up from the Bruce Weir a mile or so downstream. On reflection we boys could have been a little more charitable to our sister Denise instead of insisting she take her turn on the oars. Perhaps we were embracing gender equity before it became trendy!

My younger brother Terry, in a reminiscing email sent to me many years later reflected on our start in life:

You doubling me to school in Dimbulah for 5 miles across country after getting up early to chip weeds in the tobacco and home in time to do more.

One of the great pleasures was bringing home the hot fresh bread from Percy Collins' bakery in the bread tray on the bicycle handlebars. The temptation to pick at the crisp warm crust, rather ravenously, could not be resisted and always led to a perfunctory clip around the ears at home, to no great behavioural benefit. Even raw mince meat from the butcher (we could only afford mince and sausages) all on credit of course, was fair game too.

Tractors, and water from the newly developed Tinaroo Dam irrigation scheme, gradually revolutionised the industry. And a big step forward was the advent of aerial spraying of insecticides, replacing the backbreaking, heavy metal knapsack spray. The tobacco crop was particularly susceptible to insect and fungal attack because of the large succulent leaf. We kids used to act as markers as Harry Squires, an ex-RAAF pilot and legend of the industry, completed his spraying laps, administering the insecticide in a cloudy spray. You could almost shake hands with him in his single engine Piper Pawnee as he passed overhead. Holding a flag as a marker we would wait, shirtless, until the cool spray settled deliciously on our bare skin before hurrying, saturated with chemical, to mark out the next sortie. The insecticides were those infamous chlorinated hydrocarbons (DDT, Endrin and Dieldrin), so comprehensively damned by Rachel Carson in her iconic 1962 book, *Silent Spring,* which led to the widespread banning of DDT and the birth of the global environment movement.

It has been speculated that my political drift to the right as I aged was because of DDT contamination in those early days.

My older brother Ian fell victim to the great polio epidemic of the forties, diagnosed on VP Day 1945 (Victory in the Pacific) and spent twenty-two months as a six/seven-year-old, alone and lonely, a thousand miles from home and family (a four day train trip), in the Brisbane General Hospital.

Ian was an early beneficiary of Queensland's free hospital system, an article of faith in our household, funded by the (Hanlon) Labor

Government, largely by revenue from the State-run Golden Casket lottery. The family needed no further evidence of the benefits of social intervention, for in its absence Ian would probably have become a depressing addition to a very large statistic. Seven children of a single family in Ravenshoe on the Atherton Tableland all died from polio.

Although modestly disabled, Ian was able to get on with life and spent a lifetime in the agricultural department of the University of Queensland, still handing out Labor How to Vote cards seventy years later, his belief in his parent's collectivist doctrine undiminished by time, history, or the real world.

The salk vaccine, developed by Jonas Salk in 1953, progressively eliminated Polio and saved millions of people around the world from a dreadful disease while providing something of a balance to those millions who died from mosquito borne malaria because of Rachel Carson's success in the global banning of DDT.

Schools of Learning (and playing)

In December 1950 the whole family was in the shed, stringing tobacco leaves onto sticks to hang in the curing barn. By this time we had the luxury of a wireless. Though it was the size of a washing machine with an aerial up amongst the Kookaburras, it was still a wonder of the modern world, technology taken to its ultimate limits. It was the first cricket test series after the 1948 Invincibles tour of Britain, and the retirement of the legendary Sir Donald Bradman. My mother got the news first. 'Australia are all out for 228 on the first day, and no Bradman,' she proclaimed triumphantly as though draped in the Union Jack, belying both her anti-colonial convictions and the fact that the mother country was thirty years in her past.

That was it. I was hooked on cricket, doting on every silky word from Alan McGilvray on ABC radio – half the night when the test series was in England. As if there wasn't enough to do on the farm I fashioned for myself a crude cricket pitch from the clay of termite mounds, with a wire netting backstop. And I bowled and bowled and bowled, in the hot sun with an old cork ball, while others were enjoying their noon-day rest. I bowled leg-breaks, wrong'uns, top-spinners and whatever other mystery delivery I could conjure up.

My enthusiasm energised the Dimbulah school into a cricketing force, being the motivator, the coach, the organiser and the captain. In 1954, in my scholarship year, Dimbulah, with me as captain, entered the Far North Queensland Mullins Shield primary school cricket competition. Half the Dimbulah team was comprised of kids with not even a passing acquaintance of the game of cricket in their heritage, the children of migrants fleeing continental, war-torn Europe. Our opening bowlers were Peter Iuretigh and John Buljabasich (Italian and Yugoslav). The parents became active supporters even though the game itself greatly mystified them. The team carried all before it but was finally beaten in an epic grand final by Cairns, but I was quick to point out that the total enrolment at the Dimbulah State school was 74 *'including the sheilas!'* And Cairns would have had thousands of primary school kids from half a dozen schools to pick from, and far superior coaching facilities.

I did my Junior (grades 9 and 10) as a boarder at the Townsville Grammar School. What seemed to be my precocious cricketing talents were soon recognised and I was selected in the First XI, the rest of the team and our opponents being a minimum of three years my senior (they were in grades 11 or 12, I was in grade 9). In the first game against arch rivals Christian Brothers, I cleaned up the tail taking 4 for 19. In the second innings team captain, wicket-keeper and senior prefect Bob Cox threw me the ball to open the bowling with my leg spinners, an unparalleled show of confidence. I bowled right through the innings, 21 overs, taking 8 for 40 – a momentous victory. On Monday morning at school assembly I was called out front by the head master, and my performance proclaimed to what seemed really genuine applause of staff and students.

Apropos of nothing, I received an email from John Sourrys, an ex-Townsville Grammar colleague, in June 2016:

> You were, as Keith Oliver (a handy A grade cricketer himself and as a teacher a great coach of state school cricket sides) said, the best cricketer ever to grace the Townsville Grammar oval.

The question needs to be asked: what happened to a kid who must have been close to the best fifteen-year-old cricketer in Australia; where did all that talent go?

Well it seems it wasn't so much pure talent as pure doggedness, passion and practice that got me there, and a youthful exuberance that knew no limits and didn't understand human fallibility. Jack Nicklaus is supposed to have said that the most difficult distance in golf is the six inches between your ears. When the mind starts interfering – you see it in tennis players, golfers, all sports – instead of just letting it happen they think about it, evil thoughts invade the action.

I was still capable of missing a two foot putt sixty years later.

I largely harboured happy memories from my two years at Townsville, sport of course, and plenty of mates. I didn't get on well with teachers, a little rebellious, maybe a little contemptuous. But I got very good results, 7A's and a B in the State Junior examination, not because I was a good student but I knew how to do exams – 'you just knew what they wanted and you gave it to them.'

In the self-justification stakes I have trouble coming to grips with this attitude sixty years later when the notion of 'speaking the truth' should be more important than delivering lecturers what they want.

Three years later I took it to another level, doing the final exams at Gatton College, one three hour exam a day for three weeks; I was able to swat up the night before, memorise pages of notes, I could see the pages line by line as I went into the class room. After the exam I would shake my head, the page and all my knowledge of the subject would vanish into thin air. I got very good marks and learned nothing. And more importantly I forfeited the opportunity to contribute constructively to the teaching and learning process.

I had gone to Gatton College after Junior at the Townsville Grammar to do a three year (1957-59) Diploma of Agriculture. My life largely followed the pattern established in Townsville. I played Firsts cricket for the three years (the Lockyer Valley adult competition) and First 15 football in my final year, playing breakaway (flanker) for Gatton College in the Brisbane Rugby Union Reserve grade competition. It was the first year that Gatton College had entered this competition and we performed well. We made it to the preliminary final where we were beaten in a hard fought match by University of Queensland St Lucia.

I received some ribbing after the game as the winning try was scored by the breakaway I was marking in the line-out. I countered that *'he was a bloody good footballer!'* *'You would say that, wouldn't you?'* they countered. The breakaway was Jules Guerassimoff, who went on to play 74 games for Queensland, the best part of ten years for the Wallabies, and at his peak was considered the most devastating tackler in World Rugby and one of the best flankers Australia has produced.

Unfortunately when I was finally able to say, *'I rest my case'*, there was no one to say it too.

I think I exhibited the same lack of respect for the lecturers and the learning experience as I did in Townsville. All the students at Gatton hated what was referred to as Bails' Week, actually milking the Jersey dairy herd at 5 each morning for the seven days. But I quickly stumbled onto a lurk. I was a step in front of everyone else, if you volunteered to bring the cows into the milking bails from their paddocks you could go out at 4.30am, shepherd them in, you were excused milking and you could go back to bed for an hour or two at 5am. This worked splendidly until I attended a function one Friday evening, and in a flash of glorious inspiration, decided to bring the cattle in at midnight before going to bed to enjoy the sleep of the just. Except the cattle wouldn't cooperate, they were creatures of immutable habit. They meandered up and down every laneway on the college. It became a terrifying ordeal, I lost most of them, mooing and lowing coming from all points of the compass. I horrifyingly contemplated the prospect of fronting up to the Master in charge at 5am explaining I had lost 110 cattle, the whole bloody herd. This could be the end.

Then just before 5am the cattle started magically filing in, all of them, a little agitated by the adventure but looking forward to the milking. I survived, greatly relieved, greatly chastened and very very tired.

CHARACTER SHAPING

I teamed up with Geoff Cox who played wing in the First 15. Obeying college rules was not our strong suit. We periodically hitched a ride to Brisbane for a Saturday night-out in the state capital, usually jagging a ride home in the back of the truck delivering Sunday papers to all points west. Everybody stopped for hitchhikers in those days. One night we attended a Sammy Davis Junior concert at Festival Hall. Did they come any better than the swinging, tap dancing, impersonating, jazz singing Sammy, self-described as a black, one-eyed Jew. And only eight stone soaking wet!

What a package, laden with so-called oppression variables, heaven made to exploit the identity culture so consuming modern society. These days Sammy could have wallowed in victimhood and self pity instead of becoming one of the greatest entertainers in history.

We were of course greatly constrained in our social endeavours by lack of spending money. So early one Sunday morning Geoff and I set out to dig potatoes at a friendly farm about six miles away. We had to swim the Lockyer River, surprisingly warm in the chill morning air. We worked for twelve back-breaking hours picking potatoes, all for the princely sum of just over two pounds each. And the next week-end in Brisbane we exchanged all that hard earned money, twelve hours toil in the hot September sun, for two minutes of carnal pleasure, two inglorious minutes.

There had to be a moral. The division of labour – what would Karl Marx have thought, I wondered. Still, *'to each according to his needs'* seemed to fit the bill.

On another note, would you be a teenager again if offered the chance by a kindly genie?

We made one mistake too many. One Saturday evening we decided to have a wild night-out, eloquently referred to as a *piss-up*. We knocked off food and assorted implements from the college mess, one of our colleagues had a bottle of whisky and another a gallon of Port. We headed bush and indulged ourselves on the banks of the Lockyer River. All seemed fine except that the local farmer (the locals were called GI's [Gatton Inbreds] by college students in a display of cultural superiority unjustified by merit) reported to police that his pump belt (the large flat belt that connected the flywheel on the diesel engine to the pulley on the irrigation pump) had been stolen. The local constabulary had forensically traced the crime back to the group of college students via many clues such as broken plates sporting the college emblem. The police finally determined the students were not the belt thieves.

But the college Principal had other views about guilt, and Geoff and I were placed on very restrictive probation for the rest of our college stay. Another minor indiscretion after end-of-year exams (it seems we had accrued too many de-merit points) caused us both to be summarily expelled, *'never to set foot on the college again.'* The good news was that when pressed, the Principal promised that we would receive our diplomas 'in the mail' if we passed our exams, which we duly did. My mother didn't really buy the story I concocted to explain the fact that I arrived home in Dimbulah two weeks early. But when the diploma arrived in the post all was forgiven.

And all was forgiven at the college 41 years later when in the millennium year I was awarded the University of Queensland Gatton Gold medal in *'recognition of distinguished services to the State of Queensland and its primary industries.'* What a pity ex-Principal Briton wasn't around for the wonderful occasion, I lamented!

LIFE'S MANY PATHS – none of them paved!

After college I started share-farm tobacco cropping with my father. The Government at the same time was actively sponsoring the growth of the tobacco industry off the back of the Tinaroo Dam irrigation scheme. In my second year I won a farm of my own in the Government-sponsored, irrigation block, ballot. My contributing equity was simply my Diploma of Agriculture, and I was financed by the state-owned Agricultural Bank – capital for buildings and machinery, working capital and so on. The tobacco industry was booming, socialism was blooming. Thank you Red Ted Theodore!

Now I wasn't sure if I was a socialist or a capitalist!

In retrospect I am reluctantly prepared to admit that I wasn't quite up to it; I was too young, too unstable, and it was a bloody tough game. I not only had to manage the farm and the crop, I had to lead the workers and cook for them too. I couldn't even indulge the lunchtime siesta as was the custom (we started work at 4.30am) because I had to wash the lunchtime utensils and clean up, etc. And these obligations had to be balanced with a 22-year-old's desire to play football, impress his mates and chase sheilas!

The only farm vehicle (apart from the high-wheel-base Farmall tractor) was an old one-ton army Blitz Truck. I can remember (not fondly) driving home after a cricket celebration at the pub – no DUI in those days. I went to sleep and ended up in neighbour Fabio Petrusa's tobacco crop. By the time I woke there was no way out as the stems had slowly righted themselves behind me. Needless to say Fabio and I had some words, but we remained friends.

Perhaps the standards set by the Government for entry to farming were a trifle inadequate!

I spent a lot of time with a Catholic family in Mareeba, eleven kids. Beds arranged all along the verandas, first-in-best-dressed. An easy-going family of considerable virtue. Two golden rules, Mass on Sunday, and no meat on Friday (except for our atheist mate as Mrs Eales used to refer to me, proving there was considerable tolerance of apostates).

The Junction Hotel in Dimbulah was the biggest bar in the north, patronised by hard drinking farmers and, during harvesting, by the seasonal workforce. There were two sessions on Sunday, but largely un-policed by the two gregarious policemen, who I presume wanted just to be part of this insular community. I can remember a bit earlier when we were growing up, my brother Ian, two years older than me, drove into town (we had an old Land Rover by then) on his 17th birthday to get his driver's licence. Vic Fitch the Sergeant organised the paperwork and then admonished him: 'Make sure if you come into town and that little bugger of a brother of yours is driving (meaning me, I of course had no licence) you swap seats at Sandy Creek and do all the driving in town.'

The unwritten rules of Country Queensland. If a fight broke out between two recalcitrants in the pub, all the drinkers would immediately form a makeshift ring, and referee the fight, Marquis of Queensbury rules. As soon as someone went down: *'Stand back, let him up!'* No hardware allowed. *'Whoa, whoa, let him wipe the blood off his face, he can't see!'* So different to what you see today, knives, boots …

As luck would have it my future wife Yvonne Jarrett commenced work as a barmaid in the Junction Hotel. She came from Innisfail on the coast. I have been known to say that it was a marriage crafted in heaven – she was a barmaid and I was a piss-pot (yin and yang!)

One Sunday she visited the farm to help me clean. She was appalled by what she found, hardly the pristine kitchen of a five star hotel. She pointed out that the stew on the stove was bubbling over. Electricity still had not been connected and I said that couldn't be the case as I hadn't lit the stove. I had the habit, as you would expect from one who has had a life-long allergy to waste, of tipping the leftovers back into the pot to be enjoyed another day. The stew was boiling of its own accord!

We decided to get married there and then so that Yvonne could cook and clean. Hardly the stuff of exotic romance, but you couldn't live in sin in those days. We were married in Innisfail on 22 December 1962, had a two day honeymoon, and on Boxing Day, Yvonne, just nineteen years of age, was cooking for eight men using a wood fired stove and a kerosene refrigerator. She later said, however, that what she found most confronting was the communal, long drop dunny with a splendid view all of the way down to Eureka Creek.

And for the record, our first child, daughter Jonnie, was born on the 17 December 1963, almost exactly 12 months after the hurried marriage, thus complicating working arrangements for the next harvest, but cruelly disabusing many of the town's moral guardians who were clearly suspicious about our hurried marriage twelve months earlier! They almost dislocated their fingers flipping the pages on their calendars!

All of the seasonal workers were European migrants, predominantly Italians and Yugoslavs. The northern Italians hated the southern Italians, and the Croatians hated the Serbians – and vice versa. Communist dictator Marshall Tito formed the Socialist Federal Re-

CHARACTER SHAPING

Keith and Yvonne – wedding day, 22 December 1962

public of Yugoslavia in 1943, comprising six states, Croatia, Serbia, Slovenia, Bosnia, Macedonia and Montenegro. They existed in a relatively peaceful coalition under the iron rule of Tito until 1980, but the peacefulness of that coalition didn't manifest itself in the tobacco industry in Northern Australia with the Croats and Serbs in particular constantly at each other's throats.

It didn't manifest itself post Tito either as Yugoslavia descended into some of the worst genocidal conflicts following the Second World War.

I learned to speak Italian, initially swear words at school, but later, because I worked with them on a daily basis, much of the language too. They were wonderful neighbours. The Sicilians on the one side taught me how to make salami. The northern Italians on the other side taught me how to drink red wine. They would order sixty gallon kegs of vino rosso (red wine) from Griffiths in NSW, and invite the neighbours, apart from the Sicilians, over for a Sunday bottling. The bottling consisted of siphoning the wine from the keg through a clear plastic tube into the bottle, corking the bottle and storing it. A big percentage never got to be stored, the reward, as it were, for a job well done. But it was a long day at the office. About 8pm we were all lined up outside enjoying a communal pee when someone said, 'Look, there's a moving star.' Someone else said, 'There's another one.' In the end every star in the sky was moving, the glorious finale to a day of multicultural bonding!

These Europeans really knew how to enjoy themselves, and their food, drink and music became part of the Australian way of life. Could we live today without red wine, or coffee, or olive oil, or pasta? They still celebrated their roots, but they learned English and embraced their new country. They came to Australia to start a new life, and Australians they became. They assimilated by accepting Australian culture, based as it was on our Anglo Celtic heritage. They gradually abandoned their tribal differences and became proud Australians, and the whole country was so much richer as a result.

One of the on-going strengths of the Australian immigration system was that whilst we tend to demonise each new group for a while, we ultimately welcome them, adding and absorbing their ways to ours, their food, their dress, their music, their customs, their scholarship, to enrich and expand our culture; but we expected them to fit in.

And fit in they did. I remember vaguely hearing of the unfairness and meanness of the internment of Italian migrants during the Second World War – as though a few motley Italians, even if they did support Mussolini, could impact Australia's security. But whilst there was some resentment, they shrugged it off and got on with it – no victimhood, just gratitude for the opportunity, and they became true-blue Australians, celebrating Australia Day and opposing illegal boat arrivals.

I learned very early that being a good farmer was paramount, but the weather and commodity price cycles didn't always respect good farming. I often told the story: 'What would you do, Joe, if you won Gold Lotto?' 'Gee I dunno,' replied Joe, 'I guess I would just keep farmin' till it was all gone!'

Tobacco is an annual crop and the whole season only lasts about six months, so the farm needed financial support. As luck would have it a new underground mine opened up at Wolfram Camp about twelve miles away from the farm. It was operated by Metals Exploration Plc (referred to locally as Metals X) on an exploration basis, searching for wolfram (tungsten) and molybdenum, both metal additives. I knew the foreman George Ericson, a Dimbulah native, and I secured an off-season job at the mine, first unloading the skips on the surface, before graduating underground as a mining off-sider.

A graduation or a punishment for unknown transgressions? The first day underground was an experience not forgotten even to this day. I was issued with a head-lamp to clip on the front of the helmet, connected by a long black lead to a battery pack, charged daily, clipped onto the belt on top of the buttocks. We were working in a drive (tunnel), branching out from the shaft about 400 feet below the surface. The drive was about 500 yards long and about six foot high and five feet wide, a frighteningly claustrophobic working environment, and our task was to daily extend the drive towards a new staging point. This involved boring and firing in the morning, and mucking-out in the afternoon.

We bored (drilled) about twenty-four holes, all strategically located, into the hard rock face using a five foot steel drill with a tungsten tip, operated with a jackhammer. The jackhammer was a heavy steel implement supported on a heavy duty air leg, both powered by compressed air piped down from the surface.

I was off-sider to a large German with bulging eyes and a short temper. The off-sider's job was to pitch the drill in the anointed spot as the miner manipulated the jack hammer – easier said than done. The drill had an expanded chisel end and tended to wander over the rock face until it was properly pitched; and water cartwheeled out of a hole in the end (the recently introduced innovation of flushing the bore-hole with water during drilling reduced the dust and henceforth the common incidence of Miners Phthisis [the Ph is silent], a deadly disease of the lungs. It's funny how I can still remember the technical name for this disease – pneumonoultramicroscopicsilicovolcanoconiosis – which still rolls off my tongue more than fifty years later. There is no limit to what a show-off can accomplish!)

The secret was to hold the drill in the right hand over the shoulder like a javelin thrower, and cover the pitching point with the left hand to block off the water and stop the drill wandering. The jack hammer made an extraordinary noise, like a machine gun, positioned as it was just behind my right ear drum. In those days you never wore earmuffs, or gloves – *'What'er you, a bloody old woman?'*

We bored the whole face in the morning, and charged it with a case and a half of gelignite. The gelignite was tamped into each hole and the last plug in each hole was a primer with a small detonator on the end of a fuse inserted into it. The fuses were all cut to carefully measured differential lengths to ensure that they fired sequentially, each hole breaking to a straight surface. The last three holes, the lifters, were cut to fire last lifting the mullock onto flat iron sheets in front of the face to facilitate shovelling (mucking-out or bogging-out as it was called).

We lit the fuses with a fuse lighter just on lunchtime, scurried off down to the shaft like frightened rabbits, counted the shots as they reverberated down the corridor to ensure there were no misfires, and then went to the surface for lunch.

Mucking-out: this was the real baptism of fire. I was surprised at how competitive the workplace could be. Where was the bloody union when you needed it? But I came to learn there were unwritten rules in the workplace, even in the absence of a union: never bludge on your mate, don't suck up to the boss, a good day's work for a good day's pay, take no notice of the shiny arses on the surface, they wouldn't know if you were up them, don't lose your sense of humour, only take a sickie when the fish are biting … and don't let the bastard beat you!

The big German shovelled the first truck, a specially designed iron skip which held about two cubic metres of rock and rubble, with four rail wheels sitting on the rail line. The trick was to fill your truck with the hand shovel, wheel it back to the shaft, send it up by signalling to the platman on the drop rope, collect a clean replacement and wheel it back to the bogging point (the face) again. The goal it seemed was to get back and kick the points over while your work partner was still shovelling his truck – and register a moral victory.

I picked up all the tricks by osmosis (there was no advice, instruction program or manual), always shovel on the flat sheet, it being impossible to insert the shovel directly into the jagged rock and wet grey mullock. Drag it down with a mattock and shovel on the sheet, shovel with rhythm, in out, over the shoulder, full, kick off the brakes and tear off down the rail line to the shaft, race back again with the new skip, only to see the bastard with his truck all full, smoking, waiting ...

Ah, what a game, back breaking and physically exhausting in the extreme. Fresh air was piped down from the surface to the face via a venturi tube (all of which had to be dissembled before firing) but the drive (tunnel) between the face and the shaft was insufferably hot and humid, no breeze of course. It was two weeks before I shovelled my truck and was waiting when the bastard returned. That made me an honorary miner, but I was a good one stone lighter.

I could tell a hundred tales about my adventures, and misadventures, while working underground: exhaustion, accidents, misfires, near misses, working in a rise and boring almost straight up with the slush spewing down all over us. But the most enduring memory was the friendship I struck up with two long term miners Tony Brooks and Larry Miller.

They were refugees from the great Mt Isa industrial dispute of 1964-5. It was a dispute that captivated the whole country, hogging the national headlines for six months. The miners were led by the charismatic, base-ball cap wearing American Pat Mackie, an alleged member of the so-called Wobblies or IWW (Industrial Workers of the World).

The problem with revolutions is no one knows how to end them even when you win. As they say, the revolution eats its own children. This one culminated in a titanic struggle between the Australian Workers Union (AWU), which had traditional coverage of hard rock mining, and the craft unions, inflamed by Mackie who thrived on the limelight and the battle. In circumstances eerily similar to the cane cutters' strike thirty years earlier, the AWU, supported by the company, and the Government, finally prevailed. Forty-five AWU members who stuck with Mackie were expelled, *'never to be employed again.'* In a union mine that is. Wolfram Camp was a little back country mine not yet discovered by the AWU.

Larry and Tony were proud members of the 45, perversely celebrating the defeat as a victory. This was the Australian way. Like Gallipoli. You celebrated the fight, the comradeship, the sacrifice, the courage … I spent countless hours with them reminiscing the dispute to the extent that many years later, in 2002, I published a successful book, titled *Blood Stains the Wattle*, a fiction based on the epic strike.

On reflection I always treasured the time I spent as an underground miner. Many years later, when I was Chairman of Macarthur Coal, darling of the stock exchange in the early years of the 21st century, I reflected that I had seen the mining game, as Joni Mitchell crooned in her famous song, *from both sides now*. The message was clear: we were all in it together, we all needed each other, no matter where you stood on the ladder.

There is one other thing I should mention. Wolfram Camp where I mined was only about fifteen miles from Mt Mulligan. I knew Mt Mulligan well, played cricket there often as a kid. It was a coal mine. In those days the Government opened up as many coal mines in disparate locations as it could, to fuel the coal-fired steam engines which criss-crossed Queensland. It was a State owned mine.

Mt Mulligan is famous for the great disaster in 1921 when an underground explosion killed 75 men, Queensland's worst mining disaster. But it soldiered on. It was finally closed in 1957 and the miners transferred to Collinsville, another State-owned coal mine in central/northern Queensland, so much in the news these days with talk of anew coal-fired power station.

I can remember Nick Stump in the early 1990s, then CEO of Mt Isa Mines (MIM) which by this time had acquired the Collinsville mine, reminiscing about Collinsville. As a State-owned mine it was heavily unionised. This didn't change when the Mt Mulligan miners arrived. Most of the workers were not only members of the union, they were members of the Communist Party. They ran the town. The company had two horses that worked underground, towing heavy machinery. These horses were made honorary members of the Union. They were allowed to vote, by proxy, the right way of course. Finally technology rendered the horses redundant and they were retired (sacked) by the company. This led to a four day strike, which was only resolved when the Company agreed to provide good feed and grain for the rest of the horses' natural lives.

Nick also reminded me of an incident when I was State Treasurer. He had an appointment and was banging on about the poor quality of the State-owned Mt Isa to Townsville railway line, and the need for the State to spend more money on upkeep and maintenance. I apparently said, *'I'll tell you what I will do Nick, I will sell the whole railway line to MIM for a dollar.'* He didn't take it up.

PAPUA NEW GUINEA

I finally gave the keys to the farm back to the Agricultural Bank and went underground mining full time at Irvinebank on the Tableland, mining for tin. We lived in a lousy little one bed caravan which we rented. It was a reasonable living. But I was a restless kind of person, always have been, and I came to realise that wielding a jack hammer and a hand shovel didn't provide the platform for a long, successful and healthy life, and I accepted recruitment as an Agricultural Officer to Papua New Guinea (PNG).

Yvonne and I spent nine years in PNG, 1967-76. Two further daughters were born during this period, the second oldest Jacqui was born in the Goroka hospital in the Eastern Highlands. This was the time of Australian Administration of PNG and there was a concerted effort to bring about economic development and raise living standards. It was all well intended, though culturally challenged. Campaigns like this often bequeathed more of the worst of Western society than the best. Most Australians worked either as patrol officers (kiaps), whose job it was to preserve and institutionalise law and order, and agricultural officers (didimen) charged with the economic development task, introducing cash crops such as coffee, cocoa, oil palm, pyrethrum, vanilla, pepper …

During those nine years I served as an agricultural officer in Wabag in the Western Highlands, and Mendi in the Southern Highlands. Then I was drafted into the agricultural education sector, serving as a lecturer in Popondetta (on the top side of the Kokoda Track) and Vudal outside Rabaul in East New Britain (later wiped out by a massive volcanic eruption). I then became the inaugural Principal of the Highlands Agricultural College at Mt Hagen in the Western Highlands.

From a career point of view, my sojourn in PNG was very successful. I think it is fair to say that I was promoted beyond that of my contemporaries, and I learned for the first time to wear clothes to work which were washed and ironed!

I also felt I had made a contribution. I developed a strong affinity with the local people and worked hard to improve their lot in a culturally appropriate way, not always a major consideration of the Administration.

Another great achievement of this interlude was the successful completion of a Bachelor of Arts degree by correspondence with the University of Queensland. I was initially awarded provisional adult matriculation to do the degree, but because I had no language other than English in my prior education, I was required to do a language in my degree studies. I chose Japanese, as opposed to say French, as it did not presume prior study. I still have memories of sitting at a desk in the bedroom late at night, with a tape recorder the size of a suit case, speaking Japanese to myself – 'Konnichiwa, O genki deska? Genki des.' – while my poor wife twisted and turned in bed vainly seeking a less culturally diverse sleep!

I also remember almost going troppo. A pack of mangy dogs barking in the street, I couldn't get past the word I was reading waiting for the next bark. Then I realised I was hiding in the hedge with a three pound rock as a present for the next dog that barked. DeLacy, you are going mad I said; and I guess I got myself together.

But it was hard going, hundreds of pages of hard-copy notes each week posted up from the uni, and no assistance from modern or digital technology. However I was finally awarded a BA degree without once having set foot in UQ's hallowed halls. And on reflection, the

Japanese study, and the major I did in economics, proved very beneficial in life's later pursuits, even if the post-nominals tended to be a liability in the Labor Party in those days.

I didn't know it at the time but nine years in PNG in the 60s and 70s largely shielded me from the revolution that engulfed the West. It started off as opposition to the Vietnam war but morphed into a counter-culture that banned all inhibitions, opposed not only the war, but government, parents, the church and society itself, while embracing social permissiveness, drugs, psychedelic art, long hair, flower power and a general radicalisation involving sex and drugs and rock 'n 'roll.

Communications in PNG were rather rudimentary and it was hard to live these cultural movements. When I left PNG I couldn't tell Jimmy Hendrix from Bing Crosby, I knew more about the Goroka Sing-Sing than the peace, music and love of Woodstock, and I thought flowers simply brightened up the lounge room. Many of the survivors of this counter culture ended up infiltrating the Left of the Labor Party but I got left behind; and I blame (or should I say thank) PNG for that.

We departed Papua New Guinea early in 1976, just after PNG gained its independence, but not because of Independence. Our eldest daughter was ready for high school and we felt that our children should do their secondary schooling in Australia while enjoying the advantage of living at home. We chose to settle in Cairns, the regional capital of Far North Queensland, close to our ancestral homes as it were.

2

THE POLITICAL INCARNATION

We acquired the Railway Newsagency in McLeod Street, Cairns, just opposite the railway station. It provided a reasonable living, but 6am to 6pm, seven days a week, ensured that living was well and truly earned.

I grew to love Cairns, Australia's northern outpost, nestled on a narrow coastal strip bordered by spectacular, fringing, tropical rainforested mountains. It was founded in 1876, following the overflow frenzy from the Palmer River Gold rush which commenced in 1873. Many Chinese came to Australia chasing that golden dream, and eventually settled in Cairns. For many years a large and productive Chinese community thrived there.

Cairns was named after Queensland Governor Sir William Wellington Cairns. In the meantime the Chinese had colonised Sachs Street right in the middle of town and it became well known, mostly for all the wrong reasons being full of Chinese gambling dens and brothels. After the Second World War the city fathers decided it was time to clean up the area since it wasn't doing much for the city's moral reputation.

So they re-named Sachs Street, wait for it, after former City of Cairns Mayor, Mr JG Hoare. Sachs Street became Hoare Street. Although the spelling was innocuous enough the pronunciation detracted greatly from the cleansing benefits of the name change. All hell broke loose, and the street was finally re-named Grafton Street, which remains to this day. So as not to offend the descendants of Mr JG Hoare, a distant suburban street, with a scrupulously clean history, was named Hoare Street, as it remains to this day.

THE POLITICAL INCARNATION

The political bug had lain dormant for a long time, but it was always lurking there. The politically charged environment in which I and my siblings had been raised probably made this inevitable. I always had a keen eye for all manner of things: world events, cultural changes, social discrepancies, lifestyles, topical happenings, news, politics. I was a very judgmental individual, with an opinion on everything, whether well informed or otherwise. That hasn't changed much in all the years since!

There were so many things that needed fixing. We were living through the cold war, nuclear Armageddon was being rehearsed, there were enormous discrepancies in wealth both within and between nations, man was at war with the environment …

The newsagency was located in a working class part of town (only two blocks from the aforementioned Grafton Street), all the customers seemed to be Labor voters. Conservatives either didn't exist or pretended they didn't. I became good friends with one of the locals, Don Rookwood (Rookie), a large, avuncular man, a railway worker (linesman), and quintessentially working class. Rookie held court in the Railway Hotel, just down the road from the newsagency, after work about 5.30 each afternoon and then all Saturday afternoon. I got in the habit of joining in the Saturday afternoon session, Yvonne running the shop with her customary grace and goodwill.

Inevitably I drifted into the Labor Party. It would have been unthinkable to do otherwise in this environment, especially when coupled with the collectivist and social justice principles I inherited. Apart from that my mother would have killed me had I chosen otherwise!

I joined the Cairns Branch of the Labor Party. It was a powerful branch. Cairns was a strong Labor town, with an economy based on sugar, railways and mining. At one stage there were 800 wharfies loading sugar at the Cairns port, and it would be easier to find the stairway to heaven than a Tory voter amongst them. The electorate of Cairns hadn't had a conservative member of State parliament since 1904 (Gavin King in 2012 was the first one in 108 years, but by then of course it was a tourism town populated by small business).

Local State Labor member Ray Jones (elected 1965), an ex-railway Guard, and strong Catholic in a Catholic town, was very popular and secure, a major roadblock to a political career for an outsider young and impatient.

'Why don't you have a crack at Barron River,' urged Rookie, 'Martin Tenni's not much chop?' Martin Tenni was the National Party member for Barron River (the Party had recently changed its name from Country Party to National Party as Premier Bjelke-Petersen sought to broaden his constituency and marginalise coalition partners the Liberals).

The Barron River electorate, created in the electoral redistribution of 1971, adjoined the electorate of Cairns, taking in the northern suburbs of Cairns, Mossman/Port Douglas/Daintree to the north, and Mareeba on the Tableland. This latter made it attractive to me as Mareeba/Dimbulah was my old stamping ground, though the big population density was down on the coast. It was a marginal seat, won by Tenni from Labor Member Bill Wood in 1974.

Mind you it was easy to take a seat off Labor in 1974 because that was the election when Labor lost two-thirds of its seats including Leader Percy Tucker, and was left with the infamous cricket team of eleven, in an 82 member Legislative Assembly. The Labor brand was toxic right throughout Australia at that stage. Ray Jones, the Member for Cairns, was the only Labor member in any parliament in Australia north of the Tropic of Capricorn. What made the result all the more galling was that the election was held after Labor members of Parliament in Queensland had refused to accept a recommended salary increase in order to demonstrate solidarity with the battlers of the world.

It was noteworthy also in that the first Indigenous member of the House, Eric Deeral, was elected to the adjoining seat as the Member for Cook. He only lasted the one term.

The real issue of course was the Whitlam Federal Government, a Labor icon but about as popular in most of Queensland as the cane toads now in plague proportions. A *Crikey* journalist called the Queensland 1974 election result 'the gold standard for Australian political massacres.'

Anna Bligh was to deliver the Platinum standard thirty-eight years later.

Preselection was easier than I expected. The Barron River electorate didn't have a solid working class nucleus like Cairns, and was considered very marginal. There was no cohesive sense of belonging (no one lived in the River, only fish, and they only voted in western Queensland seats!), the branch infrastructure rudimentary at best, and there was no one splendid with numbers. And Tenni was no pushover. Though he and charisma had never been acquainted he was a hard worker, a self-made man, and very well known, having grown up in the Cairns part of the electorate. By the time he was elected, Tenni was Chairman of the Mareeba Shire Council, and owner/manager of Tenni's Hardware in Mareeba.

Meanwhile the Whitlam aroma was still heavy in the air, with Premier Bjelke-Petersen stoking it daily.

I think I was seen as a reasonably attractive candidate, well educated (not always a plus in the ALP though), with strong historical links to part of the electorate, and a variety of life experiences. The communist connection was raised in one debate but it largely simmered just below the surface.

But preselection was not the end, just the beginning. Campaigning was all done on the ground in those days, no newspaper ads, no TV commercials. It was all door knocking, public meetings, leaflets and posters, and a bit of megaphone diplomacy.

I never felt comfortable door knocking, I felt like a fraud, like a religious evangelist who didn't believe in God. However I did come away with renewed respect for Jehovah's Witnesses and their door-knocking commitment to their cause. But of course they had the reward of eternal life, while I, at best, a temporary seat in the rather less ethereal Parliament of Queensland.

Years later, my daughter, a psychologist, informed me I was an INTJ under the Myer-Briggs personality type classification – the **I** standing for Introverted, maybe explaining some of my discomfort on the footpath patrol.

Billy Eales organised a truck which they backed up to the Dunlop Hotel in Byrnes Street Mareeba. I stood on the tray haranguing the multitude via a public address system they had set up. The trouble was there was no multitude to harangue, a humbling experience, speaking passionately to no one, especially for an INTJ (at least there was no fact checking). Billy solved the problem by organising a small group from the bar to walk out the front door, stand on the footpath, clap and cheer, then disappear around to the side door, only to march out the front again cheering and clapping, and again, and again, as though the lonely address really was gaining momentum!

This was our version of megaphone diplomacy.

I reflected many times in my political career about what type of campaigning actually made a difference. How many people were swayed by a leaflet thrust in their hand or a knock on the door? Sometimes I thought door knocking was like the biblical Crown of Thorns imposed by the masters as instruments of pain and passion, nothing to do with getting votes. One stuttering utterance by Premier Joh about the evils of socialism would elicit a thousand more nods of the head than all the door knocking in the world.

The whole campaign was a baptism of fire, uncomfortable most of the time. I had big insecurities – whether I belonged, whether I was up to it, whether there was a future in this game. But I never doubted my ideological predisposition that there was so much to do to make Queensland a better place.

It could be rewarding too. I ended up with a support team that made me proud, and they were ever so confident – a confidence I suspected, based more on ideological exuberance than rational analysis.

I think I always suffered from an excess of rationality, not a good trait in an aspiring politician, especially a Labor one with a mission to save the planet. Whilst we had run a competent local campaign I wasn't convinced we were winning the big picture. Premier Bjelke-Petersen was campaigning primarily on law-and-order, but the Whitlam bogey was constantly evoked too.

Gough had a long shelf life in Queensland. It was two years since his unceremonious dismissal in 1975.

For more than ten years now law-and-order had been a hot topic in the Sunshine State, starting with the anti-Vietnam war demonstrations in the '60s. A familiar pattern developed. Protestors full of self-righteous indignation would take to the streets to protest. Joh would overreact, introduce anti-street march laws and send in the police to uphold the laws.

It was all a side show of course but they lived off each other. The protestors had plenty of issues – anti-war, ban the bomb, environmental (the historic Bellevue Hotel was demolished in the dark of night), anti-Apartheid (the Springbok rugby tour of 1971), sand mining on Fraser Island, land rights, civil liberties and so on; and there were always the generic issues, like street marches to protect street marches.

There was more civil unrest in Queensland from the mid-sixties to the mid-eighties than any other time or place in Australia. This was caused in part by a perceived shortcoming in the democratic process. The Bjelke-Petersen government was sustained in power with the help of the so-called gerrymander (some called it Bjelke-mander – though it could just as easily been called Labor-mander as the system of malapportionment was actually introduced by Labor Premier Ned Hanlon in 1949 to capitalise on AWU strength in the regions) wherein a vote in the country was worth up to half as much again as one in the city. People felt that they couldn't get true justice at the ballot box so they turned to civil disobedience. And Joh played it like a violin.

The Labor Party got sucked into participating in the protests and defending them; it was, after all, the high moral cause. I learned that one of the benefits, or was it one of the negatives, of door-knocking was you came to understand how ordinary people thought, which wasn't always comforting. I gradually, and reluctantly, picked up the vibes that the constant spectre of angry marchers taking over the streets, waving placards and red flags, and shouting with ugly faces seemed to be repelling the Mums and Dads in the suburbs, not winning them. Joh was on a winner – a sobering thought I couldn't push out of my mind. The righteousness of a cause might create a warm inner glow but it did not necessarily make it a winner.

It was a lesson for a lifetime.

Election day, 12 November 1977 – the moment of truth. I toured the booths, providing moral support and encouragement to my team handing out how-to-vote cards. There didn't appear to be much agro. I ran into Martin Tenni and we endured a lukewarm handshake, wishing each other good luck with all the sincerity of a prisoner thanking his jailer!

Six o'clock the booths closed and the dreaded count began. I didn't know how I felt. Nervous to be sure. It had been a long hard road, and it all came down to this evening – all for nothing, or the sunlit plains ahead. I wished I wasn't there. In a financial sense it was important too as campaigning became a full time, unpaid occupation.

We set up shop at our home on Kamerunga Road, the team bubbling with optimism I hoped was justified. And the first booth in, Machans Beach, ALP 62%, a roar went up with the bottles' tops popping like a fire-cracker night.

Lesson number two: a booth does not an electorate make. Machans Beach was a small, mangrove infested seaside village filled with working class retirees. It always polled in the sixties for Labor.

At the end of the night's counting the result was in the balance, with postal and absentees still to be counted. Hope and despair in equal proportions. At the end of the week, Tenni 7,663, DeLacy 7,593, a margin of 70 votes or 0.2%, now the most marginal seat in Queensland, and one might say, a result almost within the margin of error. Except in real life the margin was the Grand Canyon, with Tenni a member of parliament (and soon to become a Minister) and DeLacy chasing his tail in the streets of Cairns.

I think it was inevitable that I would saddle up again as I owed it to my supporters, and most of all, I owed it to myself. I owed it to my wife not to saddle up again but …

There were two defining events in the lead-up to the 1980 election, both rendering almost meaningless electorate level campaign efforts. Oh what a frustrating world!

Federal Intervention.

The first was the intervention into the Queensland branch of the Labor Party by the Federal Executive in 1980. It had a long genesis with years of turmoil, public disharmony and chronic under performance. Ironically this followed many years of ALP power and stability prior to 1957.

By 1957 Labor had been in government in Queensland for 39 out of the previous 42 years, punctuated by the one-term Moore Government of 1929-32. This extraordinary stability was largely attributed to the domination of the Australian Workers Union (AWU) and its power base in the regions, in the mining, shearing, and sugar cane industries of which it had coverage, the backbone of the Queensland economy.

The Labor Party as it emerged and grew since the beginning of the century was dominated by the Irish Catholic working class and greatly influenced by the Catholic Church. It seemed the AWU plus Catholic Church equalled ALP stability which equalled power. In this context it is hard not to mention Red Ted Theodore who laid out the blueprint.

There was something of an anomaly here. In the early part of the twentieth century there seemed to be a strong anti-Catholic sectarianism dominating Australian politics. I think this pointed to the fact that Queensland (is anything new?) is a bit different. The end of the Anglo-Irish war in 1923 probably helped moderate English/Irish hostilities also.

Queensland has a unicameral parliament, no upper house, unlike all other States and the Commonwealth. The Legislative Council, which comprised non-elected, appointed-for-life members, was abolished by Premier Ted Theodore in 1922. Labor saw the Council as inimical to the best interests of the proletariat but needed to pass the abolition legislation in both houses, a difficult task to achieve in the upper house which would effectively be voting itself into oblivion. The ALP formed government under TJ Ryan in 1915 (with Theodore as State Treasurer) and over the next seven years was able to progressively appoint its own members to the Council. By 1922 (Theodore was now Premier) they had a majority prepared to graciously commit occupational suicide.

The Legislative Council has been singularly unlamented ever since.

As an aside I regard EG (Red Ted) Theodore as the most significant Labor figure in Queensland history. He effectively established the Australian Workers Union and used it as a personal and party power base. In one sense I'm not sure where the 'Red' came from in his moniker, apart from its rhyming qualities, because he wasn't a militant in the normal industrial sense of the word. He believed passionately that you could do more for the worker and the less-well-off by pulling the levers of power in government, than by industrial action and protest. He was implacably opposed to those left wing unions quick to down tools.

However it is fair to say that he did deliver in government a plethora of legislation of an interventionist, collectivest, anti-free-market kind. He established State-run enterprises with gay abandon (even the Babinda Hotel was State-owned, as were most of the butcher shops and coal mines in the State), he established the State owned Agricultural Bank (which many years later financed me onto my tobacco farm); and of course he introduced a range of union friendly labour market regulations. All of these put together may have justified the 'Red Ted' sobriquet.

Theodore was Queensland Treasurer from 1915 to 1919, and Premier from 1919-25. He was then recruited into federal politics and in 1929 became Federal Treasurer and Deputy Leader to James Scullin, Labor Prime Minister. He was obviously heading towards the Prime Ministerial throne. However, he and his good friend, Queensland Premier at the time, William McCormack (the Member for Cairns), were badly damaged in the so-called Mungana corruption Affair which effectively brought both of their political careers to an end. Theodore went on to enjoy a very successful business career partnering up with the legendary Frank Packer.

Another very interesting aside: Theodore was the Member for Chillagoe when he was Premier. When he retired in 1925 he was replaced by William Gillies, the Labor Member for Eacham on the Atherton Tablelands. Ill health forced Gillies to resign in the same year and he was replaced by William McCormack, the Labor Member for Cairns. If you stood in the right spot you could kick a football into all three electorates, perhaps a measure of how much more significant the regions were in those days. This largely forgotten part of Australia provided three successive Queensland Premiers from contiguous electorates a thousand miles from Brisbane. As someone said to me, the Cairns region never had it so good again until they elected a State Treasurer in 1989 (I pretended to disagree!)

But, as they say, all good things come to an end. In the 1950s the Labor Party throughout Australia became wracked by sectarian strife. Australia in those days was a very sectarian society, you knew everyone's religion, inter-denominational marriages were frowned upon, school playgrounds hosted never-ending fist fights between Protestant (Prods) and Catholic (Cattle ticks) kids, people were even employed on the basis of their religious affiliation. The State Government Insurance Office (SGIO, now morphed into Suncorp) for instance was Protestant free. Irish Catholics dominated the police force too, though the Free Masons had a powerful, if minority, presence – a presence which exerted itself in the Terry Lewis era in the dying turbulence of the Bjelke-Petersen Government.

The Communist Party was a growing influence in the years following the Second World War. Its vision of equality and fairness was attractive to utopian intellectuals, and the Russian people were seen to be heroes in the defeat of Hitler. The atrocities of Stalinism were yet largely unexposed in the insular world of the time. Capitalism also had a dirty name because of the pain of the Great Depression.

The AWU, a non-militant union, saw the Communists as a threat to their hegemony, a threat to industrial peace and a threat to electoral success. Most of the industrial outbreaks of the time had strong Communist involvement, as with the sugar industry strikes in the 1930s. And especially the Railway Strike of 1948 when Fred Paterson, former Rhodes Scholar and radical barrister, Member for Bowen and the only Communist ever elected to parliament in Australian history, was badly beaten by a plain clothes policeman, almost certainly, according to Ross Fitzgerald, on the direct orders of ALP Premier Ned Hanlon.

Ironically, bearing in mind the draconian legislation later introduced by the Bjelke-Petersen Government in the face of widespread civil disobedience, and so vehemently opposed by Labor, ALP Premier Hanlon, in order to counter the highly disruptive railway strike of 1948, rushed through Parliament the *Industrial Law Amendment Act*, prohibiting illegal strikes and imposing severe penalties. *The Courier Mail* editorialised (10 March 10 1948): 'These powers are the most far-reaching ever given to Police in any State in Australia.'

A year after Paterson's bashing, Hanlon's *Electoral District Act 1949* created a zonal malapportionment of major proportions, illustrating once again how Labor laid the blueprint for the excesses of the Bjelke-Petersen Government which was to follow.

The Catholic Church was strongly anti-Communist, too, with good reason. Karl Marx had outed religion, and this was mainly Catholicism, from the beginning as the opiate of the masses, which he claimed caused class disadvantaged masses to become complacent in the face of injustice. After all, wasn't one opiate enough for the masses? Communist regimes, wherever they sprung up, focused quickly on eliminating the influence of the Catholic Church, sometimes in draconian ways.

Industrial Groups (Groupers) were set up under the auspices of the Catholic Social Studies Movement to oppose Communist incursions in the Labor movement. At a national level, B. A. Santamaria provided the philosophical ballast for this movement, with the strong support of Catholic Archbishop of Melbourne Daniel Mannix, first through the *Catholic Worker* newspaper, and then through weekly radio broadcasts on the ABC. I can still remember my father tuning into these broadcasts, mumbling objections, luxuriating in the revulsion he felt for Santamaria and all he stood for.

In Queensland a number of Trades and Labor Council (TLC) leaders were active Communists, but they were largely marginalised while the AWU was calling the shots. AWU heavyweight Joe (the enforcer) Bukowski chaired the Industrial Groups Committee in Queensland. Bukowski was a big man of Polish Catholic, anti-communist heritage. It seems he earned his 'enforcer' reputation in the sugar industry wild-cat strikes, doing most of his enforcing after dark (he was sometimes also referred to as Midnight Joe).

As an interesting aside – Robert Menzies and his Liberal Party were elected Federally in 1949 and in 1950 passed the *Communist Party Dissolution Act*. A motley group of unions, communists and civil libertarians challenged the legislation and it was overturned by the High Court as unconstitutional. Menzies then called a referendum for September 1951 to give him the power to legislate to ban the Communist Party. They were frenzied times, dividing the nation.

My older brother Ian tells the story that he and our father were working in the tobacco crop up near the barbed wire gate that was the entrance to our farm when a stranger arrived. Ian drew it to father's (he had very bad eyes) attention. When father went up to meet the stranger he froze. Ian claims it was Joe Bukowski (though he is not sure how he came to know this, and we have no way of validating it – probably in subsequent conversations with father). The visitor said, 'Hello Ern. I am campaigning against Menzies' referendum. Would you be prepared to organise the town?' Father peremptorily said yes, his only utterance, and went back into the refuge of the tobacco crop.

I can also vaguely remember my Dad reacting strangely every time Bukowski's name was mentioned and Ian and I now suspect that he might have been 'enforced' during the Innisfail cane strike in 1934.

On further reflection it seems passing strange for Bukowski, a staunch anti-communist, and Chair of the Industrial Groups Committee in Queensland, to be campaigning against the anti-communist referendum. Still the unions, even the AWU, hated Menzies with a passion, and united to defeat him on this issue. My enemy's enemy is my friend!

For the record the referendum was a close run thing, carrying a majority in three states but ultimately failing to gain a national majority by a very narrow margin.

Labor Premier Ned Hanlon died in 1952 and was replaced by Vince Gair, and the implosion of the ALP dynasty began. Gair was a member of the Federated Clerks Union which was pro the Industrial Groups movement. Bukowski was by then State President of the AWU but he and Gair shared a long standing enmity. They had both attended the same Christian Brothers School in Rockhampton years earlier and it is conjectured that Enforcer Joe may have done some enforcing there too. Gair refused to join the AWU when invited to do so, as was a long standing custom for Labor Premiers, and he became alienated from both the AWU and Trades Hall Group. He fought with the union movement (including the AWU) over the Shearers Strike in 1956, and then refused to adopt the State Conference policy of three weeks annual leave. Bukowski was by this time also President of the Queensland Central Executive (QCE) of the Labor Party and this executive voted to expel Gair from the ALP. Gair took twenty-five members of Parliament (including all members of Cabinet except for Jack Duggan) with him and formed the Queensland Labor Party (QLP).

This mirrored to a great extent the split that occurred throughout Australia, primarily Victoria, leading to the formation the largely Catholic, anti-communist Democratic Labor Party (DLP), and the sidelining of Labor as a political powerhouse for a long period of time – indeed until 1972 at a Federal level, and until 1989 in Queensland.

Country Party leader Frank Nicklin easily won the State election held in August 1957 when Gair was unable to secure confidence in Parliament. The Labor vote was effectively split in half. So in reality Nicklin didn't win, the ALP handed it to him, in an eerie precursor to the Nats losing power thirty-two years later.

Bukowski lost his way, the AWU disaffiliated from the ALP, and power in the Labor movement passed to the Trades Hall Group (THG), often referred to as the Old Guard – anti-Catholic, anti-AWU, anti-reform and anti 'grubs and groupers'. All of the bastions of success had been kicked asunder, Theodore just a distant memory, and so began the era of 'turmoil, public disharmony and chronic under performance'.

Jack Egerton from the Boilermakers Union became Trades Hall and ALP President, the first strong man and public identity of the new era. He personified the anti-compromise, anti-intellectual, anti-reform, anti-progressive attitude of ALP leadership of the time. This was epitomised by the reported exchange at the 1971 *Labor-in-Politics* convention on the Gold Coast where a motion from the rank-and-file to decriminalise homosexuality was debated. Bill Hayden (later to be Governor-General) had earlier moved a motion to ban boxing which went nowhere, and he also spoke in favour of the homosexuality motion. President Egerton as Chairman succinctly summed up the debate, looking at Hayden:

> It seems it's wrong to punch someone in the face, but OK to punch them in the pants. All those in favour of the poofters, raise your right hand. I declare the motion lost.

But Egerton's career ended in a whirlpool of derision when, after spending his whole life opposing the upper class, privilege and pretension, he accepted a knighthood from the Queen (in reality from Sir Joh in a Machiavellian play). Sir Jack was followed by a succession of Trades Hall presidents each a little less colourful and a little less successful than his predecessor, but all from the same mould, and suspicious of anyone who didn't fit that mould. As one commentator said, they were reactionary, sexist and profoundly anti-intellectual – hardly the people to take Labor forward in an era with a shrinking union base, a more diversified and educated City membership, and changing societal, cultural and political attitudes throughout the nation.

Hence Federal intervention on 1 March 1980, inspired by progressives (like Peter Beattie, Manfred and Barbara Cross, Di Fingleton, Kevin Hooper and Denis Murphy) frustrated by the lack of electoral success, the refusal to share power, a lack of policy position on the bubbling social issues of the day, and the continuing failure of anyone not an 'Old Guard' supporter to win Party endorsement for anything.

But whilst intervention changed some of the optics, democratised the Party processes, and led to a gradual infusion of new style ALP members and reformers both in the Executive and in parliament, it never much impressed the electorate, which saw a bunch of losers more interested in fighting each other than running the State.

Street marches.

Civil disobedience continued to dominate Queensland politics. In 1978 Premier Bjelke-Petersen banned all street marches:

> Protest Groups need not bother applying for permits to stage marches as they won't be granted – that's Government policy now.

Police became more truculent. Seasoned marchers knew to watch for police unpinning their number badges, because it signalled things were about to turn nasty. The right to march became the central issue. More than 2,000 people were arrested including 346 from one march and packed like sardines into prison cells, and denied a lawyer.

Opposition seemed to be growing, especially in the City. But was this just the commentariat, those people living in echo chambers which reinforced the orthodoxy, or the people themselves? In much of Queensland Joh was seen as a strong Christian leader resisting a communist inspired plot to overthrow normal parliamentary processes.

Coalition partners the Liberals, as you would expect liberals to be, were becoming increasingly uncomfortable with the authoritarian line, and the relationship was inevitably drifting towards fracture. It also caused further fractures in the divided ALP. In 1978 the parliamentary Labor Party, supported by the Trades Hall Group, refused to support the marches, seeing the issue as a vote loser. This led to further conflict with the progressives, the moral righteousness of their cause overwhelming mere trifles like winning elections and making permanent change.

But if the 'Old Guard' was correct in its judgment that the street march issue was a vote loser, perhaps they could have responded more critically to the wave of industrial activity that occurred under their watch. Still there is nothing like a good strike to soothe the soul. A strike by Gladstone power workers in 1978 led to the Government's introduction of the *Essential Services Bill*, full of draconian measures. This in turn led to a wave of strikes. In 1980, a State of Emergency was called, with more strikes, 38 hour week movement, and eventually a spontaneous general strike which spread throughout Queensland. And strikes were even harder to defend politically than street marches as they denied the public a range of services (like electricity) that they valued.

What was the point of campaigning on the ground back home in the lonely electorate?

And the result, the same.

The election was held on 29 November 1980. Labor picked up two seats taking it to 25 in the 82 member Assembly, but they were just about as far from government as they ever were. The impact of the gerrymander was there for all to see. Labor received 41.5% of the vote for their 25 seats, while the National Party won 35 seats with 28% of the vote (note the ALP under Annastacia Palaszczuk won the 2017 State election with 35.43% of the primary vote). And the poor old Libs, with almost the same percentage as the Nats won only 22 seats. This represented the fifth consecutive victory for the National Party under Joh Bjelke-Petersen and the ninth for the National (Country) Party since they came to office in 1957.

In Barron River not much changed either. Martin Tenni won with a marginally increased majority, 0.7%, making it now the third most marginal seat in the State. I couldn't help but notice that my Labor colleague Ray Jones in the adjoining seat of Cairns was returned with a margin of 13.9%.

That was the end, I was a failure.

Lesson No 1: a premature call of failure is not a good life skill; Lesson No 2: a failure in one test is not a failure in life; it is a learning experience.

Ray Jones dropped the bombshell. He was retiring as the Member for Cairns at the next election, expected late 1983. Ray won the seat in a by-election on 27 February 1965, following the death of his predecessor Watty Wallace, having spent almost nineteen years in Parliament, never once gracing the Government benches on the Speaker's right hand side.

'Sweetheart, guess what?'

'Oh no, not again,' she replied, with as much enthusiasm as she could muster. We had sold the newsagency before the 1980 election (surely not pre-empting a win against Martin Tenni?). Yvonne worked for a while in her old trade as a barmaid, and subsequently running a newsagency for an old colleague. I was for some time the green-keeper at the Yorkeys Knob golf club. And I worked part time as an international agricultural consultant, mostly for the Food and Agricultural Organisation (FAO) of the United Nations, working in such countries as the Philippines, Thailand, and Zimbabwe (under the so-called Zimcord agreement).

I vividly remember the first time I visited FAO Headquarters in Rome, an enormous building that wholly occupied a very large city block. I said to the driver, 'Wow, how many people work here?' 'About half of them,' he replied. Oh dear, bureaucracies, do they ever change?

Back home it was as though we were biding time, waiting for something.

That something had come.

The electorate of Cairns was a different ball game, a plumb seat eagerly sought after. It had effectively been a Labor seat since 1904 (it was interrupted from 1942 to 1945 by Lou Barnes who described himself as Independent Labor). This was the chance of a lifetime, but the last chance. I was 43 years old. I had to go for it, and go for it with every fibre of my being.

But I was effectively an outsider. I pushed the fact that I was born in Cairns but this was a technicality since Cairns was the only birthing option for my Dimbulah based mother who availed herself of the facilities of the CWA hostel next to the Cairns Base Hospital, an amenity provided by the CWA for country women. Even our present home in Freshwater was in the Barron River electorate. We of course ran a newsagency right in the middle of Cairns for four years but official blessing as a Cairnsite doesn't come that easy. I was still an outsider, and in those parochial days it mattered.

John Cleland, my main preselection opponent, was a local. He came from a local working class family, lived all of his life in Cairns, trained as a pharmacist and had his own chemist shop, his brother was a lawyer and played golf off handicap 6. He was close to sitting member Ray Jones. He was in the straight before I got out of the blocks. But favouritism breeds complacency, and complacency breeds lethargy. He expected to win. I had nothing to lose, I personally visited every branch member and made them feel special, followed up on specific requests. I think it is fair to say, based on feedback, that I came across as fresh, committed, capable and authentic.

There were a number of other candidates, but they never excited the bookies. In the beginning it was John Cleland first and daylight second, but DeLacy started to rattle the odds. Ray Jones of course was supporting Cleland, but wasn't as active as he could have been. It seems he didn't want to be seen as pushy in what was the last play of his political life. Or perhaps he still believed the State Executive would 'fix it up' as they always did. He was however quite cold towards me, an outsider, not a unionist, not a Catholic, and whose father had been a member of the ...

To the surprise of many, I won the preselection ballot, by a single vote. I received 39 votes out of the 77 which counted, and over the years at least 45 people reminded me they had delivered that single winning vote!

On reflection I now know I would not have been preselected for Cairns prior to the 1980 intervention into the ALP by the National Executive. The Trades Hall Group, with its oligarchic control of all that happened in the party, would not have countenanced a person with my credentials replacing a loyal old guard member like Ray Jones.

My older brother Ian, active in the reform side of State politics in Brisbane, worked hard to ensure that my win in the branch preselection ballot was endorsed. My memory of those days is more than a little hazy. But I understand that the preselection process (after Federal intervention) consisted of a local plebiscite and a vote of the State Electoral College, both with equal weightings. With only a one vote majority in the branch plebiscite I had to win in Brisbane. There were three factions in those days, the Old-Guard, the Socialist Left, and the AWU. Ian said the AWU was OK as they were a moderate faction and opposed to the Old Guard. The Socialist Left was the key. He tells me he largely liaised through John Sinclair of Fraser Island fame (I have no way of substantiating this) and John (we called him Bugs Sinclair, he had been a colleague at Gatton College many years earlier) was interested in my policy capabilities (whatever that means) and on this criterion I won the Socialist Left vote, endorsed by the bleeding hearts – will I ever live that down (maybe the communist heritage helped; we will never know!)

So back to the election proper. 13.9% margin. Gee, you can't lose from there can you, can you … So ushered in a period of gross insecurity. In Barron River at least there wasn't much to lose, do your best and what happens, happens. But a jewel like Cairns.

These feelings of self-doubt were greatly magnified by the reaction of the National and Liberal parties to Ray Jones' retirement. It was their best chance in fifty years to snatch the strategic electorate, and they weren't going to let the opportunity pass easily. I think it is fair to say, they didn't see me as a commanding candidate, replicating the initial response of Labor people. And what price physical appearance in political campaigning? As I sunk into a morass of morbid introspection I felt I never had that look of authoritative masculinity that marks a leader. I learned later that this sort of introspective analysis is highly counter-productive. I think I eventually learned to be myself, live your values, that's what makes you authentic, and that is much more important than some comic book notion of something like authoritative masculinity.

The National Party preselected Chris Bolton, a Cairns builder who founded the successful Bolton Concrete Pumping in 1974, part of a large and well known Cairns family group. His cousin Brian was a local legend in both Cricket and Rugby league (and a Labor man I was to find out later).

The Liberals preselected Lionel Van Dorssen, a local tobacconist with his CBD shop part of the furniture of Cairns (still is), a community man highly respected. Exchanging preferences they were a formidable combination. There were no wharfies left in Cairns by 1983 – sugar was all bulk loading.

But they were at it again in Brisbane, rendering our local campaigns virtually redundant once again.

This time it was the Government parties having a party. For once Labor couldn't out discredit its opponents. The Bjelke-Petersen Government's gradual creep (or was it a gallop) to autocracy, especially in relation to public dissent and civil disobedience, made their Liberal coalition partners uncomfortable. Were they, the Liberals, in Parliament to enjoy the mere trappings of power, or did they have a responsibility to uphold the great principles of liberalism?

A number of Liberals crossed the floor to support an ALP motion to establish a Public Accounts Committee. Among these brave souls was cabinet minister Terry White. Joh sacked him from cabinet before the Division bells stopped ringing.

On the principle, in for a penny in for a pound, White then launched a party room coup against his own leader (Sir) Llewellyn Edwards and became Liberal leader with Angus Innes as his deputy. Under the Coalition agreement this entitled White to become Deputy Premier. Premier Bjelke-Petersen, attracted to this proposition as one is attracted to a taipan snake, refused. White symbolically and ceremoniously tore up the Coalition agreement for the cameras (it was actually the Premier's press release but the theatre was undiminished). The departure of the Libs left Joh seven seats short of a majority in the Assembly, but Joh convinced the Governor to prorogue parliament (for nine weeks), protecting the Government from a no-confidence vote before the election was called for 22 October 1983. Westminster process was not the sacred road map for Queensland politics at the time.

One would have thought that the electorate would be outraged at these shenanigans. They were – outraged at the Liberals. Joh's campaign message that Labor and Liberals would form a socialist coalition after the election seemed to gain traction. The Liberals were massacred. There was a 12% swing against them, losing thirteen seats – seven to Labor, six to the Nationals. They were left with 15% of the vote and just eight seats – a forlorn rump, paying the ultimate political price for sticking to their liberal principles.

The grand conductor of the democratic symphony sometimes trashes the melody! Do you blame the politicians, or the voters? As Winston Churchill said, 'The best argument against democracy is a five-minute conversation with the average voter.'

And Terry White retired from politics, sentenced to spend the rest of his life as a multimillionaire pharmacy chain owner.

But the lesson was clear, to be learned a hundred times, in politics and in life: it is easy to signal virtue but practical outcomes are much more worthy. As Gough Whitlam was later to say, 'Only the impotent are pure!'

The other half of the once proud coalition, the Nationals, received an eleven percent positive swing, finishing with 41 seats in the 82 member Legislative Assembly, one short of a clear majority, though Lindsay Hartwig, a previous National Party member expelled for criticising State President Sir Robert Sparkes, was re-elected as an independent in the strongly National Party electorate of Callide.

This problematic majority was resolved in quintessential Queensland fashion when two Liberals, Brian Austin and Don Lane, defected to the Nationals and were appropriately rewarded with senior portfolios, and ultimately jail.

The ALP under Keith Wright as leader received a modest swing of 2.5% but won seven seats, all at the expense of the hapless Liberals, finishing with 32. It is worth noting however that the ALP received 44% of the votes cast compared to the Nationals 39%, such was the power of the gerrymander.

All eyes were on Cairns. Certainly mine were, feverishly so. I was apprehensive in the extreme. You couldn't lose with an existing 13.9% margin could you, especially with the existing Government in disarray; and if you did, the ultimate humiliation, a political career finished before it began, and a laughing stock forever. I tried to rid myself of these negative sentiments but during the campaign, when I got away from the Labor faithful, I didn't pick up the Government in chaos story line as much as a muted anger about destabilising forces.

I won by the skin of my teeth, receiving 50.6% of the primary vote and 52.2% two-party-preferred, a swing of minus 11.7% from Ray Jones' last outing. There was no elation, just an empty feeling, lamenting a victory as a loss (unlike my underground mining mates who celebrated a loss as a victory). The support team couldn't care less, we had won hadn't we? And they were right. As it settled down I knew that deep within I had something to draw upon. I followed in life a motto (most un-Churchillian I admit), 'Get up! Dress up! And front up!' That's how you deal with issues. It has served me well during life's many tribulations.

A further feature of the election in Cairns, when I was in a position to thoroughly evaluate the outcome, was the extraordinary belting the Liberals received. Lionel Van Dorssen received just 7.4% of the vote – a well known, well liked, well respected businessman. In the early stages of the campaign I thought he was my greatest threat. Chris Bolton, the National Party candidate, received 42% of the primary vote.

KEITH DELACY MLA – THE SUNLIT PLAINS AHEAD

I inherited Ray Jones' electorate office in Cairns and his secretary Elva Vaughan, greatly easing that part of the journey. Computers were a modern marvel in 1983, so I went into the office at 6 am each day to try to cultivate some computer literacy. I had never even used a typewriter before.

I later received sterling service from Lyn Gane (electoral secretary) and Mike Bailey as Electoral Chief-of-Staff during my years as State Treasurer.

Ray Jones became a little friendlier, accepting the reality of my accession as his replacement, at times lapsing back into his 'old guard' earthy affability. When I was preparing to go to Parliament for the first time he apocryphally recounted his version of his own first visit in 1965. 'And who are you?', asked the parliamentary attendant when Ray fronted up. 'I'm a country member,' said Ray, puffing out his chest. 'I'll remember,' said the attendant.

His further earthy advice was 'Look at their eyes, not their tits!'

The eyes were where the recognition was, the connection, and you had to be alert to this, not to be seen as arrogant or 'up yourself'. And the tits were, well they were where a community leader should not be looking! Oh the sacrifices those seeking high office have to make!

Including myself there were nine new ALP members elected in 1983, not one of whom fitted the 'old guard' mould, an extraordinary turnaround. On reflection the Federal intervention in 1980 had a profound effect on the profile of Labor Party parliamentary representation, whether for better or worse is for others to judge. There were some notables among the nine including Denis Murphy, leading reform campaigner and Labor historian, who sadly died of cancer before he could deliver his maiden speech. Up-and-comers like Wayne Goss, David Hamill, Paul Braddy (we made Paul an honorary 83'er as he was elected the following year when Keith Wright retired as the Member for Rockhampton to pursue a federal career), Pat Comben, and Anne Warner among others – all destined to serve substantive ministerial careers later on.

And of course me, if I fitted the description of up-and-comer.

The old guard members were still the dominant grouping, characterised as they were by strong union affiliation, conservative social values, a commitment to collective action and a fairer society. Unity and loyalty were prized above all else, a tribal grouping where the word 'mate' rather than 'comrade' was universally used. To a certain extent they modelled themselves on the NSW Right, but in the more conservative, regional, gerrymandered oasis that was Queensland, they were unable to match NSW's electoral success.

They were a long way removed from the 'save-the-world' generation that progressively succeeded them. I came to appreciate over time that most of them were true gentlemen (no ladies of course) – people like Tommy Burns, Neville Warburton, Ken Vaughan, Brian (Digger) Davis, Bob Scott, Eric Shaw, Les Yewdale come to mind.

Tommy Burns was the 'larger than life' character, indeed one of the great parliamentary characters of all time and an ALP legend, having served in all positions in the ALP over the years from National President down. He spent a stint as Opposition Leader as captain of the cricket eleven after the 1974 rout. Loyal supporters started the 'Bank on Burns' campaign but only the faithful banked. He was a much more successful deputy to Wayne Goss after 1989 where he added the common touch.

He always had a good line, earthy wisdom. He told me once that you make your best speeches on the way home. So true!

He loved fishing, a quintessential Queensland pastime, and he represented the seaside electorate of Lytton in East Brisbane where he had a small boat (a tinnie) which he aptly named *The Electorate,* so when someone rang his electorate office his secretary was able to say with a straight face that Mr Burns was out in the electorate. Instead of flowers he gave each of his electoral staff a bucket of fish for Christmas.

He probably had only one written speech in the whole of his parliamentary career (as everybody said he could talk under water), his maiden speech in 1972. He was scheduled to be first up after lunch, he had the lectern in position and was busy rehearsing. Gordon Chalk the Deputy Premier walked past, picked up the speech and said 'What have we got here young Burnsie?' With that he ripped the speech in half and dropped it on the floor. The bells started ringing with Tom in a frenzy, on his hands and knees attempting to reassemble his speech. 'I call the Member for Lytton,' said the Speaker. Tom's long term advice: 'Always number the pages, top and bottom.'

At the height of the Japanese investment boom in 1989 Tom was railing against the increasing Japanese presence, building resorts and golf courses everywhere. 'Before we know it,' he thundered, 'you will be able to drive all the way from Brisbane to the Gold Coast with a seven iron!'

Joe Kruger, the Member for Murumba, wasn't known for his sophisticated ways. He was shadow Minister for Agriculture and I was drafted onto his committee because of my agricultural background. Joe had the habit of reading whole columns from *Country Life* into the official record (Hansard) as his own speech. He also had the habit of commencing his mental fortification in the Members Bar around lunchtime each day. I was sitting in a sparsely populated chamber about 10pm during the passage of an unremarkable agriculture bill and Joe had the floor. I was busily preparing my own speech when Joe began slurring his words. I looked up just in time to see his head slump onto his chest, the first parliamentarian in history to go to sleep in his own speech!

Kevin Hooper, larger than life (both physically and metaphorically), was the Member for Archerfield, well known for his colourful turn of phrase and biting discourse. He had been part of the reform group that engineered Federal intervention in 1980. He raised many of the issues of illegal casinos and police corruption long before they were exposed by the Fitzgerald Inquiry. Keith Wright had been the ALP leader during the 1983 election. With the chiselled features of a modern day Adonis he saw himself as God's gift to everything. But he never impressed Hooper who claimed Wright 'had strong biological urges' and famously illustrated this by alleging Wright had a bible in one hand and his dick in the other. This proved prescient as Wright, a Baptist Preacher before entering parliament, was convicted and jailed for nine years in 1993 for rape and indecent dealing with two young girls.

Old guard members were all products of the union movement and the solidarity ethos that came with this. They were palpably suspicious of the newbies, their agendas, and the threat they posed to the status quo. I of course was much more at ease with the new cohort and became lifelong friends with Wayne Goss (until his sad and untimely death at age 63 in 2014), David Hamill and Paul Braddy. We drifted into a new grouping, I think faction was too strong a word, called the Centre-Left, rejecting the 'progressive' militancy of the left and the reactionary obduracy of the old-guard. We liked to think our moderate middle position was more electable.

But Joh was onto us, 'you you socialists you, just like Whitlam' (as I said earlier Whitlam had a long shelf life in Queensland), 'blow the budget to smithereens, you you rack up debt, rack up taxes.' The Left always made fun of Bjelke-Petersen but he had the intrinsic merit of carrying a narrative. No matter what he was talking about he could weave in his message. No matter what question the media asked he gave his own answer: 'Don't you worry about that!' His fulminations were water off a duck's back to some but I heard them loud and clear. I determined I was never going to be party to fulfilling his prognostications for a Queensland Labor Government.

Yet I had to secretly admit that there were some legitimate underpinnings to Joh's prognostications, beyond Whitlam. The fiasco of the State Bank of South Australia (the Bannon ALP Government) and the fiscal chaos of the Cain/Kirner Labor Government in Victoria didn't do much to add to the ALP's reputation nationally for fiscal virtue.

THE FITZGERALD INQUIRY

Premier Sir Johannes Bjelke-Petersen called an election for 1 November 1986, going for his seventh straight election victory, but seeking to once again govern without the support of the despised Liberals. And he did so, with the help of an electoral redistribution which increased the number of members in the Legislative Assembly from 82 to 89, and further entrenched the Bjelke-mander. With virtually the same percentage of the vote as 1983 the National Party increased its representation by eight seats to 49, a commanding majority in its own right. The Libs won two extra seats but did little to reverse the rout of 1983. And Labor, under Neville Warburton as leader, continued its long and undistinguished period of chronic under performance, losing a net two seats.

The electorate of Cairns on the other hand became a little more comfortable. I received a 5.6% swing taking my majority to 56.2% – helped by increasing acceptance of me as the local member, generally good press, and the National Party lapsing back into an acceptance of the political difficulty that was Cairns.

After his totemic victory against all the odds in the 1986 State election Joh had become the superstar of non-Labor politics throughout the land. Hawke and Keating were running the show in Canberra and there was a feeling in the populist Right that John Howard and his National Party deputy Ian Sinclair weren't landing enough punches. The so-called white shoe brigade in Queensland, a motley group of developers, urgers and self-proclaimed millionaires, convinced Joh that he should be running the country. He didn't take long to be convinced. On 1 January 1987 he announced his intention to set sail for Canberra, with a fundamentalist platform based on dismantling Labor's 'socialist' legislation (think medicare), and a 25% flat tax. All hell broke loose in conservative politics.

On 28 February, Queensland National Party under President Bob Sparkes declared:

> That the National Party of Australia (QLD) fully supports the move by Sir Joh Bjelke-Petersen to attain the Prime Ministership… Accordingly, all members of the National Party, in this state, both Parliamentary and Organisational, are fully committed to this cause which can be appropriately styled Joh for PM for Australia's sake.

It was civil war in conservative Australia. The irony was that the Hawke-Keating Government appeared very vulnerable going into the 1987 election due to the ill-fated attempt to introduce an Australia Card, the failed tax summit designed to gain support for Keating's consumption tax, and a declining economy.

Sir Joh's grand assault however proved delusionary. The White Shoe Brigade's promised millions failed to materialise, the Federal Nationals split from Queensland, and Bob Hawke almost took to the booze again in thanksgiving!

Sir Joh slunk back into Queensland, a greatly diminished figure, especially in his own party. I will speak later about overreach, a condition that infects so much of modern society. Maybe Sir Joh started it.

Around about this time, early 1987, Phil Dickie wrote a series of articles in *The Courier Mail* alleging high level police corruption in Queensland. This was followed on 11 May by an ABC *Four Corners* program titled 'The Moonlight State' which sensationally highlighted an epidemic of prostitution (illegal in Queensland) and organised gambling, allegedly flourishing under the patronage of corrupt police. It was like a bomb exploding in the weakened corridors of the National Party. Sir Joh was overseas and his deputy Bill Gunn, in a most un-National Party way, ordered a Commission of Inquiry the day after the *Four Corners* program went to air, a response so foreign to the way Bjelke-Petersen would have responded in his salad days.

Tony Fitzgerald QC was eventually appointed to head the Commission of Inquiry into possible illegal activities and associated police misconduct. The inquiry with limited terms was initially scheduled to last six weeks. It went on for the best part of two years as Fitzgerald used his determination, moral authority and legal skills to continually expand the terms of the inquiry.

By the time he was finished he had exposed systemic political and official corruption, and there was blood everywhere. The two most significant recommendations were the establishment of the Criminal Justice Commission (CJC) and the Electoral and Administrative Review Commission which was to review electoral boundaries.

The need for Freedom of Information legislation was noted, as was the need to review laws relating to public assembly, and guidelines for the disclosure of pecuniary interests of parliamentarians.

The notorious Queensland Police Special Bureau was also disbanded in 1989 following a recommendation by Fitzgerald (Special Branch destroyed its records before Fitzgerald could *subpoena* them).

Three serving politicians (Don Lane, Brian Austin [both ministers] and Leisha Harvey), police Commissioner (Sir) Terry Lewis and a number of other senior policemen were sentenced to jail terms, and the collateral damage was immense. Bjelke-Petersen himself was later charged with perjury but was saved by a deadlocked jury. It was later found that the jury foreman Luke Shaw was a member of the Young Nationals, but special prosecutor Doug Drummond eventually declined to proceed with a retrial on the grounds that Sir Joh, then aged 81, was too old.

My view, even at the time not widely held in the Labor Party, was that Bjelke-Petersen himself was not corrupt. He was God fearing and highly moralistic. But he was naïve in the extreme. By now the National Party was in turmoil. Sir Joh had lost his authority, the Fitzgerald Inquiry was daily wounding them, and internecine warfare was escalating.

Mike Ahern became a pivotal player – young, progressive, tertiary educated and Catholic, all attributes greatly unadmired by Bjelke-Petersen. In November all hell broke loose. Joh sacked Ahern and two other ministers when they refused to support his plan for the world's tallest building at Central Station. But he had lost his authority, and ministers/members were drifting into the Ahern camp. Kevin Lingard, the Member for Fassifern, and Gordon Simpson, the Member for Cooroora, defied the trend and shifted their allegiance back to Bjelke-Petersen. As noted in Tony Koch's opinion piece in the *Courier Mail* on 1 November 1997, following the announcement of my decision to retire from politics, titled 'Role Model for Politicians', it seems I stole the parliamentary show at that time by accusing Lingard and Simpson of 'being the first rats in recorded history to be seen swimming towards the sinking ship.'

A party room meeting (which Sir Joh boycotted) passed a leadership spill motion and Ahern was elected as leader of the National Party. Sir Joh refused to resign as Premier and, for a while, in quintessential Queensland style, the majority National Party had a leader who was not Premier, and Queensland had a Premier who was not party leader. Bjelke-Petersen eventually retired and on 1 December Mike Ahern was sworn in as Queensland Premier.

Phew! But credit where credit is due. Sir Joh, the so-called 'Hillbilly dictator', had served 19 years and won seven consecutive elections as Premier, albeit greatly assisted by serious electoral malapportionment. His uncompromising conservatism, his political longevity, and his leadership of a Government that in later years was proved to be institutionally corrupt, made him one of the best known and most controversial political figures of the twentieth century.

But he wasn't the only larger-than-life controversial politician in Queensland. Russ Hinze, the 'Minister for Everything', was truly colourful. He couldn't see any conflict of interest in owning 167 race horses while being the Minister for Racing. Tom Burns accused him of building, when he was Minister for Main Roads, a four lane highway through the bottle shop of his Oxenford hotel. He responded that if you had the power you would be a mug if you didn't do something for yourself and your electorate – shades of Tammany Hall in New York when 19th century quintessential wheeler and dealer

George W Plunkitt famously said, 'I seen my opportunities and I took 'em!'

As Minister for Police he was apprehended for speeding by an officious young constable. Russ gradually unravelled his corpulent mass from the front seat and spread a map of Queensland across the bonnet. 'This is a bloody big state son,' he said, 'How does (a posting to) Birdsville look?'

In the Government party room they were having a debate about dingoes killing sheep. The Liberal member for Salisbury Rosemary Kyburz said the dingoes should be sterilised. Hinze interjected, 'They are killing the sheep love, not fucking them!'

In a Labor pub in Tom Burns' electorate of Lytton he shouted the bar and sung the *Red Flag* in raucous off-key tones. I doubt this would have impressed his Premier, but then two characters more dissimilar in a moral sense would be hard to find.

Hinze's controversial reputation didn't fit with Ahern's plan to cleanse the image of the National Party either, and he was overlooked for Cabinet, which he didn't take to kindly, making him a focus of discontent. ALP Leader Wayne Goss and Deputy Tom Burns hatched up a plot to see if Hinze could be cajoled into joining Labor to bring Ahern's Government down. Worse still they decided it should be me to put the proposition to Hinze – I guess on the basis that if things went bad, better that the leaders weren't implicated. What could I do – 'Yours is not to reason why, yours is but to do or die!'

Arrangements for the meeting were made and down I went to his home at Oxenford on the Gold Coast in the Opposition Leader's car. I was met by his wife Faye (really his second wife after divorcing his first wife Ruth in 1981. There was a juicy story in the press that the ever generous Russ bought a new Mercedes for Faye but it was delivered to the wrong Mrs Hinze who refused to give it back.)

Faye took me into the house to meet Russ. Wearing only stubby shorts the whole 25 stone of him, hardly rippling muscle, was reclined in a Cleopatra lounge chair, a sight I will carry to my grave – reminiscent somewhat of the pics of the beer belly contest he judged on the Gold Coast when he was cajoled into doffing his own shirt and lining up with the best of them. 'What do you want young DeLacy?' he said. We had a good conversation, and he was certainly pissed-off with Ahern and the Nats, but no deal. Just an experience to be treasured, and in a strange way, I found it very difficult not to like the old bugger. He was later charged with eight counts of having received $520,000 in corrupt payments, but bowel cancer beat the judiciary to him. 'I have been sentenced by the Lord,' he claimed at the time.

Back to the real business. Ahern promised to implement the recommendations from the Fitzgerald Inquiry, 'lock, stock and barrel'. But the continuing revelations from the inquiry, culminating in its release on 3 July 1989, seriously impacted his attempt to reform the Party and rehabilitate its image. Moreover, he wasn't a convincing politician. A Newspoll released after the inquiry had the governing National Party at just 22%. Russel Cooper, much more of a National Party traditionalist than Ahern, toppled him in a party room coup and became leader/Premier on 25 September 1989. But it was all beyond redemption.

1989 was a momentous year: the Berlin wall came down, the tanks rolled into Tiananmen Square, and Labor formed Government in Queensland after thirty-two years in the wilderness. I guess it depends on your perspective which was the most significant.

There was one significant event around that time that deserves a mention. I was working hard in my electorate, aiming to consolidate my position. I never had any great strategy, but I guess it was something any good politician would do: build a team, build a network, the theory being if things turn sour you have supporters you can trust, and preferably in influential positions. Keith Goodwin under my tutelage won the Mayoralty of Cairns at the election in 1988. Keith wasn't really a politician, but he was young, good looking, intelligent and a practised and very good public speaker – a Rotary champion as it were. This was quite a coup and the existing Mayor Ron Davis was uncomfortable with the Labor Party's intrusion into Council politics. To make matters worse I had also pressed Rose Blank to join the Labor team. She was a perfect politician, mid thirties, business woman, intelligent, personable and very easy to like.

Then disaster. A chartered Cessna 500 Aztec Eagle aircraft set out from the Whitsundays, carrying nine Far North Queensland councillors returning from a local government conference at Airlie Beach (plus the pilot Stan Lindgren and Catholic Nun, Sister Nadia Del Popolo who had accepted an invitation of a ride back to Cairns). The flying conditions were appalling with heavy rain, heavy cloud. The plane crashed into Mt Emerald not far from Mareeba on the Atherton Tableland. Eleven people perished, making it one of the Far North's worst air disasters.

Yes you guessed it, both Keith Goodwin and Rose Blank died in the crash. Apart from the tragic personal loss, local government in the North lost two of its truly emerging stars. For a long time I felt guilty, full of terrible remorse as, without my interventions, Keith and Rose would probably be alive today, enjoying life and carving out exemplary careers.

I had one other close confidant in local government while I was Member for Cairns and that was Tom Pyne. Tom lived in the Mulgrave shire (part of which was in my State electorate) and became the Chairman of that Shire in 1979 (he was first elected as a Mulgrave Shire councillor in 1961). When the two shires were amalgamated in 1995 he became Mayor of the Cairns Regional Council. A very popular politician, a large and avuncular man, knockabout, personable, the ultimate politician. What you saw was what you got, no airs and graces, but under that knockabout persona there was a very good politician and administrator. He never ever went close to losing an election, in fact he was seldom challenged. He acted as my campaign manager for a number of my re-election campaigns.

I can remember attending a large fund-raising function with Tom in Cairns. Towards the end of the evening they would have a series of lucky draws donated by the business community. The MC: 'And the next prize is a bungy jump donated by A.J. Hackett. And the winning ticket is (drum roll) … Blue ticket 45. Someone said, 'I've got Blue 46 so it must be here somewhere.' Someone else said, 'I've got Blue 44, it must be you Tom.' Tom said, 'Well it's definitely not here, not anywhere', he said, lifting his plate and emptying his pockets. I had been watching Tom from the other side of the table. As soon as Blue ticket 45 was announced, he slipped the ticket into his mouth and ate it. Not very nutritious, but better than the prospect of a bungy jump, which Tom, because of his good natured and knockabout character would be under pressure to execute, a pretty tough call as he had long ago surrendered his athleticism and slim figure to the demands of public life.

It is my view Tom Pyne was the best local government operative I had the honour to meet, a man of the people, competent and ethical, a trifecta you would wish on them all.

Just to conclude this interlude, I should mention that, despite our frosty beginning, Ron Davis, who spent ten years as Mayor of Cairns prior to Keith Goodwin's accession to the throne, and myself, became good friends (and his good wife Erin), based I think on mutual respect and a commitment to Cairns. He was a very active committee man at the Cairns Amateurs Racing Carnival (Cairns' big social event of the year) for many years and I have been Patron of the Amateurs for many years.

On the subject of Tiananmen Square (mentioned above), there was another special adventure that deserves an outing. In May 1989 Wayne Goss, his legal partner Peter Carne, myself and Goss Chief-of-Staff Kevin Rudd visited China on a good-will/fact finding mission. We arrived in Beijing to an extraordinary spectacle. There were one million students in Tiananmen Square, that massive arena in central Beijing presided over by the portrait of Chairman Mao and bordered by the Great Hall of the People. The students were protesting for democracy and freedom.

It was an extraordinary experience, we had never seen so many people, really the population of Queensland in those days, and an atmosphere full of electricity. As is well known, Kevin Rudd, ex-ambassador to China, could speak mandarin. And he surely could. We spent the whole night, not retiring till dawn, speaking with the students and drinking in the atmosphere, an experience I will never forget. We had long left China when, on 4 June, they gunned down the students in the Avenue of Eternal Peace, an event played out worldwide, and a turning point in the evolution of the Chinese political scene.

Keith DeLacy – shows off his oratorical skills

The Queensland election was held on 2 December and the ALP under Wayne Goss swept into power. The National Party had effectively handed government to Labor on a platter, just as the ALP had done to the Coalition thirty-two years earlier. What goes around comes around as they say, though sometimes you can grow old waiting!

The Labor Party received more than 50% of the primary vote and won 54 seats in the 89 seat assembly – gaining a net 24, bearing in mind the gerrymander was still in place (but not for long). The Nationals suffered a 15% swing against them and went from 49 seats to 27. The poor old Liberals seemed always to be collateral damage, winning only 8 seats altogether. Within six months both Mike Ahern (National Party) and Angus Innes, Leader of the Liberals (and a very capable performer) had headed for the hills. The Coalition had gone from the most formidable political force in Australia to the most disconsolate.

In Cairns my majority increased to 12.9% putting it self-evidently into the safe seat category. For the record, the ALP's Lesley Clarke, riding the wave, defeated Martin Tenni in Barron River. Politics is a tumultuous game.

The sun was shining brightly. On the 7 December I was sworn in as Treasurer and Minister for Regional Development.

That was the easy bit. What next? Treasury and the Treasurer's office occupied Level 12 of the Executive Building, 100 George Street, the seat of power, with the Premier on the top floor Level 15. A large mahogany desk, and deep red leather lounge chairs. People were running everywhere, introducing themselves to me, some to be office staff, and some from the Treasury Department itself. Ken Maley introduced himself as my driver and said he would be down in the corner awaiting my bidding.

When the day was done I looked at all that mahogany and leather and said 'What the f--k am I doing here – a humble little tin miner from the Far North?' There is no training school, no 'how-to' manual, no induction courses on being a minister. Although surrounded by people all day I felt all alone. 'You put your hand up mate, now do the job', I said to myself. I came to learn this about politics: although you are always surrounded by people, and you go nowhere without taking the people with you, it can be the loneliest game in the world.

I had been appointed Shadow Minister for Primary Industries in 1986 (under Neville Warburton), not much competition for this portfolio in a party full of tradies and inner-city bleeding hearts. I was promoted to Shadow Treasurer and Minister for Regional Development when Wayne Goss took over as leader in 1988. That's when I had a hard look at myself.

The National Party was self-immolating, and Wayne Goss was

already presenting as a credible and electable Labor leader after so many years in the wilderness. My insecurities kept nagging me. This was not a natural progression for a boy from the bush. Could I measure up to the challenge of being Treasurer of Queensland. Parliament could be a bit of a sport, at times a blood sport, but Treasurer of Queensland … I did a Bob Hawke and gave up the booze there and then (1989). I think I always had a predisposition for the drink, based in part on my earthy upbringing (you didn't catch up with your mining mates at the school-of-arts!). I suspect there are a few genes lurking there too. And in politics, with so many obligations, I was at times not drinking and wishing I was, or drinking and wishing I wasn't. I had to make the ultimate sacrifice for the pending challenge. I never touched another drop of alcohol for eight years.

Back to the occupation of the Treasurer's office. To this day I don't know how all those staff were appointed, though I came to learn that the Premier's office was greatly involved. The Premier had a very self assured, boyish looking Chief-of-Staff who was certainly not overwhelmed by the challenge. He luxuriated in it: Kevin Rudd, future unlamented Prime Minister of Australia.

At around this time I, and other Ministers, started to hear disturbing rumours about the *Gulag*. It seems there had been something of a purge going on in relation to Departmental heads. In those days senior public servants were tenured rather than contracted, so they could not be summarily terminated and their contracts paid out. The alternative therefore was the *Gulag* – a desk in an out-of-the-way office block and a soul-destroying nothing to do.

The details were unclear and I for one never had the self-confidence or sense of authority to do something about it. I'm not proud of that because, on reflection, it was the first serious assault, in Queensland anyway, on what was known as the Westminster system wherein public servants serve the Government of the day without fear or favour. These days we have a system much more closely paralleling the American system wherein a new government appoints a new clutch of chief-executives. I'm not sure whether this is to ensure sympathetic advice, or to punish the out-going bastards for working with the other mob! It has been referred to as the Washminster system of government, a combination of Washington and Westminster. In either case I think it was a highly retrogressive development and not in the best interests of good governance.

In recent years this trend has spiralled out of control, all at the expense of merit, to be expected if senior departmental people are selected on their political leanings, and their main responsibility is to foster the political fortunes of their minister. The national interest is nowhere to be seen. It also impacts the careers of senior people, totally at the mercy of the political cycle. At the same time ministerial offices are being continuously bloated by advisers, their role theoretically is to politically filter public service advice. In the meantime the upper echelons of the public service are doing this too. You work it out.

Oh for the days of the 'without fear or favour' public sector.

In the case of Kevin Rudd (so-called Dr. Death), I think he just enjoyed the visceral executions!

ALLAN BOND CAME CALLING

I was only sworn in ten minutes when Allan Bond came calling.

Martin Kriewaldt was a partner with law firm Allen & Hemsley (now Allens Linklaters) specialising in corporate law, banking and finance. In 1989 he was consulting to Queensland Treasury with special focus on celebrity entrepreneur Allan Bond and his manoeuvrings in respect of Greenvale/Yabulu nickel project in North Queensland.

He was a brilliant lawyer having received first class honours and the university medal in his law degree. He went on to have an exceptional career as a Non-Executive Director, serving on many Boards as Chairman or Director, too numerous to mention here. He is a Life Fellow of the Australian Institute of Company Directors (AICD). He was President of the Queensland Division of the AICD, and was the recipient of the AICD Queensland Gold medal in 2014. He also Chaired Opera Queensland for many years.

I'll hand over to Martin to give his account of our run-in with Mr Bond (December 2018):

One should not judge a book by its cover. Keith DeLacy demonstrates that one also should not judge a person by their formal CV.

Yet in one incident Keith, personally, made more than $500 million for the tax payers of Queensland. Few politicians have added that kind of value, yet it will appear nowhere on his CV, his Wikipedia page, nor in City Beat.

Queensland was fortunate to have had a man of courage, common sense and practical experience at the controls at exactly that moment when opportunity came knocking. Keith took the opportunity; many would have hesitated, or declined, and lost it.

Keith came into office in 1989 on the back of the election following the Fitzgerald enquiry which found widespread corruption at the highest levels of the Police force and in Cabinet. The National Party had been in Government since 1957, effectively with two leaders over that time.

So what could be expected from a party that had not seen government for 32 years: or for that matter from a man who had been in Parliament just 6 years, with Shadow Treasury responsibility for under 2 years.

One burning matter for Queensland Treasury was the Greenvale project. That matter was to go into a crucial phase just days after the change of government, before the new cabinet had even been selected and sworn in. Things were all the more chaotic as the pilots' strike was then raging, making long distance travel a nightmare.

The Greenvale matter which was to confront the Government was complex and very unusual. To get a sense of the weight of it, it is necessary to give some background.

In the 1960s, two large mining companies Metals Exploration and Freeport Nickel held the licence to mine nickel from a deposit at Greenvale, some 250 kms north-west of Townsville. The initial exploration work indicated that the resource was vast, justifying the building of a railway line to Yabulu, 25 kms north of Townsville, and construction of a refinery at that site to export nickel matte through the Townsville port.

The project was financed through subsidiaries (MEQ and FQN respectively). The funds were advanced by banks but secured only by the project, not the parent companies. What was unusual was that the Queensland Government had agreed to become a guarantor of part of the project financing.

The project floundered through a combination of cost over-runs, low nickel prices and the resource proving to be much smaller than forecast. Accordingly, the banks sought to restructure the loans so that they might recover at least some of their loans. The hundreds of millions put up by MEQ and FQN were effectively lost.

The restructuring was done by deferring interest on the loans except where the companies MEQ and FQN generated enough cash to pay interest. Those lenders who were guaranteed by the State, expected and received their interest from that source, making the State an unsecured lender to the project.

Additionally, much work was done to improve the project economics.

Despite this work, the project rarely paid interest to the lenders and the State stoically paid the guaranteed lenders their interest each quarter.

During this time, Alan Bond (of America's Cup fame and of corporate infamy), through the listed Bond Corporation, took over Metals Exploration. The subsidiary MEQ was worthless and so Bond took it as a personal asset into his private company Dallhold. He also bought FQN from Freeport for a nominal sum.

In a stroke of pure genius, he then bought all of the debt not guaranteed by the State for 10 cents in the dollar – buying some $800 million of debt at face value for just $80 million.

As no interest was actually being paid on the debt, that may seem illogical, but Bond had a greater plan. As MEQ and FQN were in his personal assets (through his private company Dallhold) the losses they were making were all tax deductible, offsetting income Dallhold had from other sources.

In addition to more than $80 million of tax losses annually from this source, Bond got many more millions of losses arising from depreciation of the assets of MEQ and FQN. These losses saved a good deal of tax in his private company.

He then proceeded to acquire the loans guaranteed by the State at a significant discount too. The lenders were only too pleased to be rid of a troublesome loan and Bond was now receiving interest payments from the State on the full face-value of these loans.

It was a structure of pure financial genius: a massive tax loss costing nothing, as the interest did not have to be paid, the depreciation loss not costing actual cash and an incredibly high interest payment from a triple A rated State government on the rest of the loans.

The State was very unhappy at being played for a fool, but there was nothing that could be done legally. It was just an unsecured lender. It had no right to appoint a receiver.

Matters eventually came to a head when the Greenvale ore ran out in the mid 1980s. It meant that the State potentially had to pay the capital on the guaranteed loans and write off all the interest it had paid. However, stopping the Yabulu plant would deprive Bond of his very valuable tax break and many workers their jobs.

Sir Leo Hielscher the Under-Treasurer regarded the money already paid as dead money, but saw the financial benefit to Queensland of the business operating, as well as the deferral of having to pay out the loans. Sir Leo negotiated an arrangement with Bond which secured the continuation of the Yabulu refinery operation (using imported ore) but in return allowed the State to receive a 28% equity in the project if Bond or his companies were ever to get into financial difficulties.

A matter of days after the election, the NAB placed one of Bond's companies into receivership for some infraction.

Treasury had dusted off the agreement made by Sir Leo and was ready should a triggering event occur. The NAB action was an opportunity for the State to change the dynamics of the relationship completely.

It was also an opportunity which had to be grasped immediately. Whilst technically the occurrence of the triggering event meant the right to acquire the asset remained, it would muddy the argument if the right were exercised after the triggering event was cured or removed.

The 64 dollar question – would this new Treasurer, just days in the job, isolated in Cairns from his department and advisors, step up to the mark? His CV did not suggest that any of the legal or corporate machinations would be familiar to him. Tobacco farmer, tin miner, teacher, did not speak strongly of transition to Treasurer, even if they did all start with 'T'

Fortunately, his CV omitted to mention a Ph.D. from the University of Life and Hard Knocks. This is sometimes better than a Harvard MBA.

A briefing paper was quickly prepared by Treasury recommending that notice of the right to acquire the 28% be given immediately and we awaited word from the North? Would it be, as we feared, a request for more briefings or a deferral for wider consultation – with the attendant possibility of loss of the chance?

To the delight of us all, word came back swiftly to serve the notice. It was just as well. A day or so after the notice was served, the receivership was lifted as the necessary funds had been found and paid.

Serving the notice was not the end of the matter, rather the beginning. Bond was very angry that he had lost 28% of the project for what he saw as a temporary, technical breach. He decided that fronting the new Premier and Treasurer in person immediately was what was required to resolve the issue, i.e., have the Government back down.

He was in Perth, but possessing his own jet meant that the

pilot's strike did not affect his ability to travel. Keith tried to stall the meeting by pleading his inability to attend but Bond countered with the very kind offer to detour via Cairns to help Keith's travel plans.

Keith very wisely declined that offer of assistance. It was yet another indicator that here was a canny operator for a Treasurer. Most would have fallen for the allure of a private jet at a sensible hour rather than a noisy RAAF Hercules transport plane overnight arriving a few hours before a very important and difficult meeting.

Keith eventually arrived just one hour before the meeting with Bond. Half of that time was devoted to briefing him and covering any questions he had, clarifying the key arguments and the legal basis for the notice. Keith also wanted to understand why it was commercially and morally right to do this, coming to understand the history of the State involvement.

The next half hour was spent briefing the Premier, Wayne Goss. Wayne was a lawyer so the legal side was less foreign to him, but the commercial side was, of course, completely new.

The meeting with Bond and his advisors in the Executive building was titanic.

Goss was a tall man. Bond was a big fleshy man. They sat opposite each other with Keith to Wayne's right. Bond was a titan of the Australian business world, winner of America's Cup, leader of a sprawling corporate empire which held the world's largest gold company (Bond International Gold – BIG, by name and nature), the Chilean telephone company, Channel 9, Bond Brewing (XXXX, Swan Brewing, etc.) and a man used to getting his own way.

Would Wayne and Keith be up to these negotiations? They would be hard and tough. In an argument with one of Australia's foremost business men, a master deal maker advised by the brightest minds money can buy?

As he hammered his arguments at Wayne, Bond seemed to inflate and expand across the table. Wayne responded with the points prepared by Treasury, but after a time, Wayne would appear to shrink back into his chair as the barrage from Bond and his exceptionally talented support team was fired at him.

After what seemed an eternity, a witty remark from Keith punctured the Bond attack and reinvigorated Wayne. The remark was not scripted by Treasury, but drew on the script and the debate which had gone before. It neatly disposed of the point being laboured at Wayne, but with humour. It was devastating.

Bond was not done though, and he came back. He gradually recovered his bluster and pugnacious approach to Wayne. The process repeated several times – Bond getting on top of Wayne in the argument, expanding across the table, Wayne diminishing and Keith destroying the argument with a pithy and well directed comment from the side.

After several hours of this, Bond eventually left empty handed threatening litigation (commenced but later abandoned). Some additional work was required to extract the interest from Bond's empire but in this Keith was ever ready to assist by appropriate approvals where needed to achieve it.

Queensland Nickel (QNI Ltd), including that 28% interest, was floated on the stock market in 1992, leading to an enormous financial gain to Queensland – in effect more than recouping the interest losses over the years. It was a gain which would probably not have occurred had Keith not given the go-ahead so promptly and would have been lost had Wayne and Keith not held their line in the meeting with Bond.

Queensland Nickel's illustrious history does not end there. The mine at Greenvale was started with great fanfare in 1974 but it eventually proved to be a dud, and ore ceased to be railed to Yabulu in 1993. However the refinery was world class and ore was then imported from overseas (mostly New Caledonia) through the port of Townsville for processing/refining and re-exporting.

But nickel, even more than probably all other resource commodities, was subject to vast fluctuations in price. This meant that the business lurched from grand profitability to grand losses on a regular basis.

South African owned Billiton purchased the refinery in 1997 and subsequently merged with BHP in 2002. Profitability continued its wild fluctuations and, in 2009, larger-than-life Queenslander Clive Palmer made a strategic acquisition, acquiring the whole enterprise for a song.

The rest, as they say, is history. Queensland Nickel was hardly out of the headlines, as Mr Palmer with his irrepressible ego and publicity hunger, seldom drifted by in an anonymous cloud. At one stage when the project was sailing high, Palmer provided $10 million in gifts, including 55 Mercedes Benz cars and 700 overseas holidays, to the workforce for Christmas.

But nickel is nickel. The company went into voluntary administration in 2016 when nickel prices hit a twelve year low, leaving 600 people out of work and $300 million in debt, including $66 million owed to the Commonwealth Government who paid the workers' entitlements.

In 2018, in a show of extraordinary chutzpah, Palmer promoted the prospect that he would stand for the federal seat of Flinders, the electorate in Townsville where most of the sacked and unpaid (at that stage) workers lived. And he launched a $60 million dollar advertising blitz throughout the length and breadth of Australia promoting his (now called) United Australia Party.

In the past tycoons with inflated self-images bought yachts, football teams, race horses or wineries to flout their wealth and suckle their ego. So the intriguing question remains: what was there about a nickel business in far away North Queensland that attracted the entrepreneurial white-shoe wheelers-and-dealers of Australia like Allan Bond and Clive Palmer? And how come Christopher Skase missed out?

LEARNING FROM ADVERSITY.

The first Labor Cabinet meeting for thirty-two years was held on 11 December 1989. But the new parliament never got into full swing until late February/March 1990 – we had a lot to learn.

Unfortunately it seems I was a slow learner.

In the Address-and-Reply debate on 7 March, a set piece debate wherein honourable members make speeches theoretically in response to the Governor's opening address to a new parliament. I, as Treasurer, used the occasion to make a lengthy, and very critical, attack on the Queensland economy and the fiscal position inherited from the National Party. I said, amongst many other things, that Queenslanders were the victim of three great myths:

> The balanced budget myth;
> The low debt myth;
> The strong investment myth.

It bombed as somehow deep down I knew it would. You see it was not written by me, my office, or Treasury. It came as a tablet from above. Probably written by some school boy staffer imported from NSW Labor working in the more venerable office of the bureaucratic maestro. Deep down I knew it was wrong. There were so many things for which one could criticise the Bjelke-Petersen Government, but fiscal profligacy was not one of them.

Mike Ahern, ex-undistinguished Premier, made the best speech of his parliamentary career the next day completely demolishing my treatise, lambasting 'a boy on a man's errand':

> I have no doubt that a great job economically has been done in this State. No cowboy, jackeroo Treasurer can disprove that, no matter what figures he contrives. No-one can point a finger of scorn at the previous Government's long – over decades – economic record in regard to low taxation, growth and management of the debt. All those things were achieved according to the best rules in the textbooks. Today, no two-bit lad with no knowledge can discredit that record. The facts are there, and the world knows them.

The press fall-out was disastrous. Although it was traditional for new Governments to beat-up on their predecessors it still had to have a ring of verisimilitude. I was bleeding, substantially diminished, not only in the eyes of my opponents and the press gallery, but no doubt in the eyes of my colleagues too, though I am happy to say there were no overt negative recriminations.

1989 The first Labor Cabinet meeting in Queensland for 32 years
(Treasurer DeLacy RHS, opposite Premier Goss)

These things have a habit of feeding on themselves as people see you through that particular lens. Of course it is a challenge to maintain self-confidence, which in itself is performance limiting. They say the hardest shot in golf is the next one after a shank!

What to do? Such an empty feeling. There was only one way – *get up, dress up, front up,* my philosophy for life. They say life is 10% what happens to you, and 90% how you respond. I determined hard work and discipline was the way, the only way, get across the brief, keep fronting up, keep performing; there was no short cut.

And the lesson: believe in yourself, be yourself and trust yourself. I should never have made that speech, I didn't believe in it. Not a very persuasive argument in the self-justification stakes, but a very valuable lesson in life. Be yourself, live your values, challenge your beliefs but don't abrogate them.

I had learned a very valuable life lesson. At the same time, and perhaps more importantly, I gradually regained respect. At the end of the 1994 parliamentary year, Tony Koch and Peter Morley, the two crusty old senior political reporters for the *Courier Mail*, in their football-like, end-of-year ratings of the political play-makers, were able to give me 9+/10, writing:

> This failed tobacco farmer and former tin miner, after a shaky start, is in total control of the State's coffers. Lives by the motto that fiscal responsibility is an everyday imperative, not just a Budget-day buzzword. Is unchallenged in Parliament.

Reflecting, with the benefit of time, a further truism lay embedded in this priceless life lesson. Authenticity is the most valuable piece of luggage you can hump through life, in politics, in business, in the whole of life. Authenticity means being yourself, living life to your own values.

Though, as I pondered authenticity, I couldn't help but think of Russ Hinze. He was authentic, that was why 'I couldn't help liking the old bugger'. But his value system didn't measure up. So life was more than authenticity. The values on which you live your life, and base your authenticity, must also have an ethical dimension.

SIR LEO HIELSCHER.

John Hall was the Under-Treasurer (Head of Treasury) when government changed hands on 2 December 1989. I never really got to know him as he was a *gulag* victim. Henry Smerdon was appointed Under-Treasurer and I established a very good relationship with him, as indeed I did with the rest of Treasury.

Treasury was the pre-eminent department in the Queensland public sector. This was no doubt due to the long reign of Sir Leo Hielscher as Under-Treasurer, both because of his program of recruiting tertiary educated quality graduates into the Department, and because of his influence and power with governments. In the end, and during our time, very little happened without Treasury's imprimatur.

Stephen Rochester, ex-CEO of the Queensland Treasury Corporation, tells the story that when he was recruited into Treasury, Sir Leo's first words to him were: 'Your job is to provide me with the best possible advice and my job is to manage the politics!'

Manage it he did. Perhaps the apocryphal story of the way he managed Sir Joh best sums it up. Joh had a manic obsession with planes in general and the government jet in particular, and indeed pilot Beryl Young was often considered one of his most influential advisors. Sir Leo carried around a full brochure of the latest model of the right sized aeroplane, and when Joh got stroppy Sir Leo would magically produce the brochure from his back pocket and say, 'Before we get into that Mr Premier, I happen to have this info on a possible new Government jet.' And that was that.

Sir Leo is a Queensland legend. He is credited with transforming Queensland from a small backward economy into something of a growing powerhouse by utilising a focused investment strategy and a powerful fiscal position.

Apart from all that he was a good bloke, with an engaging personality which was difficult to resist. I can remember when I first met him. He visited me at Treasury to explain the role of the Queensland Treasury Corporation of which he was now chairman, and what he saw as my role going forward. When time was up he looked at his watch and explained that it was time to do the Russian General. This mystified me. 'What do you mean Russian General?' I asked. 'Pissinoff,' he said. Hardly the language of a Knight of the Realm, but indicative of the common touch and sense of fun.

He told me you always knew you'd done a good deal if both sides were equally unhappy!

The massive Gateway Bridge across the Brisbane River, out near the Brisbane airport, is now called the Sir Leo Hielscher Bridge in his honour.

Sir Leo retired as Under-Treasurer on 30 April 1988, the day Expo '88 in Brisbane opened, after forty-six years in the public service. But he retired into the position of Chairman of the Queensland Treasury Corporation, a newly established centralised borrower which managed the debt of all Queensland government entities, including the state, Local authorities and government owned corporations.

In this capacity I came to know Leo well, travelling with him often to overseas capital markets promoting the fiscal virtues of Queensland. I learned plenty from him also, and came to consider him a close friend. Sir Leo had this to say about me in March 2019:

> The Honourable Keith De Lacy. What an achiever. What a friend …
>
> Keith De Lacy has had a remarkable and one of the most extensive and successful careers of any person I know. Furthermore, he is never satisfied with being just associated with all of his varied achievements, he performs as the Chairman or President of the many organisations which he has served.
>
> *He commenced his working life with a pick and shovel job at Mt Isa mines, but while there (sic), he authored his first book* Blood stains the wattle.
>
> In politics, he was not content on the backbench – he was front and centre as the Treasurer of Queensland. And he went on to be Chairman and/or Director of a whole range of prestigious organisations both commercial and not-for-profit. His life has been a very busy one indeed.
>
> My association with Keith commenced when he was appointed Queensland Treasurer of the first Labor government in Queensland after his Party had been in opposition for over 30 years.
>
> The permanent senior staff of Queensland Treasury had some fear that after such a long time out of office, the new government would be wanting to spend up big and perhaps diminish the fiscal position of the State that we had built up over the years.
>
> This was not to be. Keith very quickly assessed the State's fiscal strength and the philosophy that got us there and defended it to the hilt. He created his own mantra of the 'fiscal trilogy' (low-tax state, fully funded liabilities including superannuation, and only borrowing for assets which can generate income sufficient to service the debt) which preserved and strengthened our hard earned fiscal position. When

Keith arrived in Treasury, Queensland had a triple A (AAA) credit rating from the international rating agencies. When he handed in his commission as Queensland Treasurer, we had a very much strengthened AAA rating.

It had been a hard fight. He didn't shirk it and he won – our budgets were balanced, our AAA credit rating was preserved and our debt level was held to a very manageable $22 billion (including Local Government and GOC's). The importance of this fiscal achievement should be noted as with a AAA rating, not only is it easier to raise the funds needed but this can be done at a much cheaper interest rate (an interest saving of up to 0.5% per annum on a debt of $22 billion is a saving in dollar terms of $110 million per annum).

It was in the raising of these monies in the financial markets of the world that I got to know Keith very well. We were raising around half of our annual requirement from overseas and it was essential that we presented to the international bankers and investors in their offices with regular updates of Queensland's good story.

As a trump card we also had with us in a hands-on leading capacity, the Treasurer of the Queensland Government. Keith excelled in this role and his presence and performance clinched many good deals for the benefit of Queensland and Queenslanders.

From a personal point of view, this overseas exercise cost many hours in aeroplanes, many hours of free time into the evening, all of which gave us plenty of time to discuss everything from football to the different lifestyles and understandings of the people we were meeting, to the present and future plans we had for Queensland Treasury Corporation and other very varied ideas, policies, idiosyncrasies of each other and the like.

Keith has a down to earth sense of humour. He looked after his good health – jogging instead of walking. I tried to convince him that walkers saw more of what was around them; other walkers were smilers and greeters with a friendly 'bonjour' while joggers seem to be hurting. He continues his morning jog today.

His favourite beverage is champagne and he blames me for enticing him away from his teetotaller lifestyle with the occasional glass of cold French champagne. This day-in-day-out relationship became the foundation of a friendship that has lasted 30 odd years. What a friend.'

Sir Leo won in the end, I no longer run and am a very committed walker, though my advancing age may have had something to do with his victory.

Fiscal prudence was going to be a very big challenge for the new Government, as it always is for a Labor government. Labor priority is social policy. And after more than thirty years in Opposition to an ultra-conservative government this priority was manifest.

I could see the fiscal precipice ahead with all these forces lining up. On top of this we had a reputation for financial incompetence even before we could demonstrate it. As I pointed out before, the spectra of Whitlam, Jim Cairns, Rex Connor hung daily over us – Bjelke-Petersen made sure it did. Some of the other Labor states didn't help either. Russell Cooper, as Leader of the Opposition said in the Address-and-Reply speech in March 1990:

> All honourable members would be aware that Mr Goss is a great fan of John Bannon and John Cain. They would also be aware that Victoria and South Australia are broke.

I think I have always had an old-fashioned attitude towards spending and financial management. My upbringing it seems inculcated in me what is sometimes referred to as the Protestant Ethic of thrift and hard work. I can remember my wife saying to me, in recent years, 'You know we can actually afford a new *kleenex* tissue every single day.' I was so allergic to waste that I had the habit of using a tissue for a week or two till it was a little hard ball. I've always found it difficult to spend my own money. I didn't find it easier to spend other people's money, an affliction it seems, which is not too widespread.

I think I learned early that debt doesn't give you more to spend, all it does is bring spending forward and, of course, passes the bill to the future. In the whole scheme of things it actually gives you less to spend because of the costs of borrowing.

Be that as it may, people say to me these days that this is not the Labor way; how could you be a Labor person with views like that? My response is that Labor doesn't have to be irresponsible with spending, it is a choice. I shared the Labor social conscience, with a genuine concern for the less-well-off and a long term goal of a fairer society. It is the means to this end where I increasingly differ from many in the Labor Party.

I believe that you deliver on your social policy commitments through efficient spending and efficient delivery of programs (rigid planning and cost/benefit analyses), well ordered priorities, a strong economy (which increases revenue) and a strong balance sheet, as opposed to splurging today and paying tomorrow, increasing taxes (which weakens the economy) and seeking to please the undeserving entitlement-seekers lining up outside the door. In the Labor Party, in fact in politics generally, there has always been too much of a tendency to measure social policy success by counting inputs rather than assessing outcomes, in education, for example, focusing on dollars spent, or class sizes, or staff-student ratios, no matter if the kids come out dumber.

As I will continue to say, I don't believe I have ever changed my values, but I have progressively over my lifetime changed the policy prescriptions needed to realise these values.

In my view, the Goss Government did deliver on its social priorities while still maintaining a level of fiscal discipline unusual in Australia. In an anniversary function speech I made on 2 December 1999 (after I had left parliament) I admitted that there was a bit of a perception around these days that we as a Government had drifted away from our roots:

> Well I make no apology for the fact that we continually stressed good financial management. You have to understand the environment in which we were operating. But people shouldn't lose sight of our real social achievements, we met our other obligations too. In six years we more than doubled spending for Health, almost doubled it for Education, quadrupled it for the Environment and for Family Services and so on. And during those six years Queensland

created almost half of all new jobs in Australia. We never finished the revolution, but we sure got it off to a good start.

My apologies for breaking my own cardinal rule and spruiking inputs as a measure of social policy performance!

SPIRALLING QUEENSLAND DEBT

We developed the Trilogy, a budget management tool designed to repel the wanton spenders: (i) fully fund long term liabilities such as public sector superannuation; (ii) fund social capital assets such as schools and hospitals from recurrent revenues and only borrow for commercial assets which can service their own debt; (iii) maintain Queensland as the low tax state. We promoted this as a government mantra, surprisingly accepted by the whole team. As they say, every galah in the pet-shop was singing the tune.

It was very successful. I can remember in 1994 Michael Roche, my Chief-of-staff at the time, in celebration mode, cavorting through Treasury offices with half a bottle of red wine in one hand and the other poised in high-five mode, proclaiming in his best Martin Luther-King accent, 'Queensland, net-debt free, free at last, free at last!' We had just officially passed the point where our cash assets were larger than our cash liabilities, i.e., our debt. It was worth celebrating as few jurisdictions around the globe have been able to claim such. And when I talk about cash assets I mean cash, I am not counting other State Government assets on our balance sheet like schools, hospitals, office buildings, railways, energy companies and so on. To the extent that we had debt at all, it belonged to the Government Owned Corporations (GOCs) which serviced this debt from their own revenue.

One further collateral benefit from this interlude of fiscal rectitude was that we removed the stain on Labor Governments generally. As Gene Tunny says in his excellent book *Beautiful One Day Broke the Next*:

> Arguably, by showing that a Labor Government can successfully manage public finances, the Goss Government made it easier for future Labor governments, which were under less suspicion of fiscal mischief.

With the benefit of hindsight I'm not so sure this was in the long term national interest.

Where did it all go so horribly wrong? Within twenty years Queensland had lost its triple A credit rating, net debt had soared to circa $40 billion, gross debt to circa $80 billion, and Queensland's fiscal performance compared to other states had deteriorated dramatically – hence Tunny's book, the title of which was a play based on well known tourism promotion campaign, *Queensland, Beautiful one day, Perfect the next*, but which in this instance referred to Queensland's fiscal and economic decline. Whilst I had by this time cantered off into the sunset, I think it is worth while trying to identify just where it all went so wrong. In this context I owe some debt to Gene Tunny for his major research project analysing and comparing state budgets and fiscal performance over a forty year period.

By and large, under the Borbidge/Sheldon administration (1996-1998) and Beattie/Hamill (1998-2001) fiscal performance remained sound. After all in Queensland it had become an article of faith. It would take a determined and capable assault to breach the fortress.

Terry Mackenroth became Beattie's Treasurer following Hamill's retirement at the February 2001 election. A formidable assault team had been assembled.

There had been some softening of the Trilogy principles by David Hamill, but he largely held the line. In 1999 Beattie introduced the *Charter of Social and Fiscal Responsibility*, which read well but crucially placed *Social* before *Fiscal* in terms of responsibility. In delivering the 1999 budget (Treasurer Hamill had been temporarily sidelined) Beattie stressed the social challenge, spruiked the Smart State big spending agenda and not so subtly distanced his administration from the rigid budgetary principles of the Goss Government.

However Beattie and Mackenroth were able to dine out on the resources boom, producing three record surpluses, to the extent that Beattie labelled Mackenroth as Queensland's best ever Treasurer. But they were planting the incendiary devices for the explosion to come.

Surpluses notwithstanding, they started building boom-time revenue into recurrent spending which by definition represents a structural deficit. It is so difficult to reverse a spending regime based on rivers of gold when those rivers run dry.

On top of this, in 2004-5 the Beattie Government was confronted by three crises, in electricity, health and water. The response to these crises represented the incendiary devices referred to above.

In 2004 there was a major electricity failure, 120,000 households without power. The response, the proverbial inquiry and a very large spending commitment to upgrade the distribution system.

In 2005 a health crisis, kicked off by the Jayant Patel shenanigans at the Bundaberg Hospital pointing to a range of shortcomings. The response, two inquiries resulting in the ambitious and very expensive *Health Action Plan* involving 'a major transformation and renewal of Queensland's public health system'.

Then the millennial drought, with dam levels dangerously low. By now the global warming mantra was in full swing with Tim Flannery from the Climate Commission declaring drought was the new normal and the dams would never fill again. Beattie declared a water supply state-of-emergency and committed billions to a desalination plant at Tugun, which remains effectively a white elephant to this day, a monument to the folly of allowing self-appointed climate change activists with an agenda, but no skin in the game, to determine government policy.

Anna Bligh, first as Treasurer (2006–7) and then as Premier (2007-12) presided over the explosions which followed Beattie's time bombs, unable, and arguably ill-equipped, to deal with the challenge, exacerbated as it was by the Global Financial Crisis and a number of natural disasters. In February 2009 rating agency S&P downgraded Queensland's much cherished triple A credit rating.

How the mighty had fallen.

New Premier Campbell Newman and Treasurer Tim Nicholls (2012-15) made a valiant, if ham-fisted attempt to reverse the slide. They were rewarded for their platform of fiscal responsibility by being booted out of Government, worryingly a measure of the general public's concern about debt. And Annastacia Palaszczuk and her

Treasurer Curtis Pitt, according to Gene Tunny, would 'learn to stop worrying and love the debt.'

Then, of course, the final debasement, the second Palaszczuk Government, with a Treasurer presiding over massive debt, representing a green electorate in inner city Brisbane, where survival meant toeing the Green line: anti-coal (our biggest export and revenue generator), anti-mining and anti-economic just about everything. With some clever footwork a coal industry in the Galilee Basin could have been nurtured producing upwards of sixty million tonnes of coal per annum, generating thousands of regional jobs and billions of dollars in royalties, a royalty stream which could have been used to fund the Treasurer's favoured project, the (unfunded) cross river rail, then the Olympic Games, and so on, while simultaneously reducing debt.

If only. Imagine Sir Leo Hielscher with this opportunity in the halcyon days!

As I have said in a dozen speeches over the years, and this refers equally to the Commonwealth, another shock will come, whether it comes from God, or nature, or human perfidy, or the international economy, or wherever, and the only defence is a strong balance sheet. Queensland, and for that matter the Commonwealth, now have no defence, as they stand vulnerable before the slings and arrows of outrageous fortune. (Note, this was written before the COVID19 pandemic, but nicely makes my point).

The timeless lesson is so clear: debt doesn't give you more money to spend, it just brings spending forward. The current debt is seriously impacting present day spending as debt servicing costs eat deeply into the budget. And it constitutes a serious violation of Edmund Burke's so-called social contract between those who are dead, those who are living and those yet to be born.

How I despair at the lack of real focus on debt in current political conversations and election campaigns.

WAYNE GOSS, PREMIER

On reflection, the six years and three months I served as Treasurer of Queensland was a fantastic experience. It was a time of many challenges, interesting ventures, many learnings, personal fulfilment, and hard work. I was now largely Brisbane-based luxuriating in an elementary bedroom in the Parliamentary Annexe and my office in the Executive building. I tried to return to Cairns each Friday as one still had to occasionally represent one's electorate and reacquaint with the family. I religiously travelled to Brisbane each Sunday afternoon and spent until the wee hours in the Executive building trawling through the cabinet papers – the Treasurer had to be across every submission no matter from where it emanated, and very often a plan to respond to an unapproved departmental excursion. Early next morning a meeting with the Under-Treasurer to again go through the papers, and then with the Premier to ensure we were on the same page on the big issues, plus Cabinet every Monday at 9am sharp.

I greatly enjoyed working with Wayne Goss. He was a leader who led from the front, greatly respected by the whole team, even by the so-called hard guys. Bob Gibbs was supposed to have said, in a weak moment, that he would die for Goss. Then realising what he had said quickly qualified it, 'Let me re-phrase that, I would kill for Goss!'

Goss was a hard task master, very orderly, very focused, very articulate and of course, incredibly capable. Cabinet was very disciplined under his watch, and to a certain extent so was parliament. Once, a commitment in Canberra required him to seek leave from the hurly burly of State Parliament for a day. The parliamentary discipline evaporated like the early morning dew, a bit like primary school kids when the teacher walks out. Bob Gibbs made some unflattering comparisons between Joan Sheldon and a German Shepherd dog. Deputy Premier Tom Burns went recidivistic reverting back to the Tom we knew and loved. Everyone was gesticulating and shouting – chaos personified.

Goss read all about it in the *Courier Mail*. I'll never forget him coming into the Chamber the next day and tapping both Burns and Gibbs on the shoulder and saying in that deceptively polite rasping voice he sometimes used: 'Could I see you two in my office for a moment please.' Apparently Burns, Deputy Premier, twenty years Goss's senior and with an impeccable Labor pedigree, as soon as they were inside, blurted out, 'It was all Gibbsy's fault!'

Premier and Treasurer: Wayne Goss and Keith DeLacy

Robbie Schwarten, the Minister for Housing, used to refer to Goss as the headmaster, and I understand why.

He had an acerbic sense of humour, though he did come across as a little aloof and he was fiercely competitive. I was a regular jogger, and I went for a 10k run with him late one evening. Never again, I said. He couldn't just jog along and enjoy the breeze, he had to win.

He was invited to open the new Paradise Palms Golf course in Cairns, built by Japanese Developer Daikyo. The ceremony involved Wayne, who was not a golfer, teeing off on the first hole. I looked at him; he couldn't just enjoy it as good fun, as perhaps Peter Beattie may have done. His knuckles were white as he clutched the club and the veins were sticking out on his forehead. He unleashed a mighty swing and the ball trickled off the front of the tee into the water hazard.

I was very close to him and I like to think we were a good team. But I didn't always win. Matt Foley, Attorney-General and Minister for the Arts, tells the story that he took a submission to Cabinet for the establishment of a Gallery of Modern Art at South Bank in Brisbane. He said he argued against it with considerable vigour, citing his two (tiresome) favourites: where was the money coming from and, speaking as a regional Queenslander, why was everything going to Brisbane? Wayne listened respectfully to the whole debate and finally said, 'I think we need a Gallery of Modern Art.' So we have this very fine facility, referred to as GOMA, in Brisbane today.

We remained good friends, and as I said before, enjoying a regular coffee together until his untimely death in 2014 at age sixty-three.

A question from left field. People have asked me how I dealt with the stain of communism: was it used as a weapon against me, was it a major negative? After all, in politics it is not uncommon to build a mountain out of a mole-hill. Surprisingly it didn't raise its head too often, perhaps because I was the most unlikely communist you would expect to find while trawling through the corridors of power!

DAWSON PETIE

Dawson Petie was the General Secretary of the Queensland Council of Unions from 1991-1995, Queensland's peak union body. He grew out of the union movement having served time as State Secretary of the Finance Sector Union in both NSW and Queensland.

He went on to have a meritorious career as both an Executive and Non-Executive Director. Over the years he has served as Chairman of Uniting Care Queensland and Indue Ltd. He has been a Director of QIC, Queensland Rail and Mandis Roberts. At the time of writing he serving on the Queensland Council of the AICD. Dawson Petie offered these thoughts in 2020:

> Yearning for change from the decades of repressive and ultra-conservative years of National/Liberal Party governments in Queensland, I and fellow Labor supporters working on successive campaigns endured disappointment after disappointment. We hoped that under the leadership of decent and capable people like Ed Casey and Nev Warburton the time for change had come but more disappointment followed the early hope of these campaigns.

When I met the next Opposition Leader, Wayne Goss, at the Australian Workers Union Queensland Branch State Conference, it seemed that any hope of ever winning government in Queensland was futile. But change did finally come. Goss was impressive and fitted the mould of other successful State Labor leaders – Don Dunstan, John Cain, Neville Wran, Peter Dowding. All were lawyers, articulate, middle-class and with attractive wide-spread electoral appeal.

However, the dominance of the unions on the Labor Party made it difficult for this new breed of Labor leaders to effectively manage these complex power relationships with Labor in government. Goss was no different and seemed uncomfortable in union gatherings. His inter-state counterparts often relied on a Deputy/senior minister who could capably assist with union relationships e.g., Jack Ferguson Deputy to Wran. Ferguson had been a building union organiser.

Undoubtedly, the success of the Goss Government was anchored by the support of his Treasurer, Keith DeLacy. DeLacy was similar to Ferguson with hard-graft work experience and the ability to relate well with unions and their members. On a personal level, I immediately felt at ease with Keith and appreciated his open and honest 'no bullshit' approach.

Much has been written about Keith's work ethic and ability which I fully endorse. He quickly won widespread respect within Government and the business community. The Goss Government's significant and wide-spread reforms are a matter of public record but it is easy to gloss over the strength of their economic management. DeLacy lead a highly disciplined Treasury team who developed a prudent, clear and consistent direction for the State's finances. An example is the *Economic Strategy 1992 Queensland Leading State* policy.

Trying to balance the often competing interests of a reformist Labor Government and the union movement is challenging. One mechanism to help manage this was the Queensland Labor Advisory Council. This forum brought together the leaders of the Queensland Council of Unions, AWU, ALP and

Goss and De Lacy. The glue in these often difficult meetings was DeLacy. My impression was that this forum was more of an irritation for Goss where DeLacy sought to gain maximum benefit from these important interactions. Discussions often continued over a beer with DeLacy after the formal proceedings concluded.

The Labor Party and the ACTU face similar challenges at a national level. Writing about these challenges Ray Markey (Macquarie University) said 'The Australian Labor Advisory Council (ALAC), which previously brought Labor and ACTU leaders together for policy discussion, has been dormant for some years; its revival could be an important step in this direction.'

Despite some serious disagreements, the relationship between the Goss Government and the union movement was open and constructive and contributed to the extensive reform agenda driven by the Government. Key to this was QLAC and the personal relationships fostered by De Lacy with the unions.

Keith and I have followed similar non-executive director career paths following our time with the labour movement. I am pleased that this has allowed us to maintain our personal relationship forged during the years of the Goss Government. I am equally impressed by his significant contribution in government as his continuing outstanding contribution in the private sector. The latter was recognised by the ultimate recognition from his peers with the Australian Institute of Company Directors Gold Medal Award in 2019.

THE REFORM OF NON-BANK FINANCIAL INSTITUTIONS (NBFIs)

Over the years, as Treasurer I had primary responsibility for the delivery of a number of policies with far reaching consequences for the people of Queensland, policies like the national regulatory reform of Non-Bank-Financial-Institutions (NBFIs), the reform of Government Owned Corporations, the introduction of casinos in Brisbane and Cairns, the introduction of Poker machines, and the redevelopment of the Gabba Cricket ground, all character building challenges.

The late 1980s and early 1990s exposed serious shortcomings in the regulation of NBFIs nationwide. These comprised state-based building societies, friendly societies, credit unions and co-operative housing societies, all of which operated under state legislation and regulatory supervision.

In 1990, a number of building societies in Victoria collapsed with debts of almost $2 billion. These included the Pyramid, Geelong, and Countrywide Building Societies. Ultimately, depositors were bailed out by the Victorian Government, funded by a 3 cents per litre levy on fuel.

Around the same time, the State Bank of Victoria (SBV) collapsed with $1.5 billion of losses by its wholly owned merchant banking subsidiary, Tricontinental. The SBV group was rescued by the Commonwealth Bank of Australia (CBA) which acquired it in 1990, and also ended up acquiring the State Bank of South Australia.

Each of these institutions was supervised by a state-based regulator. In Queensland, the regulatory supervision was provided by a small unit within the Department of Justice. In this context, I asked Treasury to establish a commission of inquiry (the Brady Committee) to examine the regulation of non-bank financial institutions in Queensland. The fundamental principle recommended by the Brady Committee was that supervision of NBFIs be undertaken by an organisation at arm's length from government, effectively based on the Reserve Bank system.

We began a push for national reform and, through the Ministerial Council comprising Federal, State and Territory Treasurers, successfully advocated for a uniform national scheme.

With Queensland driving the reforms, the enabling legislation (the *Financial Institutions Act*) for deposit-taking NBFIs was passed by the Queensland Parliament and adopted by all other States and Territories through *Application of laws* legislation. The Act established a new regulatory regime and provided for a national regulator, the Australian Financial Institutions Commission (AFIC) as well as State-based regulators in each State and Territory. In May 1992, the Queensland Parliament also passed the *AFIC Act* which established the headquarters in Queensland as we were instrumental in driving the reform.

Pivotal to these wide-ranging national reforms was the drive and policy leadership of Queensland which had a longer term objective of transitioning to a Federal regime based on Commonwealth Government legislation and the eventual displacement of the state-based regulators. This did occur in 1998 with the establishment of the Australian Prudential Regulatory Authority (APRA) to oversee banks, insurance companies and deposit-taking NBFIs.

The whole process represented a major reform, based on modern prudential supervisory principles, almost completely authored by Queensland, to the benefit of the whole nation.

GOVERNMENT OWNED CORPORATIONS

One of the determining factors that pointed me towards the director-world on retirement from politics was my role in shepherding through Cabinet/State parliament the *Government Owned Corporations (GOC) Act* in 1993, aimed at modernising the governance and accountability of GOCs in Queensland. It was a foreign language to most members of parliament, but we persevered finally delivering comprehensive legislation based on the principles of management autonomy, clarity of objectives, strict accountability for performance and competitive neutrality. This formed the basis for major reform of public utilities during the term of our Government.

Of course, as Treasurer and responsible Minister I was a shareholding Minister of all Queensland GOCs. I was almost anal in my determination to appoint competent and independent directors. I learnt a lot from some of these people, and became good friends with many of them. Jim Kennedy is an example. He was one of Australia's most distinguished company directors. His Board appointments included the Australian Stock Exchange, GWA International Ltd, Queensland Investment Corporation and the Commonwealth

Bank. He was named a Queensland Great in 2006 by then Premier Peter Beattie for his outstanding contribution to Queensland's accounting, banking and finance, business and tourism industries. He was also inducted into the Business Leaders Hall of Fame in 2009. Jim is known for his major achievements in the tourism industry, including the establishment of the Queensland Tourist and Travel Corporation.

Jim Kennedy recalled the following in 2019:

> When Wayne Goss became Premier of Queensland, he appointed the Member for Cairns, Keith DeLacy, as Queensland treasurer in his first cabinet.
>
> At that time I was chairman of 'the Queensland Investment Advisory Board', which had been established by a former premier Mike Ahern, to attempt to recover nearly half a billion dollars that had been invested by the former Government of Sir Joh Bjelke-Petersen, into a number of Queensland companies. All these high profile Queensland based, public companies, shortly afterwards went into liquidation, owing the Queensland taxpayers hundreds of millions of dollars. It was strange that the Queensland Government had put taxpayers money into this 'investment', nor do I think did the public.
>
> The new premier Mike Ahern was outraged when he discovered the extent of the potential losses and phoned me personally for my help. The companies into which the government money had been invested were: Ariadne Ltd, headed up by Bruce Judge; Quintex Ltd headed up by Christopher Skase; Kern Corporation headed up by Ron Paul; and a start-up called Southern Cross Airlines – which never got off the ground.
>
> Premier Mike Ahern asked me to put together a board to assist in trying to retrieve some of the money. We did all we could, but had little success. The companies all went broke and shut down.
>
> I appointed Treasury official Ian Macoun to work with us. He was a highly qualified executive and joined the Kern Corpo-

ration Board, to see what if anything could be done to save that company. He was an invaluable recruitment. I don't think the public or the media had any knowledge of these matters and ultimately most of the funds were lost and the companies were delisted and/or closed down.

In the meantime, Wayne Goss won the election and one of his first appointments was Keith DeLacy as the new treasurer. DeLacy is a competent and intelligent person and has had plenty of prior experience in public affairs in North Queensland. He was an excellent appointment as Treasurer.

I clearly remember my first meeting with Keith. Because of the change in the government, every member of the advisory committee had agreed to resign, so I asked the new Treasurer to come to the meeting and to discuss what should happen in the future with the advisory committee. We all felt it was the right thing to do to offer our resignation, having been appointed by a former Government. To my surprise, Keith asked us to continue on and we did, with his continuing help and support.

He was an excellent Minister and Treasurer and ultimately, we became good friends and remain so to this day. After a time we realised that we could no longer do much about the lost millions and suggested to Keith that none of us were happy working under treasury staff in an advisory role in financial matters. Public Servants are best involved in administration and government matters and advice, so after discussion with DeLacy and Premier Goss, it was decided to form a permanent Government investment organisation with the Premier and Treasurer as the two shareholding ministers, and with a refreshed board and staff. We recruited extensively and former Treasury official Ian Macoun became CEO and Laurie Brindle, also from Treasury, established our property portfolio which has been a very successful division of what is now known as QIC. Keith asked me to help draw up an act of parliament to establish a government owned investment organisation, free of government interference, with the government appointing its Chair and Board.

The Queensland Investment Corporation was then born and continues to remain an important part of the Queensland Government. I became the first Chairman of QIC and retired after 12 years. The *QIC Act* specifically prohibits anyone, including members of parliament, to in any way, try to influence investment decisions by the QIC. The QIC has always been happy to work with its shareholding ministers for the benefit of Queensland and Queenslanders.

Keith is now out of politics, but he then had another successful career, as a public company director and was chairman of the Australian Institute of Company Directors in Queensland.

We need more Keith DeLacys in the Queensland Government.

Seems a bit of crony capitalism was running rampant for a while!

What GOCs needed was deeply embedded cultural reform, not just legislated technical reform. If I was asked a question as shareholding minister relating to a particular GOC, I always responded that I would contact the Chairman and revert back. Sometimes there would be excitable accusations that I was passing the buck. I surely was. You don't have an independent Board with full management autonomy and accountability and then muscle into their territory. My simple counter response was that you wouldn't want a politician running the show would you?

But the reform didn't endure. I am eternally disappointed at the bastardisation of these principles over time by later governments, clueless as to their substance and value; to see a shareholding Minister fronting the media to explain the shortcomings of Queensland Rail for instance, or to take credit for some reform. Being the public spokesperson is the responsibility of the Chairman and/or the CEO as this emphasises independence and accountability – principles so poorly understood these days.

As for stacking the Board with cronies… no wonder some ministers feel the need to answer on their behalf!

INTELLECTUAL HORSEPOWER

It is worth noting that the early cadre of advisors to the Goss Government were people of considerable stature and intellectual horsepower, attracted it seems to the challenge of helping the new Government navigate the ship after so many years lost in the swirling seas.

Kevin Rudd of course was a singular intellect, with a self-advancement agenda bigger than the Gulf of Carpentaria. He commenced as Chief-of-Staff in the Premier's office later moving to Director-General of the Office-of-Cabinet, before he was preselected, and elected, to the Federal electorate of Griffith in 1998, subsequently to rapidly move up (and down) the political ladder.

Glyn Davis was appointed Director-General of Office-of-Cabinet under Wayne Goss. Glyn went on to have a stellar academic career serving as Vice-Chancellor of the University of Melbourne from 2005 until 2018. He presented the 51st Boyer lectures for the ABC in 2010.

Peter Coaldrake became the inaugural CEO under the Goss Government of the Public Sector Management Commission. He went on to be Vice-Chancellor of the Queensland University of Technology (QUT) from 2003 to 2017. Although QUT metamorphosed out of a technical college it became a substantial university under his tenure, with 50,000 students and occupying prime space beside Parliament House and the Botanic Gardens in Brisbane.

Michael Roche was my chief-of-staff, recruited from Sydney where they had the unusual experience of a Labor Government within recent memory. He went on to spend eleven years as CEO of the Queensland Resources Council. Michael sadly passed away in August 2019, way too soon.

Gerard Bradley was one of the most accomplished public servants of his generation, having spent sixteen years as Under-Treasurer (i.e., Head of Treasury). Two of these were spent as Under-Treasurer in South Australia when he was banished from the Queensland job by the Borbidge/Sheldon Government because he had been a Labor appointee, proving this mob were as bad as the mob they replaced – who will remain nameless!

He has been Chairman of the Queensland Treasury Corporation

since 2012, Chairman of Q-Super, and Chairman and Director of a range of other prominent entities – all of which he served with distinction.

The following are his reflections on my role as Treasurer:

> After a career of over 10 years in Queensland Treasury by the late 1980s I had reached the level of Assistant-Under-Treasurer in the Budget Division. Initially this was in a new role leading Budget reforms including the introduction of program management, and shifting the focus of budgeting from inputs (i.e., salary and admin expense items) to outputs – or programs with increased flexibility for individual departments if they could perform efficiently.
>
> Then everything changed. I recall I had taken leave from Treasury in late 1989 to drive my family including my young son to Cairns for a family wedding. Following the election of the Goss Government, Treasury, along with the rest of the public service, was in turmoil, with the Under-Treasurer and other Director-Generals stood aside. I was recalled urgently to Brisbane so I put my car on the train and flew back with my family. Little did I realise I would be spending a lot of time with the local member for Cairns, Keith DeLacy over coming years.
>
> The first exposures to the new Government were difficult and tense. There was a real sense of mistrust and lack of confidence in the public service. The new Treasurer Keith DeLacy and his office reflected this with stern briefings given to us to abide by the new Government's policy agenda and priorities. The old system where Treasury was pre-eminent and dominant in preparing the State Budget was over. The new world had a whole new machinery of Government with a Cabinet Budget Review Committee including the Premier and Treasurer, influential Ministerial Advisors, new central agencies including the Premier's Office led by Kevin Rudd, the Cabinet Office led by Glynn Davis and the Public Sector Service Commission (PSMC) led by Peter Coaldrake. Treasury was

one of the first agencies to be subject to the PSMC review process.

The new Treasurer however also had a sense of urgency to commence the Budget process and to set a clear strategy to guide its preparation. The view that a Labor Government was inexperienced and likely to be unable to soundly mange the State finances needed to be dispelled. There was already an election commitment not to introduce new taxes but more was needed. Keith DeLacy was quick to see the need for a guiding set of principles. The Budget 'trilogy' was devised i.e., fully funding of long term liabilities, funding of social capital from recurrent revenues and borrowing only for economic assets with income to service the debt.

Once the strategy was clear, gradually the new Treasurer and his Office became more comfortable with Treasury as they came to understand the complexity and tensions involved in Budget preparation and documentation and the professional role played by Treasury officers. It is fair to say however that the level of confidence and communication took some time to evolve.

More importantly, the personal relationships started to build as we faced the reality of economic challenges including the recession of the early 1990s. Queensland faced successive years of real reductions in Commonwealth funding and weak tax revenues. So there was a need for regular savings rounds and micro reforms. The latter included the development of Corporatisation Policy. Here again Keith DeLacy supported the development of clear principles to guide governance of Government Owned Corporations i.e., clarity of objectives, management autonomy and authority, strict accountability for performance and competitive neutrality. This formed the basis for major reform of public utilities during the term of the Goss Government which was timely as the national competition policy agenda was adopted at a national level.

It is hard to capture succinctly all of the cut and thrust of some six State Budgets developed under Keith DeLacy's leadership. Perhaps the key thing I learnt from him was the need for each Budget to contain some new initiative to provide a positive economic benefit. Other Ministers were quick to claim ownership of spending initiatives in their Department which then left the bad news on savings or revenue measures to the Treasurer. So each Budget there was usually a special announcement, perhaps a revenue relief measure. In early Budgets this started with modest tax concessions but towards the final Budgets, bolder initiatives such as the abolition of share duty featured.

For me personally, my best moment came when Keith advised me in early 1995 that I had been appointed as permanent Under Treasurer.

Fortunately I had the opportunity to travel with Keith on a number of QTC Investor Roadshows which allowed me to get to know him more informally. The feature of these two week around the world trips was usually the spare weekend where we could relax from the grind of relentless investor meetings. I recall some pleasant stays in the English countryside near Bath. Perhaps the most memorable weekend involved a drive from Zurich to Venice and back. Along the way we dropped into Keith's old Italian neighbour who insisted we try his home made wine. Keith was a great travel companion.

Keith was generous in his support of hard working Treasury staff which saw him each year address our post Budget staff function. Over the years we developed a strong bond and friendship which remains today.

At a personal level I felt his compassion when I had to take urgent leave late in 1995 as my brother was terminally ill overseas. Shortly after I returned, the change of Government occurred and my term as Under Treasurer was over too quickly. It had been a great privilege to serve with Keith DeLacy and Wayne Goss during their term in office.

CASINOS – BREAKING DOWN THE BARRIERS

The Australian public was always somewhat apprehensive about casinos, loosely associating them with organised crime. Strange thing is, the first legal casinos in Australia were in Tasmania, constituting something of an aberration, as Tasmania is usually referred to as Australia's national park – no need to pursue economic progress, live off the rest of Australia!

The Wrest Point Casino in Hobart was opened in 1973, to be followed by the Country Club Casino in Launceston.

In another aberration, the Bjelke-Petersen Government in Queensland actually approved the Conrad Jupiters Casino (to go through a number of naming iterations throughout its noteworthy existence) at Broadbeach on the Gold Coast in February 1986. I say aberration because an evil gambling den was the last thing you would expect from a Government presided over by such a puritanical Premier. This puritanism was ameliorated somewhat by not allowing the entry of the dreaded poker machines into the casino – just a big space for future governments to address.

The Labor Party had no such qualms about gambling, with both casinos and poker machines in pubs and clubs part of our election policy platform. This was part of our plans for the liberation of Queensland, though it has been pointed out that becoming a problem gambler was hardly liberating. Of course, it is relevant to point out that the Hanlon Labor Government employed the Golden Casket lottery to underwrite the free hospital system in Queensland in the late 1930s.

Although Bob Gibbs as the Minister for Tourism had much of the early carriage of the introduction of gaming machines, formal responsibility for both gaming machines and casinos resided with the Treasurer, that is, myself.

I recognised early on that in order to overcome the public disquiet in relation to casinos, there had to be a regulatory regime which ensured they were squeaky clean. The *Casino Control Act* of 1992 delivered: a dedicated regulatory body (Office of Liquor and Gaming Regulation – OLGR), a probity regime that assessed the character, honesty, integrity, and business reputation of a proposed casino operator, all employees licensed, an extensive network of CCTVs throughout casino premises, regular audits, and so the list goes on. The bribe was a Community Benefit Fund set at 1% of revenue to be distributed to sporting clubs and charities throughout Queensland.

I think I can say the regulatory regime has been very successful indeed, with few instances of improper practice in Queensland during the last thirty years, at least since Brisbane Broncos Star Julian O'Neill was sprung pissing on the carpet under the roulette table at Conrad Jupiters in 1995, extending considerable free publicity to that establishment – and himself!

Brisbane of course was the logical destination for the first casino under our regime. Expressions of interest were called, probity completed on applicants, and the selection process commenced. It became very clear to me early on that the so-called Treasury Building occupying the city block bounded by Queen, George, Elizabeth and William Streets was the place to go, as one consortium had proposed. It was Brisbane's finest building, a sandstone spectacular Italian renaissance style, heritage listed in 1992. But it was nearing the end of its useful life as a public administration building, the upkeep being enormous, with restoring and retaining its heritage values more expensive by the day, and in the end we couldn't get public servants to occupy it, so clumsy a venue had it become.

With Cabinet approval there was just one more obstacle, to secure Heritage Council approval. The Goss Government had introduced the *Heritage Act* in 1992, another feel-good intervention to separate Queensland from its philistine past. I was confident that Council approval would be forthcoming because part of the approval process was for the casino operator to restore, and maintain, all of its heritage values, a very expensive exercise; as well as paying an arm and a leg to lease the building.

The trouble is, if you give well-meaning people a responsibility, they sometimes take it seriously. The Council rejected the proposal on the grounds that the Treasury Building's use as a casino was not consistent with its traditional use.

I advised Goss of the bad news. He was somewhat bemused as I knew he was hardly a supporter of a casino from the word go. 'What do you propose to do?' he asked. I pointed out that we (Treasury inspired) had enough common sense to insert a clause in the *Heritage Act* allowing government (and no one else of course) to decide whether or not to abide by the Council's findings.

'Oh,' he said, 'Good luck Comrade!'

By the time I called a media conference to announce the Treasury Building consortium as the successful bidder, the Heritage Council's decision was common knowledge (it seems a variant of social media existed even in those days). I reckoned it would have been easier to convince Hitler to pardon the Jews than to convince a cynical press gallery that I had taken a decision in the best interests of Queensland.

All that I had going for me was that I actually believed I had. The media conference went on forever. 'Why do you have a Heritage Council if you take no notice of them?' 'We take notice of them but sometimes the Government has to make decisions in the broader public interest.'

'The Council says that the use of the building as a casino is not consistent with its heritage values?' Where does the Press get all of this bloody information from? 'This will provide us with an opportunity to restore and maintain all of the building's heritage values at no cost to the taxpayer.' 'Is it cost that determines heritage values?'

It went on for an hour. Finally they started to wind up their cameras. Geoffrey Boycott would have been proud of me. I had straight batted my way through a full session with a fading light and a swinging ball.

Cathie Job, presenter of the ABC's *7.30 Report*, asked conspiratorially. 'Com'on Keith, why have a Heritage Council if the Government ignores them?' I was reasonably good friends with her. As all the cameras were gone and I was exhilarating in a sense of relief, and it seems, ill-discipline, I said: 'Good question Cathy, good bloody question.' There must have been one camera lurking, as that comment was featured on all the evening news bulletins!

The Treasury Casino has been very successful and, as promised, all of the physical heritage values have been assiduously restored and maintained. It will now be incorporated into the new $3 billion Queens Wharf Casino and Integrated Resort development as a high-end shopping complex.

The second Casino went to Cairns, my home town. The principle was manifest: if Government issues a money-making, exclusive casino licence to a private consortium then there must be a substantial public benefit associated with it. I had that figured in Cairns – we sold the land, the licence, the Customs House, and in return we funded the Convention Centre, the single most successful tourism driver in the city, a city which was enjoying a rapid transition from an industrial to a tourism economy, with the casino a great tourism asset in its own right, which it still is (as well as employing more than 500 people, many of whom have been there more than twenty years).

There was a small activist group that opposed the Casino, and specifically (or as a convenient focus) inclusion of the Customs House in the basic Casino footprint, 'turning our heritage buildings into grubby casinos!' It wasn't unusual for a Customs House to be the grandest building in a port city because in the early days it was really the only tax collector. The trouble was that the Cairns Customs House was only built in 1938, just two years before I was born, and I hardly saw myself as approaching heritage status. This is quintessential Australian cringe: if the Cairns Customs House was a heritage building how do we classify say Buckingham Palace, or Notre-Dame?

But all's well that ends well. And it ended better still. A couple of years after I retired from parliament I was invited to join the Board of the Reef Casino, and have remained there ever since.

POKER MACHINES – COMING OF AGE

As referenced above, the introduction of Poker Machines in clubs and hotels in Queensland was a conspicuous plank in the policy platform Labor took to the 1989 election. It wasn't just that revenue from the machines in NSW, where they had been legal since 1956, provided facilities and recreational opportunities that we could only dream about in Queensland, the fact was that much of the revenue actually came from Queensland. The throngs heading across the border to the Tweed each weekend to enjoy their facilities and play the pokies had to be seen to be believed.

Peter Cummiskey is the CEO of QSport, the industry peak body for sport in Queensland, and has held that position for 22 years. His previous background includes nine years as Chief Executive of the West Australian and Queensland Football Leagues. He is also secretary of Community Sport Australia and was awarded an OAM in 2018 for services to sports administration.

Peter had this to say (April, 2019):

> Born, bred and educated in Brisbane, I arrived back in Queensland in March 1990 to manage the Queensland Australian Football League (QAFL) after nearly 12 years working interstate.
>
> One of the factors influencing my return was the impending introduction of gaming machines in Queensland, a plank in the policy platform of the Labor Party that won government in December 1989.
>
> Having lived in Queensland during the sixties and seventies, I was well aware of the impact on the Brisbane rugby league scene of poker machine funded Sydney rugby league clubs poaching many of our best locals, widening the gap in performance between the two States, 'knocking us' as Queenslanders. It was particularly galling that NSW teams contained top line Queenslanders lured south with poker machine money.
>
> Holidaying here in the eighties it was hard not to be aware of bus loads of people tripping off over the border south of the Tweed to play the pokies, a pursuit denied Queenslanders in Queensland, together with the services and facilities that poker machine revenue provided in NSW.
>
> *I realised that my code of Australian Rules football with its Gold Coast based Brisbane Bears in the expanded VFL competition (soon to become AFL) would not prosper without a flagship presence and support in the State capital for the development of the code at grassroots levels.*

As well as revenue for the local club, Poker machines guaranteed annual revenue to the State Treasury. This convinced me (and the Government) that a venue in Brisbane at the Gabba, shared with cricket, was a realistic proposition, as was substantial additional support for grassroots development.

Thanks to the Goss Government, its Treasurer Keith DeLacy and its Sports Minister Bob Gibbs, poker machine receipts started to flow in 1993 to State sporting organisations like the QAFL which had its financial support trebled in two years with a resultant jump of some 20% in code participation over the same period.

Significantly though, the surge in funds available to the State Government ensured the progressive upgrading of the Gabba, enabling the Brisbane Bears to relocate from Carrara to the Gabba and share the venue with first class cricket.

A few years later the Bears merged with cash strapped Fitzroy to become the Brisbane Lions and just five years later, win the first of three consecutive AFL premierships – none of which would have been possible without upgrading of the Gabba.

While there is the inevitable debate about whether gaming machines have been a good thing for our communities, the fact is the revenue obtained by State Governments and licensed clubs and hotels have made a significant contribution to the well-being of many Queenslanders over the nearly three decades since their introduction.

Sport at all levels has been a major beneficiary of the decision Queensland voters took 30 years ago that resulted in more services and better sporting facilities large and small becoming available for the enjoyment, health and well-being of Queenslanders.

I had the honour, some say dubious honour, of pressing the button on the first poker machine in Queensland in February 1992, so to the extent that people raise the negatives about machine gaming I cannot plead innocence. Wayne Goss was never a supporter, and made this known publicly prior to his untimely death. 'Although it was long-standing Labor policy, it was a mistake to bring in gaming machines in 1992,' he said in 2008. While most of us know of problem gamblers whose lives have been sadly blighted by an addiction to poker machines, in defence I would say firstly, as Peter Cummiskey has pointed out above, that there were many benefits that accrued to the community. In casinos, in particular, but also in clubs and hotels, there are strict requirements to deal with and assist problem gamblers. Finally, is it really up to government to remove all sins from society? After all there is only one person who can ultimately control your moral depravities, and that is YOU (with a capital Y).

THE GABBA'S GRAND TRANSFORMATION

Don Nissen is a former General Manager of the Commonwealth Bank in Queensland, Director about town, and Chairman of the Brisbane Cricket Ground Trust. He guided the redevelopment of the Brisbane Cricket Ground, the Gabba (so-called because it is situated in the near south-eastern suburb of Woolloongabba, said to mean meeting place in local aboriginal dialect, although it seems the meeting place was for fighting, which fits in nicely with the many cricket tests played there). Don takes it from here (1 November 2019):

> I met Keith DeLacy in the early 1990s when he was Treasurer of Queensland, the Goss Government having been elected at the end of 1989. I occupied the position of General Manger, Queensland of the Commonwealth Banking Corporation which had won a tender for the transaction banking of the State Government. As Treasurer, Keith had responsibilities for this area of activities.
>
> We shared mutual friends & a deep love of sport soon becoming close friends ourselves. This friendship has grown over the 25+ years since & remains something that I treasure today.
>
> In 1993 Keith invited me to become Chairman of the newly constituted Brisbane Cricket Ground Trust. The Goss Government had recognised the need for the Gabba to undergo a

Keith DeLacy plays the first poker machine in Queensland, 1992.

major face lift as well as an important update to it's management structure. Earlier trusts had been made up predominantly of representatives of the users of the facility. Changes included the need for the trust to manage in a way consistent with sound commercial principles producing an annual cash surplus after meeting operating costs & committed debt repayments.

Trust functions required the maintenance of the Gabba as one of the major sporting facilities comparable with other Australian sporting grounds. Standards should be suitable for international & interstate sporting events as well as encouraging public attendance. Importantly Management needed to have due regard for the requirements of tenants with the view to achieving mutual benefits & the improvements of Sports generally

Selection of the Board of Trustees was careful & considered with particular skills in mind. This saw specialists in the areas of Venue Management, Construction, Hospitality & Catering, Finance & of course that typical Queenslander trait of being lovers of Sport.

Early priorities included the development of a Master Plan for the redevelopment of the facility which arrived at the following 6 stages to be completed over a number of years.

Stage 1. Removal of the Greyhound racing track & reconfiguration of the playing surface to the same dimensions of the Melbourne Cricket Ground.

Stage 2. Construction of a temporary stand together with installation of terrace seating & provision of corporate suites & boxes.

Stage 3. Completion of a Northern stand, installation of lights for night sport together with new electronic scoreboards.

Stage 4. Completion of an Eastern stand & 5 bays of a Western stand the achieve a capacity of 26000.

Stage 5. A 15 bay Southern stand taking capacity to 37600 & replacement of the ground surface with a USGA sand profile.

Stage 6. Replacement of the Brisbane Lions social club with a fully seated grandstand taking ground capacity to 42000.

It is to the credit of all stakeholders that the total program of redevelopment was completed within the planned time frames & more importantly within budget. That is not to say that a number of interesting challenges did not arise at times. An unplanned event during the program of redevelopment arose when Queensland secured the opportunity to participate in the 2000 Olympic games by hosting the International Soccer competition at the Gabba. This saw our proud venue in the World's view & required careful planning & delivery.

Unlike most major sporting grounds around the world the Gabba is not situated in parklands surrounded by open space. It is in fact located in a densely populated residential & commercial area. The footprint of the site is therefore contained & quite small by comparison to other similar facilities. This demanded special consideration of the matters of ideal ground capacity & flood lighting.

In order to meet 42000 seats target whilst complying to health & safety standards as well as patron comfort levels, the overall design required the grandstand extremities to overhang the airspace in Vulture street in particular. This required the airspace to be 'leased' from the local authority which was forthcoming & gratefully accepted.

As far as the flood lighting was concerned the location required a redesign following considerable community consultation. Light towers needed to be much taller in order to focus specifically on the playing surface without leakage outside the ground to any material extent. This added significantly to budgeted cost. For a start the head frames were then reaching high wind areas with the result that ladders to reach them were located inside the towers rather than by external ladders. Towers were much larger structures as a result. To address the added budget issues further redesign was able to arrive at reducing the towers to 4 rather than the 6 towers which were the norm at similar venues worldwide.

The facility enjoys a number of revenue categories such as public attendance, catering rights, ground memberships, signage, licensed clubs, corporate suites & special entertainment events.

For years it was known internationally as the venue for the first test of the cricket season (and an Australian fortress), and the home of the Brisbane Lions, especially during their glory years of three successive AFL premierships from 2001 to 2003.

All in all this story is a proud one with all stakeholders having contributed with energy & enthusiasm. The Gabba remains a special place in the hearts of Queenslanders. Time moves on quickly however and it is interesting to note the number of major sporting venues around Australia have since then been either refurbished or seen new facilities built. It is worth noting that a positive response has come from the Authorities with talk emanating of another program of redevelopment in the wind.

It wasn't all plain sailing. For many years the Gabba was noted for its famous 'Hill', a grassed slope on the western side, home of the barrackers, the experts, the boisterous and the drunks, but a rite of passage for many Queenslanders. Folklore has it that it was from the Gabba Hill that one of the legendary barrackers let fly during the 1931/32 Test series against the English, the particularly bitter body-line series. Bodyline was a strategy dreamed up by English captain Douglas Jardine to contain Donald Bradman after he massacred the Poms on the 1930 tour of England. It featured short pitched bowling by the English fast bowlers led by Harold Larwood, and a packed leg-side field. As an uneasy silence settled over the ground and Larwood ambled back for his run-up, Jardine was in the slips swatting away flies. *'Leave our bloody flies alone Jardine you Bastard,'* bellowed the voice from the hill (time plays games, and so do legends. This quote may have come from the legendary Yabba from on the Hill at the SGC, or it may not have happened at all, but I like the story).

The Hill however didn't fit in with the modern concept of a major sporting complex as it was inefficient in both access and numbers, and crowd control was difficult. But it didn't go painlessly. Rupert McCall, famed Queensland poet lamented the wanton destruction of heritage in the following poem. He was generous enough to present me a signed copy of his poems after it all settled down – no hard feelings:

The Gabba Hill

I'm feeling very sad today
I've lost a faithful friend
I never thought I'd see him go
Until the very end
My sorrow burns with angry tears
I can't believe he's dead
'tis only just a memory now
That floats around my head
In hidden rooms they made their plans
They sharpened up the knife

Then when his friends had turned their backs
They took away his life
And it's hard for me to swallow
It's a very bitter pill
The day they hired plastic chairs
To kill the Gabba Hill

* * *

It was home to Queensland wildlife
It was part of every game
Cricket in this State of ours
Will never be the same
And I cursed the wretched bulldozers
That took away its grass
And I curse those wretched plastic chairs
They'll never see my arse
And I curse them in the suits and ties
For making this decision
In the dreaded name of progress
They have murdered a tradition
The wind that blows this summer
Will be christened with a chill
So long old friend, I won't forget
My mate – the Gabba Hill

(8 October 1993)

There was one other pleasant memory of the Gabba for me. On 28 March 1995 the Queensland cricket team won the Sheffield Shield after 68 years of trying, the greatest drought in Australian sporting history (if it happened today they would blame climate change!). Parliament was in session and half-way through the final day of the match it was clear Queensland was going to win, after scoring 664 in response to South Australia's first innings of 214 in the grand final. I ran into Premier Goss in the corridor and he said, 'What are you doing here DeLacy, you're our Gabba man, you should be out there!' I'll forever remember that moment in history, the capturing of the holy grail. I was invited into the players' dressing room celebrations after the win. There were 400 people crowded in there, many ex-Queensland representatives openly crying.

THE MEMBER FOR CAIRNS.

On the surface it is not easy to be both State Treasurer and a hands-on local member at the same time, especially if you hang out at different ends of a pretty big State. Inevitably the priority had to be the Treasurer's role, complex and time consuming as it was. But it had its pluses too, as one's hands were close to the levers of power. Unlike Russ Hinze I would never countenance improper deployment of government funds into my electorate, or any expenditure at the expense of other electorates. But I quickly came to realise that there were massive gains to be made by creatively managing State assets. I developed the view that the public will condone the sale/privatisation of public assets if they could see the proceeds directly going into alternative purposes of greater value – the public generally I am talking about, not the noisy few, God's gift to humanity, always ready with a megaphone to promote a noble cause!

As I pointed out previously, by selling the land, including the Customs House and the Casino Licence, we were able to deliver the Cairns Convention Centre, a wonderful facility and the greatest tourism enabler it was possible to conceive.

One of the big electoral challenges I had as the Member for Cairns was the courthouse/police station complex on the esplanade. It was a disgrace, an indictment on the State Government and, indirectly the people of Cairns. The Courthouse was a quaint little structure in a tropical garden setting, but totally inadequate for purpose. We ended up with makeshift courtrooms all over town.

The enduring memory I have is of the Monday morning line-up spilling out onto the lawn in front of the courthouse, awaiting their judicial destiny, all of the weekend miscreants in great public view, the poor and the prosperous intermingled, Cairns' contribution to egalitarianism.

I discovered a replacement complex was not even on the capital works forward estimates, many, many years away. So deploying those levers I spoke about earlier I organised the sale of the whole complex, an attractive private development site on the Cairns esplanade. The proceeds were to fund the construction of a new state-of-the-art courthouse/police station/watch-house complex on Government land down the road on Sheridan Street. Special conditions were imposed on the sale: the old courthouse was to be retained together with the historic open space on the Abbott Street side. I was able also to wangle $1 million to upgrade the Public Trustee building (part of the complex) into a Regional Art Gallery. A wonderful deal for Cairns yet the naysayers were out in force. I must have been smarting at some of the opposition to the proposal, and in this context I publish part of my speech at the opening of the Cairns Courthouse and District Police Headquarters on 20 November 1992, reflecting some of my exasperation:

> [T]he reason I am doing this (giving the historical perspective) is because I am aware of calls being made to make the old police station available for a museum, or public open space, or a habitat reserve, or some other grand purpose. Some people are saying as it is public land it should be used for public purposes and that the Government shouldn't be selling it off in pursuit of the mighty dollar.
>
> Well let me say this – it has been used for public purposes, the very best kind of public purpose. It has provided the wherewithal for the establishment of this magnificent facility in which we stand today. Without the deal this wouldn't have occurred, at least not for many years.
>
> It's called managing your assets.
>
> We could have left it another five or ten years and redeveloped on site when it found a place in the capital works queue. But that wouldn't have got us a museum either, or open space, or for that matter a regional art gallery.
>
> It doesn't make you a hero to call for a museum on the police station site – anyone can do that.
>
> Anyone can call for the Government to spend money or

renege on a deal, especially if that person doesn't have to account to the taxpayer whose money is being spent.

I think it is widely recognised now, that Queensland's financial performance is a long way in front of the rest of Australia. As the debt of every other State is spiralling out of control, ours is heading towards zero.

As every other State is grappling with financial problems which they can't solve, as they continually increase taxes, increase debt, sack public servants and sell off assets, Queensland has everything under control.

But we have things under control because we are committed absolutely to a disciplined approach to financial management. But fiscal management is not just some nice sounding rhetoric around budget time. It is an attitude practised year in year out, month by month, week by week, day by day – it is an attitude, an ethic practiced program by program, project by project.

It means if the revenue situation changes, then your expenditure plans change. It means that if a budget was exceeded or an agreed off-set not achieved, then other projects will be cut or delayed.

The point I am making is that we have done a deal, and the deal has to stand. But it is a bloody good deal for Cairns, a win, win, win situation.

The old courthouse and its heritage garden will be preserved; a magnificent building will be provided free of charge to the people of Cairns as a regional art gallery, with one million dollars thrown in for restoration; and we now have this magnificent facility – dare I say the best in Queensland, to replace that abomination on the esplanade.

It gives me very great pleasure to welcome you here today for this historic occasion. In more ways than one the coming of age of Cairns

I included that speech and details of the transaction because I think it illustrates a number of essentials:

My attitude to financial management – now I can understand why the Socialist Left was not a great fan of mine!

Keith DeLacy turns the first sod on the Cairns Convention Centre

I think it fair to say that I wore my heart on my sleeve, generally not a recommended character trait for a politician. But some say it reflects authenticity, so I'll humbly go with that one!

I think it gives a good illustration of my electorate modus operandi, especially in relation to asset management, and the benefits it can deliver.

There are quite a few other examples of where I was able to manage public assets to great benefit, but I think these examples tell the story.

With the benefit of hindsight I believe I could have done more. The Cairns Base hospital was crying out for some urgent and expensive upgrading. I had this brilliant idea: sell the hospital footprint, ten acres of absolutely prime real estate overlooking Trinity Bay and the Pacific Ocean, and build a new, truly world class, university teaching hospital on government-owned land off Anderson Street, still in the centre of Cairns, but from a real estate point of view, quite nondescript. Well then it started: flogging off our hospital to greedy developers; the hospital patients deserve a view of the ocean just as much as the high and mighty; why should sick people only have Brothers' Leagues Club to look at? And so on. I was of the naive view that if a hospital patient was well enough to sit on the balcony and enjoy the ocean views they were bundled into a taxi and sent home. What a hospital needed from a capital point of view was state-of-the-art facilities, state-of-the-art medical hardware, and easy access and ample parking. I kept up the fight for some time but I think I was getting a bit punch drunk. Too many battles, too many scars. So I surrendered, and in my view Cairns is the poorer for it.

In regard to James Cook University, I was instrumental in securing the land at Smithfield for the Cairns campus, and it has worked out well, with a scenic almost rustic setting, but a long way on the north side of Cairns. It should have gone slap-bang in the middle of town, on the vacant railway land available after the railway station was closed. But oh gee, how it would have revitalised the CBD, with five or ten thousand students and a thousand staff right in the middle of Cairns, living, shopping, eating, entertaining, and not clogging up the main northern arterial traffic way. Cairns has always had a problem with a daytime empty centre with all the tourists out on the reef and the rainforest, and the CBD shops empty monuments to hope. It comes alive in the evening of course, but even that life is mostly confined to the esplanade. I don't know how many times the City Council has attempted to establish a town mall over the years but all floundered because of a lack of people. A mall doesn't work unless it is busy, full of people and life – like Brisbane, one of the best in Australia. I didn't push this one as I should have, so it was an opportunity missed.

One of the other great developments during my tenure was the international airport. This required firstly assuming local ownership of the existing domestic airport, owned by the Commonwealth Government, who had a policy of encouraging local ownership by providing capital for upgrading works prior to the transfer. It was finally proposed that the Cairns Harbour Board (later re-named the Port Authority) would be the vehicle for local ownership. It turned into an almighty brawl, with the town divided into pro's and anti's. Long time editor of *The Cairns Post* Alan Hudson said, 'This has split the town as we have never seen it split before.' We even had the spectre of National Party Member for Barron River Martin Tenni and Labor member for Cairns Ray Jones, both sworn enemies, united in their opposition to the proposal.

Much of this battle occurred before I became the local member, but I supported local ownership, though to become involved before one found one's feet was dangerous politics. Townsville, Cairns' bête noir and eternal competitor, was angling for international airport status, and they even secured the right to some international flights. Whilst we in Cairns knew that Cairns was the obvious destination for overseas flights because of its tourism potential, Townsville had more political ooomph. Should they have won this pseudo battle Cairns would have been relegated to satellite status, and Townsville would have consolidated what they saw as their rightful position as the capital of North Queensland,

Suffice to say the Local Ownership brigade won the local battle. The Cairns Port Authority became the owner, the Commonwealth honoured its capital contribution commitment, and Cairns became a serious international airport and a booming tourism centre. For this I salute people like George Chapman (later to build the Skyrail Rain Forest Cableway just north of Cairns) whose unfailing determination saw the mission through, at times at great cost to his reputation and peace of mind, as the battle was quite brutal.

I think it is fair to say that the international airport and subsequent direct flights between Asia and Cairns provided the greatest boost to tourism and the economy in the whole history of Cairns.

There was one other accomplishment that is worth a mention. We, the Labor Party, established a Workers Club in Spence Street in the old Brewery Hall, the prime movers being myself and a small cohort of Branch members. My wife and I were bar staff every Friday night. We, the Cairns Branch, eventually sold it and invested the money under my tutelage. With the best part of half a million dollars in an investment portfolio we were the richest branch in Queensland, self-funding elections (all from earnings, never the capital, a KDL imposed golden rule) as well as making donations to neighbouring electorates. The State Branch couldn't take its greedy eyes off the honey pot, and I think they finally got it (after I had moved on).

The Verdict

Please allow me to invoke the Bob Hope defence for what might seem to be a lack of modesty as I furnish some verdicts on my political career: when he was being presented with the Congressional Medal of Honour, Bob Hope said, 'I feel very humble but I think I have the strength of character to fight it!'

In the parliament elected in 1995, Lyn Warwick the newly elected Coalition member for the neighbouring seat of Barron River, asked, apropos of what I don't know, 'What did Keith DeLacy ever do for Cairns?' It brought the house down, and became a satirical meme – 'What's DeLacy ever done for Cairns!' People say it to me as a greeting even to this day.

When I announced my retirement *The Cairns Post* dedicated the whole editorial and op-ed page to me under the Editorial headline 'Golden Age for Cairns' (28 October 1997). And this perspective has endured. John MacKenzie, who has hosted the morning talk-back on Radio 4CA Cairns for more than thirty years, still beats it up as the Golden Age, reflecting that eternal adage, 'The older I get the better I used to be!'

Not to be outdone, Tony Koch, Senior political writer at *The Courier Mail* wrote an op-ed in reference to me titled 'Role Model for Politicians' (1 November 1997).

THE SUN SETS ON A POLITICAL CAREER

The trouble with democracy is that the people keep wanting to be part of it, or, as I have heard said, democracy only works if people vote the right way! Premier Goss chose to go a little earlier for the scheduled 1992 election, I think on the basis that the 2 December anniversary was a little close to the holiday season, with people already loading up their four wheel drives.

During our first term, acting upon the EARC (Electoral and Administrative Review Commission) Report (inspired by the Fitzgerald Inquiry) the Government established the Electoral Commission of Queensland as an overseeing body; eliminated the zonal system; reintroduced optional preferential voting; and provided for future redistributions which would maintain electoral equality.

There were few major issues going into the election: a relatively small hiccup when two ministers resigned because they misused electoral allowances, and the small weight of incumbency. Rob Borbidge, the National Party member for Surfers Paradise, was leader of the Opposition. Labor was returned, after a small swing against it (1.59%), with 54 seats in the 89 seat assembly, the same as in 1989. The Nationals lost one seat and the Liberals gained one.

In Cairns I suffered a slight swing, registering 61.1% of the two-party-preferred vote. It was a good result considering the demographics of the electorate were slowly moving away from Labor, and both Liberals and Greens stood candidates, unlike 1989 when the National Party candidate was my only opponent. I settled down for another term as Treasurer, having jettisoned the Regional Development part of my portfolio.

It was a different ball-game in 1995, referred to sometimes as the Koala Road election, to be followed by the baseball bat by-election. The Queensland Nationals and Liberals were fighting their first election as a formal Coalition in fifteen years, a factor which reversed Labor's perceived advantage from the introduction of optional preferential voting (OPV). As the Liberal and National parties were now a coalition there were no leaked preferences on that side (this was prior to the One Nation emergence). On the Left side however the Greens, gathering some strength, initially would purloin their votes from Labor, but under OPV not give all of them back. They didn't formally allocate preferences, as they hated everyone!

In Queensland incumbency began to bite also, even though our record of economic and fiscal management was world beating. The following stats come from a speech I delivered to the new parliament on 20 February 1996 defending the Goss Government's record against claims by the newly elected Borbidge/Sheldon Government that they were inheriting a basket case. It was a wilful disregard for reality (we would call it fake news these days!) that made my imprudent criticism of the previous National Party Government's economic performance six years earlier seem quite mild by comparison:

- Since 1990/91 Queensland Real Gross State product grew by an average rate of 4.4% in real terms, while growth for the rest of Australia averaged 1.9%.
- Queensland exports grew by an average rate of 6.3%, compared to an average rate of 4.2% for the rest of Australia.
- During this same period Queensland generated 171,200 or 55% of all the new jobs created in Australia.
- Total net interstate migration into Queensland totalled 215,530. This contributed to the fact that Queensland accounted for 41% of Australia's population growth over the five year period.
- Queensland consistently delivered structural budget surpluses, leading to net-debt-free status being achieved in 1994.

- Queensland's AAA credit rating was enhanced setting Queensland apart from most other jurisdictions around the world.
- Queensland not only retained its status as the low tax State but increased the differential between Queensland and the rest of Australia.
- Our good financial management allowed Queensland to increase spending in service delivery by 39% in real terms since 1989/90.
- Bain and Company's Chief economist Don Stammer reported, after hosting a mission of investors from around the world, that the mission's official comment was 'that the Queensland Government has among the strongest finances of any Government in the world';
- Access Economics Budget Monitor (1993) said 'Queensland is in easily the strongest financial position of any State';
- In the same year International Ratings Agency Standard and Poors predicted that while relative economic performance of the rest of Australia will catch up a little, Queensland should exhibit annual GSP growth rates about a percentage point above the national average until at least the end of the decade.

As an aside, according to ABS, interstate migration reached 52,290 in 1993, allowing us to boast that 1,000 Mexicans (southerners) were migrating to Queensland each week, heading for the sun, surf and sand, or as Goss put it, to God's waiting room on the Gold Coast.

This record notwithstanding however, sentiment had begun to turn sour. Australian PM Paul Keating, after famously stealing the 'unlosable' election' from John Hewson in 1993, had outlived his welcome with Australian voters, poisoning ALP sentiment Australia-wide. As a ministerial colleague recounted to me, a constituent told him while he was out door-knocking, 'I like Goss, but I am not voting for him this time.' 'Why?' 'I can't stand Keating!'

Isolated protest movements began to gain traction. 'Send Goss a message,' became a catch-cry, the subliminal point being that you could send him a message without sacking him. And then there was the Koala Road.

The Pacific Motorway, linking Brisbane to the rapidly growing Gold Coast, was fast becoming a traffic nightmare. In fact it was so bad that Transport Minister David Hamill commanded that no maintenance work be carried out during daylight hours. He became incensed one day when a mammoth traffic jam led him to the conclusion that the edict was being breached, only to discover that the malefactor was an Ashton Circus elephant peacefully grazing roadside at Coomera, seriously distracting drivers.

Four lanes were grossly inadequate, with modelling showing that eight lanes, although horrendously expensive to deliver, would be at capacity by 2012. The Department of Transport came up with a solution: construct a second highway along the so-called Eastern Corridor. As a new parallel road it could be tolled, thus mitigating fiscal constraints, and provide the wherewithal to manage traffic in the case of pile-ups.

Wow, we ran into an electoral pile-up. The road had to traverse Koala country, or what soon was referred to as Koala habitat. The megaphone mob had a picnic. I have a view, referred to earlier, that while the inevitable naysayers can make a lot of noise and appeal to the nimbys as it were, the general public outside looking in, and not directly affected, silently nodded their head but took no notice. But the koalas generalised it, Australia's national icon being trampled, and so easy to sensationalise. There were reports of dead koalas being brought in from outside to be 'discovered' in the habitat. It seems they were dying at the prospect of extinction. Hetty Johnson, the founder of Bravehearts, led the campaign, and a formidable campaigner she proved to be. She attacked us all as just a mob of lying politicians, who say one thing and do another. She has since spent the next twenty years vainly trying to join that reviled assemblage, at various local, state, federal and Senate elections.

The prospect of a toll on the road didn't help either. Altogether, great politics just prior to a general election.

I can remember walking around the electoral booths in Cairns on election day. Although a million miles from the koalas, you could feel the negativity. I thought it was unfair then and I still do. The abuse I received at one booth, full of smears and falsehoods, was unbelievable. Still politics is politics. My mother used to say, 'Life isn't fair, get used to it.' And so the day went on, and into the night, a very unpleasant one, a numb feeling in the pit of the stomach, watching the vote-count on TV at the Workers' Club.

In the wash-up, the Goss Government suffered a swing of five percent and just stumbled across the line, winning 45 seats in the 89 seat assembly. The coalition won 43 seats, while Liz Cunningham was elected as the Independent member for Gladstone. A paper thin majority to the Goss Government.

In Cairns I suffered an 8% swing finishing with a two party preferred margin of 2.3%. Phew! I of course was seen as one of the prominent faces of the Goss Government, so if there was a retribution to be delivered then I had to expect it.

Then real disaster struck. Ken Davies had won the new Townsville seat of Mundingburra for the ALP by the skin of his teeth, but the Court of Disputed Returns threw out the result on the basis that twenty-two overseas military personnel were denied a vote. Davies had won by a measly 16 votes.

A by-election was scheduled for 3 February 1996. It became a picnic. On the basis of internal polling, and an on-going legal case between Ken Davies and the Commonwealth Bank (there was a concern he would be bankrupted, which would result in automatic disqualification) the ALP decided to drop Davies as its endorsed candidate, selecting Tony Mooney, the Mayor of Townsville, in his place. Davies went feral, nominated as an Independent and kept releasing damaging internal attacks on the ALP. It became clear he had one objective, not to win himself but to ensure the ALP didn't win.

Anybody in Townsville with a grudge, or a warm-inner-glow, hopped on board; in the end there were twelve candidates.

Then came the baseball bat. Prime Minister Paul Keating, in an act of collegial bastardry, called a Federal election with one week to go in our absolutely critical by-election campaign. Goss pleaded with him to delay the announcement for a week. However Keating wasn't noted for his sentimentality. He had a memory too as Goss had supposedly supported Bob Hawke in the preceding Federal leadership tussles.

Keating was by this time pure toxicity. He had some sterling qualities, noted for his famous declamations and insults, and is generally held in high regard these days because of the micro economic reforms he helped pilot through parliament. But in 1996 his welcome had well and truly run out. His signature aggression, and previous grand pronouncements like 'This is the recession we had to have!' turned to poison. In the ensuing Federal election, held on 2 March, Keating suffered a massive defeat, with John Howard finishing with a forty-five seat majority, the second largest majority in history, behind Malcolm Fraser's fifty-five seat defeat of Whitlam in 1975. The ALP lost thirty-one seats altogether, and all but two of its seats in Queensland.

What is the message here: two Labor icons, Whitlam and Keating, worshipped within the party, charismatic and flag-waving heroes, but finishing their political careers despised and rejected by the general public?

Whatever, Keating's intrusion into the Queensland by-election was ruinous. Goss famously said that the voters were waiting with baseball bats. It was Keating they wanted to clobber, but we would do as an entrée! And I think the protest vote was significant; nobody expected Goss to lose so you could send a message with impunity. It was widely referred to in Labor ranks as the Munding-bloody-burra by-election!

There was one other issue that never surfaced for some time. During the by-election campaign, Rob Borbidge and Russell Cooper (Shadow Minister for Police) had signed a secret Memorandum of Understanding with the Queensland Police Union, guaranteeing that a Borbidge Government would repeal unpopular measures (introduced by the Goss Government on the basis of Fitzgerald Inquiry recommendations), introduce a power of veto over senior police appointments, and increase police funding, in return for a campaign donation of $20,000, and campaign support. Every little bit counts as they say.

So much for the integrity lessons learned from the Fitzgerald Inquiry.

Frank Tanti won the by-election for the Coalition (2.8% margin), Independent Liz Cunningham threw in her lot with the Coalition, Goss submitted his resignation and Borbidge/Sheldon were able to form a minority Coalition Government. We headed for the dark reaches of the chamber, on the Speaker's left hand side.

It was time to take stock on my future. Goss was doing likewise. We both came to the conclusion that it was time to move on. Peter Beattie was ready willing and able to lead the chosen people out of the wilderness, this willingness being no secret for quite a number of years, which wasn't always helpful to us as a government. Once I came to the decision, and a very big decision it was, I would like to have closed the door and walked out into the night immediately. I'd done my bit, I was fifty-six years old, I had a close family, and there were other things to do in this rich and exciting world. I had enjoyed a good innings: fifteen years in Parliament and more than six years as State Treasurer. My predecessor as the Member for Cairns, Ray Jones, spent nineteen years in Parliament without once gracing the government benches. But you don't rat on your party and bequeath them a by-election in such unstable circumstances. So both Goss and I retreated to the Opposition back-bench and formally retired at the next (1998) election, won by the Beattie led ALP.

I was succeeded as the Member for Cairns by Desley Boyle, a Cairns City Councillor and a clinical psychologist, who served until 2012. Gavin King, who succeeded her in 2012 (in the Anna Bligh rout), was the first non-Labor member for Cairns in 108 years.

During this interregnum I focused my political attention on the electorate (without the assistance of the levers of power of course), but I must confess that I spent much of my time and all of my passion writing the book *Blood Stains the Wattle*, published by Central Queensland University Press in 2002. The title came from that immortal poem by Henry Lawson, 'Freedom on the Wallaby', composed after the great Shearers' Strike in Barcaldine in 1891:

> *We'll make the tyrants feel the sting*
> *O' those that they would throttle;*
> *They needn't say the fault is ours*
> *If blood should stain the wattle!*

I was obsessed with writing, reading, researching, interviewing, travelling (Mt Isa is where the story is based). I can remember Christmas day at home, dinner ready to be served and my daughter asking her mother, 'Where is Dad?' 'Where do you think he is,' my wife replied, with just a hint of sarcasm, 'upstairs with his head stuck in the great Australian novel!'

It was published to some acclaim, and I still get an annual stipend (which I didn't seek) from the Australian Lending Rights Scheme for its use in public libraries.

Masterminding the craft

During reflective moments I pondered ministerial performance. What qualities do you need to be successful? First of all, I think it is to have a set of values, clear, consistent, transparent, and ethical, a value system based on enduring principles. But values aren't values unless you live those values. As we have discussed before, living your values is what creates authenticity. The biggest crime in egalitarian Australia is to be inauthentic, to big-note yourself, or in the Australian vernacular, to be up yourself, the unforgivable sin. In this respect the Australian public are perceptive, and quick to judge, possessing what is sometimes referred to as a highly refined 'bullshit detector'! They can pick a 'shit-eating grin' from a hundred paces (meaning an insincere one).

A bit of advice – hard earned. In public life one has often to assume the responsibility for moving a condolence, paying tribute to the dearly departed. One thing I learned early in life is that a good and memorable condolence can quickly be crash-tackled by too much emotion early on. Emotion can quickly build on itself, take over, and debilitate the speaker. The solution: if ever you are going to use a written speech this is the occasion. Secondly, don't commence on an emotional note, so easy to do. Start with something light, even humorous; friends and relatives love hearing amusing, character defining anecdotes about their loved ones. This enables the speaker to progressively move into the tribute with the subject matter, and the emerging emotion under control.

After leaving politics and making something of a mark as a Company Director I was asked by Ray Weekes, convenor of the CEO Institute in Queensland, to present to his Institute on leadership. This surprised me. It is not the way I saw myself. I hadn't studied leadership at university, or been to a leadership school, or rose through executive management ranks, so I hardly knew the vernacular. I got to thinking, and articulated a set of my own principles along the following lines, principles that I learned from the real world (which some refer to as the University of Life) and some from politics, a list which I think has served me well as a company director, and which provided an informative adjunct to the many presentations on corporate governance I subsequently delivered, especially as President of the Queensland Division of the Australian Institute of Company Directors (AICD). Some are original, and some no doubt plagiarised – after all these years I have trouble remembering which is which:

- All of life is politics: understanding people, their egos, and what motivates them.
- Pick the best, and stick with them.
- You're on your own, but you go nowhere without people.
- Don't burn bridges, it is a luxury you can't afford. As Fred Daly said, 'I have never had an enemy that I couldn't be friends with!' or legendary socialite Zsa Zsa Gabor, 'I never hated a man enough to give the diamonds back!'
- All of your enemies aren't on the other side.
- Forgive but don't forget. As John Wayne said, 'Always forgive your enemy, but don't forget the bastard's name!'
- Perceptions are realities. Right or wrong, what will it look like on the front page of the *Courier Mail*?

- Embrace the struggle – success will look after itself.
- There will always be obstacles, but there will be solutions too.
- Learn every day, it's called experience. When you stop learning you start dying.
- Experience is something you get just after you need it.
- Intellect is not wisdom.
- Ethics isn't something you do only when someone is watching.
- Do the right thing – deep down you know what it is.
- Don't be greedy – always leave something on the table for the other person.
- Life is ten percent what happens to you and ninety percent how you respond to it.
- Authenticity is difficult to fake. Groucho Marx said to the effect, 'the secret of life is honesty and sincerity. If you can fake these you've got it made.'
- Be anything you can, but don't try to be something you're not.
- Take responsibility for your own choices, and your own problems.
- Don't lie, especially to yourself.
- Embrace change – if the world outside is changing quicker than you, then you are going broke.
- Values are the bedrock – clear, consistent, transparent and ethical.
- Trust is mutual. Let it grow.
- You always know you've done a good deal when both sides are equally unhappy (thanks Sir Leo).
- Listen, don't talk. Respect the power of silence.
- Under-promise and over-deliver.
- Get up, Dress up, and Front up.

In respect of the public service I noted that the best ministers were those who had a close and positive relationship with their department, but retained their own mind, their own circle of contacts, and value system as well. The second best were those who simply surrendered to the public service and did their reckonings – not all bad as most departmental people genuinely desire to deliver good policy – though I must make the proviso that increasingly these days the public service is becoming isolated from the 'real world' as they retreat into their bubble. Finally the worst performing ministers are the ones that know everything, and take no notice of departmental advice. I could name a few people in each of these categories but that would take the fun out of it for the reader.

However you can't beat the discipline of being across the subject. You have to be able to tell if the advice being tendered is on the mark. In this context, knowing whom you can trust is the most intuitive skill of all.

But at the end of the day, having a well thought-out philosophical overview, and always testing your decisions, reactions and policy approaches against this philosophical foundation, is the essence of good ministerial performance.

While we are on the subject of the public service, and I had a close working relationship with Treasury, I figured there were two ways the public service could get its way in the face of ministerial obstruction. The first was that old Sir Humphrey Appleby admonition, 'Gee it would be a courageous minister who did that!' Secondly, they would acquiesce and then produce enabling legislation that was extraordinarily complex and indecipherable and which in no way delivered the intent of the trusting minister. Is that how red tape multiplies?

3

THE CORPORATE ADVENTURE

I've always believed that life was a journey, not a destination. R.L. Stevenson memorably said: 'To travel hopefully is a better thing than to arrive'. As they say, if you are building a life resumé don't get stuck holding a single trophy for the rest of your life.

But life can be a strange journey too, one that goes we know not where. I didn't know what I wanted to do, I was only ever focused on the moment.

One of the determining factors that pointed me towards the director world was my role in shepherding through Cabinet/State parliament the *Government Owned Corporations (GOC) Act* in 1993, aimed at modernising the governance and accountability of GOCs in Queensland (see p. 88). This required me to be right across the principles and philosophy of governance.

Also, as State Treasurer my main external constituency was the business community. It was therefore possible to gain some cred in that community, and some valuable contacts – not inevitable of course. Without actually mentioning names I could nominate a few treasurers throughout Australia who began with no credibility went downhill from that point on.

Before the turn of the century I was appointed as Chairman of Ergon Energy, Director of Queensland Investment Corporation (both Government appointments), Chairman of Trinity Property Group and Director of the Reef Casino in Cairns (both of which were subject of an IPO on the Australian Stock Exchange). I was on my way.

As per usual I soaked myself in it. If I wasn't swatting up on a particular Board or industry issue, I was swatting up on corporate Governance, it's theories and practices, and the politics surrounding it.

Over the years I have served on almost more boards than I care to remember, many of them iconic Queensland companies. For the record I have been Chairman of Ergon Energy, Macarthur Coal, Queensland Sugar, Cubbie Group, Trinity Property Group, CEC Group, Hynes Lawyers, Nimrod Resources, COFCO Australia, and IFED (Integrated Food and Energy Developments, the company seeking to develop the bio-futures projects).

I have also served as a Non-Executive-Director of Reef Casino, Queensland Investment Corporation, SEGC (Securities Exchange Guarantee Corporation – an ASX subsidiary which administered the National Guarantee Fund), QER (Queensland Energy Resources, charged with developing the oil shale reserves at Gladstone).

In terms of NFPs (Not-for-Profits), I have been President of the Queensland Council of the AICD (and served four years as a Director of the national Board of AICD), the Global Sugar Alliance, Advance Cairns (the peak body for economic advocacy in Far North Queensland), Cairns annual Red Shield Appeal, QUT's Creative Industries Precinct at the Kelvin Grove Campus, and the Centre of Contemporary Arts (COCA – Cairns theatre complex). I've also served on the advisory Boards of Queensland Leaders and the QUT Graduate School of Management, and finally Patron of the Cairns Amateurs Racing Carnival for the last ten years.

I will focus on just a few of these, the ones that provided the enduring memories.

MACARTHUR COAL – is coal a stranded asset?

In 2001 I was Chairman of Ergon Energy and had a visit from a fine looking, and very personable man-about-town who introduced himself as Ken Talbot. Ken explained that he was going to float his new coal company and invited me to be Chairman. Gee I said, what made you come to me? He said he initially approached Jim Kennedy, but Jim was too busy and recommended me. I was flattered of course. I knew Jim well and considered him Queensland's most accomplished company director and a great practitioner of the art. He was the Australian Institute of Company Directors' Gold Medal winner in 1999.

Jim was Chairman of QIC when I was shareholding Minister, so we knew each other well and I learned much from his congenial style and unshakeable independence.

In respect of Ken Talbot I accepted his offer before he got out the door. Ken had been part-owner of the Jellinbah Mine, and when he split from there he said, channelling the legendary General MacArthur, 'I shall return!' Hence the name Macarthur Coal.

It turned out to be a lucky call and a wonderful ride. We floated in June 2001, 128 million shares at a dollar each, market cap $128 million. There were of course a number of share placements as we continued to expand. We were taken over by Peabody Energy ten years later, in late 2011, for $4.9 billion. The final figures at takeover have not been computed. But in a speech I gave at the ten year anniversary I pointed out that Total Shareholder Return (TSR) is the best measure of investment performance, combining dividend payments and capital appreciation. Those shareholders that invested in the IPO on 5 July 2001 would have received a TSR of 1,141% over the ten years, which ranked us third overall in the ASX 300 this century.

Ken was a wonderful person with whom to be associated. He loved wealth, and to a certain extent he flaunted it, but he was generous to a fault, and had a strong working class demeanour; with thanks to Rudyard Kipling, 'he could walk with kings – nor lose the common touch'. He liked to ingratiate with important people, a trait which later caused him considerable grief.

He was a magnificent host and a great personality. He had a haunt in every centre, be it Paris or Sydney, Mackay or Brisbane, a special feast, a special experience that he could parade, worldly and gratifying. Although he was happy to ply others with drinks he didn't consume very much himself. At his corporate box at the Broncos he would assume the role of waiter all evening, assiduously topping up the glasses of his guests.

He had some shortcomings as a CEO, though intelligent, a super optimist, a great motivator and a risk taker, for he was somewhat erratic, ill-disciplined, delegated too much, and paid insufficient attention to detail. He'd start work at 6am and staff were expected to follow. But then they would pack up at 2pm and adjourn to the pub.

You could be threatened with a rum and coke at any time or any place!

However, it was obvious as a listed company we didn't have the processes and the discipline that were so essential to achieve the top 200 standards to which we aspired. We promoted Nicole Hollows, the meticulous CFO, to the position of Deputy CEO to drive the compliance and processes. It was the perfect yin and yang (the universe is composed of competing and complementary forces of order and chaos, dark and light, male and female).

There were two events where Ken's impetuosity got the better of him. For some reason he raised the issue of his will in discussions with me, with a third to go to charity via The Talbot Family Foundation (he was worth a billion dollars when he died). He explained all of the contortions he had insisted be included in the will, especially in relation to bequests to the children. I said, 'Jesus Christ Ken, you can't run the world from your grave, just do a vanilla will and rest in peace.' Unfortunately, he never acceded to my wisdom, and the last will and testament became a financial fiasco still unresolved ten years later.

In 1998 Gordon Nuttall, Member for Sandgate and Minister in the Beattie State Government, made a speech in State Parliament, highly critical of Ken and alleging shady dealings, all of it mindless defamation protected by parliamentary privilege, consolidating Parliament's reputation as Coward's Castle:

> Honourable members do not need to be reminded of the very close and personal links that existed between the now disgraced Mr Bond and his close associates of whom Mr Talbot was one, and the corrupt National Party Government that was thrown out of office in 1989. Nor do honourable members need reminding of the days of deals done in brown paper bags between corrupt National Party figures and shady businesspeople of the ilk of Mr Talbot and Mr Bond.

A classic case of the pot calling the kettle black.

Sometime in the early noughties Ken asked me to put him in touch with Nuttall (I had been in Parliament with Nuttall) presumably to establish a relationship which could erase the negative smear hanging over Ken's head as a result of the parliamentary speech (I was not aware of the speech as I had left Parliament before it was delivered). I willingly made the arrangement.

This led to a second incident where my advice went calamitously unheeded. Ken confided in me, probably in 2005, that Gordon Nuttall had asked him for a loan. I said very quickly, 'Jesus Ken, don't go there!' But with the benefit of hindsight I suspected from the look in his eyes that he may already have committed; and one of Ken's enduring character traits, for good or for ill, was that his word was his bond. It is history now that Nuttall was charged, convicted, and jailed for corruptly receiving payments worth almost $300,000 from mining tycoon Ken Talbot. Nuttall was also subject to another layer of charges, and ended up serving a full seven years in prison.

In January 2007 the CMC (Crime and Misconduct Commission) charged Ken Talbot with corruptly making payments to Gordon Nuttall, the flip side to the charges proven against Nuttall. Ken stood down as CEO of Macarthur Coal, Nicole Hollows was appointed acting CEO, and eventually CEO.

It is hard to see how Ken could have avoided conviction. If the payments received by Nuttall were legally found to be corrupt it is logical to assume that the same payments made by Ken would also be found to be corrupt. Though I must admit that as a likeable and generous entrepreneur, a well-known philanthropist, and with the best legal support money could buy, he was batting on a better wicket than on-the-make politician Gordon Nuttall.

Let me say that it is my fervent belief that the payments were not made for corrupt purposes. There was nothing Nuttall could provide to Ken or Macarthur Coal and nothing that we sought or required. Ken's indiscretion, in my mind, stemmed from his desire to clean the slate and ingratiate with important people.

After some years wheeling and dealing in the resources industry after resigning from Macarthur Coal, exploiting his contacts and expertise and wealth, Ken sadly lost his life in 2010 when, as a director of Sundance Resources, he, and the rest of the Board, perished when a small plane crashed while travelling to a mine project in the Republic of Congo. There is some irony in this also. Ken was not a good flyer and was largely terrified of flying, especially in small planes. But there was one positive, if one can be so disrespectful to use the word 'positive' in relation to such a dreadful disaster, and that was he went to his grave a free man. And the funeral service at St John's Cathedral in Brisbane, with more than a thousand people paying respects, was testimony to a life well lived, and a person greatly admired – 'just a simple coal miner', and of course, rum and coke on the menu.

Vale Ken Talbot.

Nicole (Nikki) Hollows was continually burdened by increased responsibilities, but she took them all in her stride. In the reverse identity politics of the mining world at the time she had three strikes against her before she began: she was female, she was young (circa 40) and she was not an engineer (she was an accountant), all career threatening road blocks on the way to becoming a mining company CEO. What she had going for her was a supportive Board without those biases we are often accused of embracing. She was a hard worker, a quick learner, and an infectious personality, with an attention to detail, a frankness almost to a fault, and a focus on what drove the company. She would work late into the night. I was an early riser and sometimes on important issues we would be exchanging emails at 4am. I used to mock her: I was a day in front of her, I was in tomorrow, she was still in yesterday!

But all jokes aside, she built a $5 billion listed company which became one of the darlings of the stock exchange in the first decade of this century. And she never once boasted a gender victory; she only boasted a victory for shareholders.

I think it might be worthwhile at this point to reflect on the coal industry, an industry on which everyone these days has an opinion, or a prejudice. Me too. As former Chairman of Macarthur Coal, as an

Australian, and as an old member of the ALP, I, of course, have a bias in favour of the coal industry. I hope to explain why.

Prior to the 2019 election, then Federal Shadow Minister for Defence Richard Marles said:

> The global market for thermal coal has collapsed and at one level that's a good thing, because what that implies is that the world is acting in relation to climate change.

Greens leader Richard Di Natale said in the Senate in 2018, 'The reality is that coal is dead.' He went on to say, 'Coal has no long term future.'

In early 2019 Queensland Deputy-Premier and Treasurer Jackie Trad said in State Parliament:

> Markets are moving away from thermal coal, communities are moving away from thermal coal, nation states are moving away from thermal coal. What we need to do as a coal exporter is understand that and equip our communities with the best possible chance of re-skilling.

I wonder where these people get their facts from, they must delve deep down into their kit-bag of prejudices searching for phony stats that support their preconceived views. Let's look at China. When it comes to coal and power consumption they love playing games with the rest of the world. In 2014, for instance, 'after weeks of intense negotiations' President Obama of the US signed a much heralded agreement with President Xi Jinping of China to cut CO_2 emissions, and save the world. In the agreement Obama pledged to cut US emissions by 28% below 2005 levels by 2025. China agreed to take action starting in 2030, giving itself 16 years to increase carbon emissions before promising to think about curbing them. Sometimes you can hear from here the laughter as it tinkles through the corridors of the Great Hall of the People.

When the choice is between growing the economy and fighting the phantom menace of 'climate change,' the answer, from a Chinese point of view, is straightforward. Obama, on the other hand, chose to burden his economy with a massive clean-energy dictate, killing growth, adding to the cost of energy, lowering standards of living – all for no benefit to the environment.

I admit getting stats out of China depends a bit on which ideological bucket you dive into. And I do accept that some new HELE (High Energy Low Emissions) coal-fired power plants are actually replacing older, dirtier plants. Having said that I think the following demand projections reflect reality. And to the extent that there are discrepancies, China's predisposition was always to underestimate its coal consumption and coal-fired power capacity. That is their game. For instance, according to Chris Buckley in the *New York Times* (3 November 2015) just before the heralded Paris Agreement, China had been burning 17% more coal than it had claimed for the previous 15 years.

Fortune reported (28 November 2016) that China was currently building $500 billion worth of new coal-fired power plants. According to *Infographics* (March 2019), after explosive growth in China and India, the world has increased its coal-fired power capacity since year 2000 by around 2,000 gigawatts (as a comparison, note Australia's total output of coal-fired power is 23.6 gigawatts). A further 236GW is being built and 336GW is planned. *Bloomberg* reported earlier in 2018 that China's five-year plan calls for a 19% increase in coal-fired generating capacity, almost ten times Australia's total capacity.

The latest market demand study prepared for the Minerals Council of Australia forecasts that demand for imported coal in Asia will increase by 55% by 2030. Asian thermal coal import demand was forecast to increase from 740 million tonnes in 2017 to 1,147 million tonnes in 2030 (an increase equivalent to twice Australia's total annual thermal coal exports).

In Asia there is a new coal fired power plant built every week. The Federal Department of the Environment (2019) has China locked in for 150% emissions growth by 2030.

China keeps announcing proposed cuts to coal-fired power, and the free world climate change apostles go delirious. In 2017 that bastion of climate alarmism, *The New York Times,* under the paradoxical headline 'Beijing Joins Climate Fight' admitted that plans were underway to build over 1,600 new coal plants in the next decade, nearly half of those plants being built by Chinese companies. The article continued:

> Overall, 1,600 coal plants are planned or under construction in 62 countries, according to German environmental group Urgewald, which uses data from the Global Coal Plant Tracker portal. The new plants would expand the world's coal-fired power capacity by 43 percent.

It further made the point that,

> India will more than triple its electricity generation capability in the next decade and the majority of power plants needed to achieve this growth will utilise fossil fuels. India, like China, enjoys the same Paris Climate Agreement holiday on emissions reduction and has no CO_2 reduction requirements through to year 2030, with no reduction requirements provided even after that date.'

Following the nuclear disaster of Fukushima, Japan has reverted to coal, committed now to 21 new coal fired power stations.

Good luck to net zero emissions by 2050. I have just read that every 16 days China emits more carbon than Australia does in an entire year (new research released by free-market think-tank the Institute of Public affairs). This means the annual effect on global emissions from Australia mandating a net zero emissions target would be cancelled by China in just 16 days.

In summary, the idea of saying the world is moving to zero net emissions by 2050 is a sick joke and reflects the typical Australian (and Western) inability to understand Asia.

In 2017-18 Australia exported 200 million tonnes of thermal coal and 180 million tonnes of metallurgical coal, worth $60 billion in export revenue. The IEA forecasts that Australian coal production will rise from 409 million tonnes in 2018 to 444 million tonnes in 2024.

Yet according to all coal-hating experts in Australia it is a stranded asset. It seems to me the only thing stranded are those experts forecasting the end of coal.

Yet the nonsense is being perpetrated that renewables are now cheaper than coal. Is that why electricity prices in Australia doubled over the last ten years since the renewable orgasm was triggered? Apart from the subsidies, renewable energy gets priority despatch so as to meet government imposed renewable targets, which means cheaper coal plants have to close down for much of the day, destroying their business model (coal can't turn on and off like gas). I can tell you this, if we never had the renewable boom (based on government intervention not cheaper electricity), power prices would be much cheaper, power supply more secure, consumers more relaxed and industry more competitive.

When promoters of renewable energy start talking cost they omit to take account of the cost of the back-up, the fact that renewables (sun and wind) have a capacity efficiency of around 20-30%, i.e., they only despatch an average of 20-30% of capacity over time. I am often amused that when extolling the virtues of a new solar farm, claiming it can power x number of homes, the promoters conveniently ignore the fact that this is only for eight hours a day on average. Big deal! I can't live sixteen hours each day without electricity – can you? Can your local hospital?

However I must confess the coal industry, if not stranded, is certainly under siege, not from a lack of demand but from socio-political forces around the world, from progressive elites, political parties under the thrall of the progressive elites, social activists, the climate change zeitgeist, virtue signallers, sustainability mandates, funding denial, and over-zealous regulators. And perhaps from China's sometimes capricious attitude towards international trade.

Let's talk about over zealous regulators who, under the spell of progressive evangelists, keep challenging common sense. It seems, like cane toads, red tape will keep multiplying until it eats out its environment. Macarthur Coal's first mine, Coppabella, took just fifteen months from resource identification to mining licence (commencement of mining), and cost $100 million. Today it would take at least five years (or ten if you are Indian) to do the same thing, and cost $1 billion. An Environment Impact Study (EIS) these days costs millions of dollars and takes thirty months and two tonnes of greenhouse gas emissions to complete. In the good old days it took less than six months and cost at most a couple of hundred thousand dollars.

George Jones, well known mining entrepreneur, writing in AICD Insights Paper No 10 said, 'Not only are Australian approvals taking twice the time as anywhere else in the world, they now come with hundreds of conditions that must be monitored and documented.' He cited one project approval with 1400 conditions, including the requirement to relocate any red-back spiders on the site (the dunnies will never be the same again!).

An EIS is now not just about the environment; we have to do cultural heritage studies, social impact assessments, social impact management plans, workforce planning studies, strategic cropping land impacts and what have you. We need to consult with the government, local councils, landholders, the public, other stakeholders, the Brisbane Broncos and the Secretary-General of the United Nations.

Then there is the mining lease application, with more hurdles than the Tokyo Olympics.

In a report prepared for the Minerals Council of Australia by Port Jackson Partners it is posited that the capital spend to build a tonne of new capacity of steaming coal has increased from $61 in 2007 to $176 in 2012, a staggering increase of almost 300% in five years. Even if only half right these are frightening figures.

If Adani is a guide, years of so-called 'lawfare' from activists are mostly funded by domestic governments or off-shore behemoths like Greenpeace. Have you ever wondered about the incongruity of governments funding environmental groups to subvert government policy?

As I write the New Acland Coal mine (New Hope Corporation) on the Darling Downs has been waiting 4,736 days for mining approval, despite the pressing need for jobs in the Covid-19 hit state of Queensland. The project has been shovel-ready for years, ready to create 487 direct jobs immediately, but another victim of lawfare, where it is the process which is the punishment, not the Court ruling. I regret to say that the State Labor Government seems to have thrown in its lot with the anti-mine terrorists. Is this action based on true Labor principles? I ask you, who has surrendered fidelity to the cause?

A Social-Benefit-Cost-Analysis of the project commissioned by the Queensland Department of Natural Resources and Mines demonstrates that the NPV of the project is A$1.747 billion, after taking into account the foregone use of agricultural land ($36 million), and negative value of greenhouse gas emissions. It demonstrates the folly of reserving land such as that at Acland for agricultural purposes, as opposed to extracting the valuable coal and undertaking the rehabilitation after mining.

New Hope also farms 11,500 hectares of land around the mine site (irrigated cropping and cattle raising). This farming, intensive as it is, employs eight people (full time equivalents). Each hectare of land therefore supports 0.0007 jobs. The mine when operating at a normal production rate of 5Mtpa of coal employs 350 people directly and utilises approximately 40Ha of ground annually. So over eight jobs are sustained for each hectare of land mined (compared to the 0.0007 jobs per hectare for farming).

Revenue from one hectare of coal mining at New Acland (at present low coal prices) generates $8.6 million. Revenue from one hectare of Acland land from agriculture generates $304 in total. Therefore mining generates over 28,000 times the revenue from the same area (one hectare) of land.

There are well known community concerns over the potential drawdown of groundwater. However, given that relatively few bores are expected to be affected and that the mine is required to make good any potential water loss to landowners, and the mine has long term access to water from the Toowoomba City Council via its own water supply pipeline, this is not considered a significant impact.

I can only summarise by asking, are the inmates in charge of the asylum? But then maybe Queensland does not need the jobs (high paying blue collar jobs at that), or the Government revenue, or the commercial boost to the regions.

I recently attended a retirement celebration for New Hope Managing Director Shane Stephan. It seems he has had enough. He concluded his address-in-reply to the multitude, a very big crowd, with the following words:

> We have senior federal Labor politicians in our National newspaper calling for Acland Stage 3 to be approved. We have both the CFMEU and the AWU calling for Acland to be approved. The LNP State opposition has been calling for Acland to be approved. It would appear that the only people who are deaf to these calls is the current Queensland Labor State Government. Our Premier Palaszczuk is: Deaf to the calls from employees progressively losing their livelihoods; deaf to the calls from our customers who are forced to use poorer quality coal at a much higher price; deaf to the calls from regional Queenslanders looking for job opportunities. So we will have to shout louder over the next couple of months so that even the deaf will be forced to hear the voice of the voter!

Could you ever have imagined that a working class mob like this would cheer so uproariously at such anti-Labor rhetoric? Is it any wonder that the working class is heading for the door?

Away from Acland and back to the challenges of developing the regional economy. Port and rail access is just as problematical as securing the mining approvals. If coal companies want new port infrastructure they have to sign take-or-pay contracts going out 10 or 15 years, never mind the fact that they don't have the proven reserves to underwrite it, nor do they have contracts with customers for anything like that period of time. Under these policies mining companies have paid for all Queensland's mining related rail and port assets, and took all the risk. Then, in respect of rail, government sold it off and pocketed the money on behalf of all taxpayers. Not so in the sugar industry. Although funded on a similar model the industry clings fervently to ownership of the bulk sugar terminals – farmers have always had much more political muscle than miners.

Everyone has their hands out. Miners are fair game, after all they are all wealthy and are destroying the planet. Before mining can commence we have to purchase the land, twice as much as we need because of environmental requirements for things like dust and noise buffers. And again, because we are miners we pay twice the going rate per hectare.

Land access agreements are a giant headache although coal exploration drill holes have virtually no residual impact on the countryside. In the old days we would talk to the landholder and come to a mutually beneficial arrangement. Now lawyers are involved, and these lawyers demand $40,000 up front, or you don't even get to talk to the lawyer, let alone the landholder.

No wonder they say that 99% of lawyers give the rest a bad name!

It would now take a billion dollars to start up a five million tpa coal mine. It is no longer a game for the little guys. It's sad isn't it. The irony is that all those people who rail against so-called 'Big Coal' are creating circumstances where there can only be big coal – small coal can't cope with the burden and costs of regulatory impositions.

Of course 'Big Coal' is highly misleading too. Most coal companies are listed on the stock exchange. This means they are owned not by some big ugly capitalist, but by the people of Australia, just ordinary people, Mums and Dads, largely through their superannuation funds.

Further, just in case you think from reading all of the above, that miners are greedy capitalists and environmental vandals who need to be corralled by governments in the public interest. Let me say from a Macarthur Coal point of view that whilst it was always our primary objective to grow shareholder value, we always accepted that we could not do this if we offended against what we called (before the social engineers appropriated the term and hurled it back at us) our licence to operate.

This licence in our view was more than a statutory obligation, it was a moral one, something we owed to our community and our country. At all times we needed to be focused on the sustainability of our operations which included leaving no stone unturned to minimise our environmental impact, rehabilitate our footprint, foster a very strong culture of workplace safety, and promote the welfare of our workforce and stakeholders generally. All this was central to Macarthur Coal's vision and values.

But despite our commitment to broad based sustainability, a commitment which I am sure is shared by most other coal companies, we are still perceived very negatively by many Australians, especially in the big cities. In fact some of the attitudes emanating from these so-called progressive elites are quite scary. Elizabeth Farrelly, a prominent columnist with the *Sydney Morning Herald* wrote on 14 April 2011:

> Mining provides a tiny fraction of Australian jobs, just over 1% compared with 11% for health care which the Government happily trashes. We could drop the whole mining sector and still keep unemployment well below the OECD average.

The Lord have mercy on her soul! Imagine if we abolished the whole mining industry in Australia and the hundreds of billions it contributes to national wealth. Ms Farrelly wouldn't have to worry about the Government trashing the health care system because there wouldn't be a health care system to trash. But this is the sort of ignorant proselytising coming from the leafy suburbs. What so many people fail to understand is that someone has to create the primary wealth which sustains the rest of the economy, which sustains prosperity, which sustains Elizabeth Farrelly's lifestyle. Without the productive sector, without industries like mining, farming, manufacturing, tourism, without the exporters, there would be no service industries where the bulk of our citizens are employed. These service industries, private or public, are very important, but it must be understood they do not create wealth, they consume wealth, or re-distribute it. I guess what I am saying is we cannot continue to undermine with impunity the productive sector of the economy because that is an attack on national prosperity, and on the living standards of all Australians.

As they say: Before wealth can be redistributed, it has to be created. But you wouldn't expect this fundamental truth to be understood by the virtue pedalling dreamers in the leafy suburbs. It seems they think the nation's wealth is created by public servants. Or floats down on the moon beams!

Miners are fair game, always subject to unrelenting negative propaganda. The Greens consistently accuse the fossil fuel industry of being subsidised. I spent ten years looking under every rock for these subsidies but I couldn't find one. Some claim the diesel fuel rebate is a subsidy. But it is not. It is an on-road tax introduced to recover from road-users the cost of road maintenance and construction. Off-road use (mining, agriculture, fisheries, power generation, etc) is therefore not subject to the tax. However any on-road use by miners and others is of course subject to the tax.

In 2010 the then Rudd Government announced it would introduce a Resources Super Profits Tax (RSPT) on the mining industry, the only one of the 138 recommendations in the Henry Tax Review to see the light of day. All hell broke loose. It was based on the so-called Brown Tax, devised by a Mr Cary Brown in the US in 1948. And what a wonderful pedigree it had, sixty-two years old and not a child anywhere in the world, until Treasury Secretary Ken Henry convinced Rudd and Swan it was time to procreate (in a policy sense).

It was a doozy. It was very complex and actually amounted to a 40% nationalisation of the industry. It also turned into an issue of sovereign risk (a massive retrospective increase in taxation). The resources industry responded with a massive campaign and ultimately Messrs Rudd and Swan capitulated. They replaced it with the Mineral Resource Rent Tax (MRRT) which was also a doozy, wildly discriminatory (it only applied to coal and iron ore production), massively increasing accounting costs, but forgot to increase government revenue. It was discretely placed in the trash mailbox in 2014.

In order to justify the imposition of the RSPT at the time, Federal Treasurer Wayne Swan claimed that Australian mining companies only paid 17% corporate tax rate. I suspect he may have been under the spell of those economic illiterates (ABC journalist Emma Alberici in her April 2018 analysis of corporate tax comes to mind) who calculate tax liability as a percentage of revenue instead of a percentage of profit.

At that time I analysed Macarthur Coal's tax position. In 2008-09 we made net profit after tax of $169 million, after paying $73 million in corporate tax and $66 million to the State in royalties. Our effective rate of taxation (company tax plus State royalties) was therefore 43%. This is why we bridled when the Treasurer accused the industry of not meeting its fair tax obligations We did a further exercise; had the RSPT been introduced (2009-10) it would have increased Macarthur Coal's total tax paid by a further $67 million, leading to an effective tax rate of just under 60% – grossly uncompetitive globally, and surely a career ending injury to the industry. The high tax urgers ask what's the problem, resources like coal and iron ore are not internationally mobile. True, but the investment capital sure as hell is.

On top of these taxes Macarthur Coal paid $40 million in rail freight charges to State owned QR, $27 million in port charges, $76 million as dividends to shareholders, and $65 million in wages to our 600 employees, who of course paid a good slice of that in income tax.

Those people calling to close down the nation's coal industry would do well to reflect on these numbers. Regrettably their powers of reflection seem to be smothered in the thick smoke of prejudice.

Managing Director of Macarthur Coal Ken Talbot, and Chairman Keith DeLacy ink another contract

In my address at Macarthur Coal's tenth anniversary I outlined the benefits the coal sector brings to Queensland, in my view all consistent with long term Labor principles:

Mining generates enormous primary wealth – the rest of the economy lives off the primary wealth creators;

Whilst the number of direct employees is not great, an RMIT study (released at that time) showed for every job generated in mining, 6.5 associated jobs were created in the rest of the economy;

- Our dividends bolster the superannuation earnings of all Australians.
- We create jobs, commerce and wealth in regional areas – away from the overcrowded cities.
- We pay good wages.
- The mining industry pays very large taxes which underpin the social framework in Australia.
- Our exports greatly contribute to funding the nation's current account.
- Mining is a very sophisticated industry in which Australia has expertise, technology and equipment which gives us a competitive edge, and which we also export to the world.
- And we are true blue Queenslanders!

CUBBIE – THE TRAIL BLAZER

The late Des Stevenson was one of the first Australians to understand river hydrology and the future value of water. In 1984 he started to gradually amalgamate cattle and sheep properties (and their water licences) to form Cubbie Station. He co-opted John Grabbe (formerly a farm advisory officer with Queensland Water Resources Commission), to the journey and they established a massive irrigation project on the Condamine-Balonne River system, on the upper reaches of the Darling River system close to Dirranbandi in south-west Queensland, about six hours drive from Brisbane.

I became friends with John Grabbe, and we worked together on a number of projects. In my view no one in Australia understands water hydrology and storage better than John. Where other people see only trees, or rocky hills, or a desolate landscape, John could see a water storage and reticulation centre. He strongly believed (as I do now) that off-river storage is far superior in terms of efficiency, cost and ecological sustainability, to in-river dams. Cheaper to construct, they do not impede in-river aquatic movements, and water could be harvested in a more environmentally friendly way (i.e., the first wet season flush could be free to fill the downstream ponds, and harvesting could occur from the later more sustainable flood flows).

In 2005 Cubbie Station merged with the Blache Cotton Group situated in St George to form Cubbie Group Ltd, an unlisted public company of which I became Chairman.

Cubbie is a state-of-the-art irrigated farming system, deep water, multi-celled (to reduce evaporation) gravity fed, off-river storage capable of storing 500,000 megalitres of water on 9,000 hectares of storage infrastructure. Water is harvested under licence, based on environmental sustainability, from flood flows. Production is principally furrow irrigated cotton which provided the highest gross margin. Cubbie had 22,000 hectares of developed irrigation land, capable of producing 200,000+ bales of cotton worth $100 million+ per annum. It was some operation.

Super efficiency was the key. High production per unit of water was the objective, representing the best environmental use of the scarce commodity. All storm water and tail water was captured and recycled; there were 88 laser levelled, irrigated fields with furrows 1,000 metres long; GM (genetically modified) technology was deployed – 'roundup-ready' and 'Bollguard' (a GM variety that eliminated the need to use broad spectrum insecticides for heliothis control thus sparing non-insect predators in the farm ecology); and precision farming generally, including GPS guidance and crop monitoring, and continuous in-house research and development.

Cubbie's full-time-equivalent workforce was 150, a massive input to the remote economies of St. George and Dirranbandi.

However because of its size and consumption of the precious and highly political resource, water, Cubbie became a scapegoat for all that was wrong with the management of the Murray-Darling system. The myths perpetrated were outrageous.

The shrill cry of assorted politicians, commentators and save-the-world activists was that Cubbie Station sucks the Murray-Darling system dry. Say that again! On average the Darling River contributes 16% of the Murray-Darling flows; the Condamine-Balonne, in the upper reaches of the Darling and whence Cubbie draws its water, contributes 15% of the Darling flow (i.e., 2.4% of Murray-Darling); Cubbie accounts for 15% of the extractions in the Condamine-Balonne, which represents 0.2 % of the total Murray-Darling flow. Yes that's right, one-fifth of one percent, yet Cubbie is blamed for all the drought reduced flows and environmental degradations in the whole system.

Cubbie was even accused of starving the Narran Lakes of water, ignoring the fact that the Narran River branches off the system 20 kilometres upstream from the Cubbie boundary. But when you've generated the ogre of a water guzzling, environmentally destructive behemoth like Cubbie, why confine yourself to the facts.

As it turned out, we didn't need the megaphone mob to bring us to our knees, that happened independently. They say in the bush that properties change hands because of one of the four D's – death, debt, divorce or drought. We were spared the divorce, but tangled with the other three. Des Stevenson had died and in a messy family trust his children were able to take much of their equity share as cash, pushing the gearing levels of the public company into dangerous territory.

Then the millennial drought hit. It was horrendous. Peter Beattie even squandered billions of dollars on a desalination plant. But he was OK, he was only playing with taxpayers' money. Cubbie had virtually no production from 2006 to 2009. By 2009 we had debt of approximately $320 million, interest and overheads were $30 million a year, and drought was forecast to last another three years. We went into voluntary administration.

But who said the good Lord doesn't have a sense of humour? We went into administration in October 2009. In March 2010 we had the biggest flood on record, in January 2011 we had a bigger flood, and in February 2012 we had another big flood. And cotton prices reached record highs.

In the crop grown in 2010-11 under administration, Cubbie produced 245,000 bales of cotton and 80,000 tonnes of cotton seed. 10,000 semi-trailers of raw cotton left the property, gross value $260 million. Ebit was $80 million.

But the banks, NAB and Suncorp, had turned, like unrequited lovers. They were charging usurious penalty interest rates and communicating only with the administrators McGrathNicol, who were completely unsympathetic. We pleaded we could trade out of administration, repay the debt; the dams were full, three years production guaranteed, forward cotton markets were strong, we had excellent and proven management, we could virtually guarantee NPAT of $30 million per annum even after servicing the high levels of debt. Cubbie Group was independently valued at $450 million. There was the prospect of selling $33 million worth of water entitlements (1,400 mgls) to the Federal Government under the buy-back scheme. We had been approached by a major Australian banking institution to provide both debt and private equity capital to restructure the balance sheet. Win, win, win!

Thanks but no thanks. The administrators weren't interested (I guess they were making more money with the course they were on), and in respect of the banks it seems we had been transferred from the sales department to the debt collectors, the friendlies to the miserables. The business was sold to the Chinese firm Shandong RuYi (with a minor interest to Australian firm Lempriere to satisfy FIRB requirements).

There were some winners: Shandong RuYi because they got a $400 million asset for (reportedly) $240 million, the Administrators who pocketed around $10 million, and the Australian Taxation Office – there was $68 million worth of accrued tax losses, not transferable to the acquirers. The losers were the banks and of course Cubbie shareholders.

I have calculated that under the contrived settlement approximately $140 million was, excuse the phrase, pissed up against the wall:

- $10 million to the Administrators;
- $50 million in forward sales were lost as the Administrator steadfastly refused to forward-sell even in the most propitious of circumstances (with the benefit of our long term risk management policy);
- $68 million in accrued tax losses;
- $10-$15 million commission on sale, legals, etc.

The foreign Investment genie then jumped out of the bottle as campaigners rushed to point out that Australia was flogging off its birthright to foreigners. Nick Zenophon among others rang me seeking information which would allow him to jump on the anti-foreign investment bandwagon. But whilst I harboured considerable resentment about the way we were treated, the foreign sale was not one of them. It was business as usual under the new ownership, Paul Brimblecombe was retained as General Manager, so Cubbie prospered under the same management, the same workers, same contractors, same suppliers and same tax regime.

But as an observation, to overcome the resistance to foreign investment, I think the Federal Treasurer should legislate that any foreigner purchasing Australian property and taking it home be subject to 100 strikes of the cane!

While the Cubbie story is very sad there were many learnings:

- Banks are bipolar, Administrators are … (I've forgotten the word!)
- Rural businesses should budget on a ten year basis, factoring in the actuarial incidence of droughts (we did ten year budgets, but we were over-geared at the start and were then overtaken by a once-in-a-hundred-year drought).
- Gear conservatively.
- Australia is a land of drought and flooding rains.
- Scale is the way of the future. It delivers efficiencies, productivity benefits, environmental best practice, market power

- (both buying and selling), internal research and the capacity to provide and maintain necessary infrastructure and on-farm processing.
- It consolidated my view that the best defence against misfortune is a strong balance sheet – whether we are talking about governments, businesses or individuals.

Bearing in mind we need to consume water and land to feed and clothe a hungry world, the best thing we can do for sustainability and the environment is increase production per unit of these scarce resources – as Cubbie was doing. On a related subject, I am dubious at the feel-good claims of organic food evangelists saving the world. Organic farming requires a third to a half more land and water per unit of production than conventional farming. The march of global organic farming therefore, believe it or not, seems to me to represent the biggest threat of all to the Brazilian rain forests. In fact to produce the same agricultural output today utilising organic farming we would have to increase agricultural land availability by a factor greater than the size of the United States.

QUEENSLAND SUGAR – AND ITS CHEQUERED HISTORY

Another of my politically incorrect forays, after gambling (Reef Casino), coal (Macarthur Coal), large scale irrigation (Cubbie), not to mention politics, and now sugar (the one all the obesity police want to tax out of existence).

Queensland Sugar Limited (QSL) is an institution in Queensland. It is owned by the growers and the millers and has traditionally marketed the entire Queensland cane sugar crop. The sugar industry has had a strong collectivist bias since its inception well over a hundred years ago. Many of the mills were grower owned co-operatives, and all of the sugar output was marketed by a grower owned marketing body, and stored, blended and shipped through grower owned bulk sugar terminals.

This is not surprising as the sugar industry matured under State Labor Governments, notably 'Red Ted' Theodore's reign in the nineteen tens and twenties. There were regulatory controls over production, marketing, pricing and even wages and working conditions. I think I have mentioned before that the Babinda Hotel, in the midst of the wet tropics cane belt, was government owned too.

The sugar industry has been the backbone of the Queensland regional economy for the last 100 years, and accumulated a mass of political, ideological and financial muscle. I was pleased to be invited to be involved with the industry as my father had been a cane cutter, and after spending most of my life in Cairns, sugar was in my veins. You wouldn't be game to drink coffee without sugar; if asked if you wanted sugar in your tea/coffee the politically expedient response was, 'Yes please, I will have two spoonfuls but don't stir it, I don't like the sweetness!'

In round terms Queensland harvests 35 million tonnes of sugar cane producing 4 million tonnes of raw sugar, worth $1.7 billion per annum, 90% of which is exported. There are 4,000 farms and from 10 to 15 thousand employees at any one time. Most of the cane is rain grown (in the wet tropics), the exception being the Burdekin district irrigated from the Burdekin River Dam system.

I have mentioned before that in the nineteenth century, Pacific Islanders (Kanakas) were recruited to the cane fields as it was considered that white men were genetically unable to cut cane in the ferocious tropical climate. The conventional wisdom they would go troppo!

Much of the oral history seems to conflict with official documentation as to the amount of force and coercion involved in the recruitment process (referred to as black-birding which some see as a synonym for slave trading). The *Polynesian Labourers Act 1868* was introduced in an effort to regulate the labour trafficking of Pacific Islanders into Queensland, but there is little doubt many of them were treated badly. Between 1864 and 1904 approximately 60,000 South Sea Islanders were recruited to the industry.

However there is no doubt that institutionalised slavery was never part of the Australian ethos, despite claims to the contrary by some of the self-flaggelisers today. One of the key figures in Federation and the most influential of our early prime ministers, Alfred Deakin, clearly enunciated the position of virtually the entire political class: 'No slave is to be allowed to tread Australian soil at all. The mere suspicion of the taint of slavery is leading to the prohibition of the Pacific Island labourer.'

The Federation planner took ruthless steps to outlaw slavery in the cause of white egalitarianism, the essence of Australian nationalism. Their conviction was absolute: our nationalism would not tolerate slave or cheap coloured labour.

Growing resistance to immigration, especially cheap (and coloured) immigration, from unions and the emerging Labor movement, especially in Queensland, led to the new Federal Government in December 1901 enacting the *Immigration Restriction Act* and the *Pacific Island Labourers Act* – 'to Provide for the Regulation, Restriction and Prohibition of the Introduction of Labourers from the Pacific Islands.' This document enacted a law to deport the vast majority of the Pacific Islanders in Australia from 1904, marking out the racial boundaries (the white Australia policy) of the new nation. However quite a few Pacific Islanders remained and carved a life for themselves in Queensland. Evelyn Scott, Faith Bandler and Mal Meninga come to mind as successful individuals of South Sea Island heritage.

It is surely ironic – perhaps beyond belief – that Black Lives Matter activists in Australia these days try to link this country with the American experience of slavery that ran for centuries, that was based upon the transportation of Africans to America, that became pivotal to the Southern economy, provoked a civil war and represents today a legacy far different from the challenges faced by Indigenous Australians.

The South Sea Islanders were largely replaced by Italians and other Europeans seeking a better life, and not hung-up on the notion of doing a black man's job, or going troppo. But they were not welcomed fondly either by the largely British/Irish working class, perhaps spooked by that Mediterranean olive skin. However the Italians developed a strategy of clubbing together as a gang to cut cane and the surplus earnings pooled to buy the first farm; till they were all farm owners. Towns along the Queensland sugar belt are these days known for their cultural diversity.

The march of technology, as with most other industries, has greatly impacted the production of sugar cane in Queensland. Bulk sugar terminals were progressively established over the years. By the 1960s all export sugar was finally stored and processed through these terminals. Australia has six terminals representing the largest bulk raw sugar storage and handling system in the world. Export of bulk sugar spelled the end in North Queensland of the iconic wharfie who loaded export sugar manually in bags. What a great loss to the causes of militant unionism and left wing activism! They did their best to sabotage the war effort during the Second World War because they saw Australian service men and women as 'puppets of American capitalism'.

After years of inventiveness, design, and trial and error, mechanical harvesting became the way of the land, spelling the end of that other legendary worker, the cane cutter by the 1960s.

Finally, after years of activism and strikes in the 1930s saw pre-harvest burning of cane become widely employed (when the cane was burnt it was much easier to cut [absent all the trash] but the main objective of burning was to eliminate the rats, carriers of Weil's Disease, a severe form of leptospirosis).

The wheel turned in the 1960s when years of ecological activism (and the advent of harvesters) ended with cane burning phased out, thus depriving the tourism industry in North Queensland of one of its great attractions, the cane fires lighting up the early evening sky.

In the year 2000 Queensland Sugar Corporation became Queensland Sugar Ltd (QSL) with me as Chairman. It was a time of some tension as there were great stresses in the industry, with the privatisation of some of the mills and challenges to the statutory single desk selling system, with progressive deregulation being the order of the day, though a political flash point.

At this time QSL was largely instrumental in bringing together all of the major cane sugar exporting countries, notably Brazil, India,

Thailand and Australia, to form the Global Sugar Alliance, to lobby for freer trade in sugar on world markets. As Chairman of this body for the first three years, I think we made some progress. From a producing and trading point of view, sugar is one of the most corrupted commodities of them all, plagued by subsidies, tariffs, quotas and government intervention. Apart from real progress in liberalising markets, it was a great honour to lead the group and make friends with producers around the world.

I have the view these days that governments everywhere have kept farmers poor. Rural producers the world over have wielded a large amount of political muscle, and when things turn bad governments are coerced into providing all kinds of assistance, from specific aid programs (think drought relief), subsidies, price controls, tariffs, and statutory support mechanisms. But what these measures ultimately do is intercept the structural adjustments necessary to move with the times, as happens in the business community, sometimes referred to as creative destruction. Commercial sectors cannot remain competitive without these forces at work.

I read one statistic that all drought relief in Australia goes to the bottom one-third of farms. Eighty percent of Australian wheat is grown by twenty percent of farmers. As a result we have so many rural producers locked into non-profitable and non-competitive commercial enterprises. It is even worse in that bastion of free enterprise the US, and much more so in the EU (I can remember walking through the French countryside on the Bon Camino Pilgrim track observing beef producers farming twenty head of cattle).

I retired from Queensland Sugar in 2004 but maintained links with the industry and its leaders. In 2010, I was shanghaied to assist the giant Chinese company COFCO (China Oils and Foodstuffs Corporation) invest in the Australian sugar industry. We set our sights on the Tully mill, one of the largest mills on the east coast, and which was on the market. We had to cultivate grower acceptance and at the same time beat off other potential buyers. I was virtually back in politics again, door knocking the farms. At one farm where they were advised I would be visiting, the lady of the house had baked a sponge cake in my honour. So lovely, old fashioned hospitality not so common these days. But what do you do if you don't eat sweets? I had to make an exception and tucked into it, bringing back memories of my dear mother fifty years ago, an accomplished and proud sponge cake maker, and that was nice.

The other memory I have was of the farmers all whinging about the volume of red tape they had to grapple with, not like the good old days: two days a week doing the paper work when all they wanted to do was get out on the tractor. I doubt that it has improved, as it seems red (and green) tape is a runaway locomotive.

We were successful in acquiring the mill in 2011. I didn't feel too guilty. It was on the market. The mill had changed from a grower owned cooperative to a public company, but with effectively the same grower owners. Maintenance was not up to scratch, and the injection of the selling price (circa $130 million) into the community would provide a great boost to the economy and individual wealth. And COFCO had pledged to honour the cane supply agreements negotiated with growers.

COFCO set up a subsidiary company called COFCO Australia to further invest in Australian commodities and asked me to be Chairman. We made a play for the Proserpine mill but were beaten by Wilmar Sugar which had taken over the CSR (Colonial Sugar Refinery) assets, and now represents half of the Australian sugar industry.

I left COFCO because we couldn't agree on governance. They were wonderful and friendly people; we agreed on the mission and strategy, but they kept interfering with delegated responsibility. In other words they set up an independent company but kept calling all the shots, with no concept of accountability for performance.

And you won't believe this one, but I also found them too democratic. At one broad-based meeting we had in Beijing, including both the President and Chairman (who was apparently a member of the Central Committee of the Communist Party), we talked all night, and we couldn't come to a resolution even though there seemed to be no opposition. We needed a bit of totalitarianism, we needed the Chairman to say, 'I think we have had enough discussion, and we have come to such-and-such a conclusion,' as any good Australian Chairman would have done. But my parting from COFCO was convivial and we maintained contact for quite some time.

LAZY BALANCE SHEETS IN AN ERA OF ASSET INFLATION

I was Chairman of two property management companies in the early noughties: Trinity Property Group (including Trinity Funds Management) and the CEC Group, based in Cairns and involved in construction, property development and management, both of which, as Chairman, I helped navigate through the ASX as successful IPOs. Initially both prospered in the asset boom days. It was so easy to grow wealth in those days with asset prices galloping ahead of interest rates by a substantial margin. We were accused from time to time, by analysts, shareholders and investment bankers, of having a lazy balance sheet, in other words they were encouraging us to increase gearing to increase profits.

I felt uneasy about this, something wasn't right. It shouldn't be so easy to make money (if it looks too good to be true it probably is!), and the notion of excessively increasing debt went against everything I believed. But I was new to the property industry, the groupthink was overwhelming, and as a business strategy it seemed to be delivering. Then the inevitable happened, by virtue of the contagion that swept the world following the US sub-prime crisis in 2007. Both companies got into considerable trouble, and I resigned from both, effectively accepting my share of the responsibility.

The inviolable lesson: there is no such thing as a lazy balance sheet (note how it has disappeared from the lexicon), it is much more appropriately re-termed a strong balance sheet, something so sacred in my set of values, yet surrendered to the groupthink of the time. As I have said one hundred times, values aren't values unless you live them, a valuable lesson re-learned.

They say experience is something you get just after you need it!

BIO-FUTURES – A BLUEPRINT FOR THE FUTURE.

This is the way of the future, of this I am certain. But it is a complicated concept and hard to explain in a few pages, but I will endeavour to give you the flavour of it.

In recent years I have become involved with agri-business start-ups, the most exciting being the bio-futures projects. The first was proposed on the Gilbert River system which drains into the Gulf of Carpentaria at the southern end of Cape York Peninsular. It was to be a greenfield development of a privately funded, large scale, world-class, vertically integrated and sustainable agribusiness.

In respect of the proponents I would like to recognise some of my colleagues. Stewart Peters, whose capacity to research, analyse, understand and present complicated commercial, agricultural and engineering concepts is as good as any I have ever seen. And John Grabbe, of Cubbie fame, who, as explained earlier, has an extraordinary capacity to identify, design, and evaluate water storage and reticulation solutions, even in the most unlikely of topographies. My brother Ian, a plant breeder and denizen of the Agriculture Faculty at the University of Queensland for sixty years, and dare I say it, a tub-thumping Labor voter, has embraced the project with extraordinary enthusiasm, and has been very active in the CO_2 life-cycle assessments.

The inputs for the project were water (approx. 600,000 mgls per annum), land (40,000 hectares [Ha] of irrigated sugar cane and 25,000 Ha of Guar bean) and capital. Although a large and complex project it would have employed all off-the-shelf technology.

It hasn't proceeded at this point because approvals in respect of the environment, water allocations, tree clearing, etc, are so difficult, so sensitive, so political, and so expensive. The Wilderness Society opposed the project because that is their mission, to oppose everything that creates wealth, and of course challenges the capitalist ideal. When they couldn't find a plausible environmental justification for their opposition, they cited economic issues. It nearly brought tears to my eyes: their heart-felt concern that the proponents might lose a quid!

Venture capital providers we approached to fund the pre-establishment costs, while excited at the project, were sceptical that governments, handcuffed to the Green militia, would ever come to the party and provide the necessary approvals.

Seed capital is much harder to access than development capital, because it carries so much more risk. We never had any doubt that if we negotiated all of the regulatory approvals and took the project to bankable feasibility, equity and debt finance for establishment and working capital would be available by the truck load. This was confirmed time and time again.

Do you think we will ever have a bureaucracy that says 'Why not' instead of 'Why?' As was the case in the halcyon days of Sir Leo Hielscher.

We have now made our IP available to a consortium proposing a carbon-copy project on the Mitchell/Coleman River catchment a little further north (the Mitchell River has an annual outflow of 12 million megalitres, second only to the Murray Darling, but none of it used commercially). This project is referred to as the Kowanyama BioFutures Enterprise (KBFE). Anthony Penrith, a resourceful Indigenous entrepreneur is now, in conjunction with the traditional Kowanyama owners, pursuing the project, with our support. They are hopeful of government seed capital support in the early stages to establish the business case, secure regulatory approvals and complete due diligence. If they can take it forward it will be a game-changer for remote and regional Australia of extraordinary proportions.

Under Anthony's proposal, the Government stands to redeem its seed capital investment by two times at financial close.

Just think. There are potentially ten or more of these projects in Northern Queensland, on streams with large monsoonal flows (there are 90 million megalitres of water flowing into the Gulf of Carpentaria each year, about four times the run-off capacity of the Murray Darling which drains half of Australia). Ten projects would result in $20-30 billion in investment, $5 billion in net profits, $3 billion in company taxes, 20,000 direct jobs, all in the most remote, disadvantaged areas in Australia, and no cost to the taxpayer, and no net carbon dioxide emissions.

The fundamental underpinnings of the concept:

Scale. Scale enables provision of on-farm processing, water infrastructure, economies in both buying and selling, high level on-farm research and development, and practical environmental protection. It can't work small.

Horizontal integration. Water storage and management, primary production, and processing are all part of the same entity, ensuring cooperation and perfect alignment. And of course this relieves what is referred to as the *tyranny of the farm-gate* (being at the mercy of middle-men with product still to be fully processed).

Vertical integration. So fundamental. The waste from one process becomes the feed-stock for the next process, nothing is wasted and everything is value-added. The primary product is sugar cane, selected because it is a familiar crop, it not only produces a cash flow in sugar/ethanol, but enormous amounts of bio-mass, effectively captured solar energy.

Sustainability. In terms of water and land management, generation and sale of renewable electricity, positive Green House Gas sequestration, it provides a roadmap to sustainable agri-business unlike anything attempted in the world.

Off-the-shelf technology. Although it appears to be a very complex enterprise, all the components are off-the-shelf, like sugar farming, a sugar mill, or a feed-lot, or meat processing facility – all done a hundred times in Australian ag.

Water is flood harvested into lakes and gravity fed to the co-located farming, aquaculture and processing facilities. The water is used multiple times, most notably in the processing facilities, for fish ponds (Red Claw and Jade Perch) and irrigation. No water is wasted.

The bagasse from the sugar cane, apart from co-gen electricity, is mixed with cane tops and guar waste to produce stock feed, which leads to a feed-lot, which leads to a processing facility (abattoir) which is economical because the feed-lot underwrites twelve months continuous supply of livestock (unlike other abattoirs in Northern Australia wherein the return on capital invested is compromised by the fact that they are closed for three or four months a year as the cattle supply dries up in the dry season). Sugar cane tops and trash are also turned into energy pellets (stored electricity) for sale.

The final modelled outputs from the single project are:

- Raw sugar – 535,000 tonnes per year (t/y).
- Jade Perch 20,000 t/y, Red Claw 10,000 t/y.
- Ethanol 100,000 mega-litres per year (ml/y).
- Dimethyl Ether (a cleaner burning alternative to diesel) 190 ml/y.
- Energy pellets 340,000 t/y.
- Guar gum 32,000 t/y.
- Meat products 53,000 t/y.

Financial modelling computes the capital cost to be just above $2 billion, and NPAT $450 million per annum.

To summarise, the significant strengths of the project are:

- An off-river, privately funded, water storage system that minimises the ecological effects of in-river dams.
- 100% reliable – storage is based on 100 year river flow records.
- Harvests less than 8% of the Mitchell/Coleman catchment water (environmental sustainability is usually predicated on 30% off-take).
- Uses water multiple times massively increasing the production per unit of water compared to traditional farming.
- 100% powered by internally generated renewable energy through a balance of biomass (co-gen) and pumped hydro.
- Precision application of nutrients via state-of-the-art trickle-tape irrigation. No nutrient run-off.
- Improved pest management (weeds and destructive feral animals).

- Creates in excess of 2000 jobs, mostly indigenous, in one of the most disadvantaged regions of Australia.
- A full Green-House-Gas (GHG) Life Cycle Assessment has shown that the project removes more GHG from the atmosphere than it produces, the first for any agro-industrial project in the world.

The project will address much of the inherent disadvantage experienced in these regions: distance to market, poor land management/feral infestation, unreliable and expensive energy, almost non-existing rate-base for councils, very low weaning rates for domestic stock and so on.

Social benefits are spread across communities:

- Guaranteed indigenous employment and ongoing procurement of services from indigenous providers.
- Creates a local market for cattle, reducing trucking costs.
- Creates skilled jobs which help to retain younger generation.
- Creates a platform for new technology start-ups in broad-acre tropical agriculture.
- In climate change terms it cools the planet by being a nett sequesterer of CO_2.
- The genius is in delivering mature, processed commodities, avoiding the so-called tyranny of the Farm Gate.
- This is the road map for the future, completely sustainable in terms of water use, soil and Green House gases – potentially transferable to other countries with available broad acres, such as South America and Africa. The first cab off the rank is so important to set out the pathway. A Government which helps bring this concept to life would own the regions in Queensland in a political sense for at least for twenty years.

Whilst I am sympathetic to the concept of the Bradfield Scheme being promoted by my good friend Sir Leo Hielscher and others, it is hard not to be sceptical about its economic viability. I can't see any reasonable return on the billions of dollars of investment. And because of its commercial unviability it would have to be completely funded by government. The bio-futures projects I have discussed above are privately funded, and the water is used where the good Lord provides it.

In summary the bio-futures projects are completely different in concept to the way we have always farmed. But in my view we need to look at new ways of doing things as technology and new learnings evolve. But to do this we need a change in mindset, policy, regulations and incentive. Because if we do what we always did, we will get what we always got.

AUSTRALIAN INSTITUTE OF COMPANY DIRECTORS (AICD)

In 2005 I was invited by then President Jane Wilson to fill a vacancy on the Queensland Council of the Australian Institute of Company Directors (AICD).

The AICD is the largest Institute of Directors in the world with more than 41,000 members throughout Australia, more members it is suggested, than the ALP. In 2010 I became the Queensland President and a Director on the National Board. I retired in 2014 (under the constitution members serve a maximum of nine years on State Council and three years as President). Because of transition arrangements I actually served ten years on State Council, four of these as President.

During this period I became a passionate practitioner of the theory of corporate governance and delivered many presentations on the subject throughout the State. I was also an AICD sponsored, top 200 mentor of aspiring female directors for four years.

On 26 September 2019 I was awarded the Queensland Company Directors' annual Gold Medal – for 'commitment to excellence in corporate governance.'

The award meant a great deal to me for, as I said in my acceptance speech, 'This award is final confirmation that I did indeed make a successful transition from politician to company director – or as some might say, from the darkness to the light!'

By the time I accepted the award, I was becoming increasingly despairing of the direction of corporate governance in Australia, the increasing focus on social justice (or woke) issues at the expense of shareholder value, and the increasing, unnecessary, and counter productive intrusion by regulators into corporate behaviour.

I addressed some of these issues in my gold medal acceptance speech (26 September 2019):

> That brings me to the sobering message I have for you all this evening, something I have been banging on about for some time now. I have never seen the business sector held in such low regard. It seems to me that more than half of the Australian people now see the private sector, the business sector, as the enemy. Taking cheap shots at business is par for the course – from mainstream media, social media, politicians, the public, social activists and so the list goes on.
>
> The question is, is that our fault or someone else's? Of course some of the fault lies with business itself; there are times when business performance has been less than perfect, and this has been exposed in various ways, most recently in the Royal Commission into Banking. But in my view the negative perception is greatly over-stated. The vast majority of businesses in Australia, under the guidance of their Boards, act ethically and competently, as good as anywhere in the world.
>
> We have just completed an election where one party campaigned on an anti-business agenda. They didn't win but the point is it would not have been conceivable to even run a campaign like that twenty years ago. The ideological opponents of the private sector and free markets continue to gather strength.
>
> As we move into the first half of the 2019-20 financial year it is therefore prudent to review the challenges ahead. The old challenges are still there: technology and disruption, and what is called the Fourth Industrial Revolution, the national and global economies, and the uncertainties caused by trade wars, sovereignty issues and political rivalries.

But there are a whole range of new challenges emerging, and mostly in what I call the socio-political environment. Directors are no longer primarily being held to account for their commercial performance, but increasingly for what is referred to as Corporate Social Responsibility (CSR), or as ESG – Environmental, Social and Governance criteria. Some say the social activists have finished their long march through the obvious institutions and are now turning their attention to the Limited Liability company, the fundamental driver of wealth creation and living standards in the Western world.

Now I know I swim against the tide here, and I am very conscious of a Director's ethical and legal obligations, of Corporate Social Responsibility as it were, and emerging sustainability mandates around the world. But in my view these are taking us in a direction that is not good for wealth creation, corporate performance or even public approval.

Feedback tells us that an unprecedented number of AGMs last year were invaded by people with social, as opposed to commercial, agendas. And they are having a real impact. BHP, the Big Australian, that icon of global resources, was hijacked at their AGM a couple of years ago by an activist group called Australian Centre for Corporate Responsibility (ACCR), demanding that the company withdraw its membership of the Minerals Council of Australia, a body they accused of vociferous and influential lobbying in favour of coal. Strange they would do that: advocate on behalf of their industry.

The ACCR is at the fruity end of climate policy. The Minerals Council under its then CEO Brendan Pearson argued for an evidence based policy on climate and energy, recognising the importance of coal and resources to Australia. Yet within weeks BHP was demanding Pearson's resignation, and got it. BHP with a market cap A$170 billion cowered in the corner and threw its hands up when challenged by a two-bob activist group. My message to BHP, and other woke capitalists as they are sometimes called, is that social media or noisy activ-

Keith DeLacy receives AICD Gold Medal for services to Corporate Governance (pictured here with daughters Jonnie and Jacqui, with the Story Bridge in the background)

ists don't provide a reliable compass capable of guiding mainstream business behaviour through difficult times.

Some of the banks decided to do their own virtue signalling too, announcing they would no longer finance new fossil fuel projects. A fat lot of good that did them in the public eye.

Our regulators have joined the cause celebré, banging on incessantly about culture. APRA has written a large thesis on the culture of the Commonwealth Bank (incidentally worth reading). And ASIC is singing from the same hymn sheet. You're not going to believe this, but ASIC now proposes to install a psychologist in the board rooms of our biggest companies, to ride shotgun on the culture. Yes Boardroom shrinks, imposed from outside. Can you imagine how distracting this will be to innovative decision making?

The trouble with an imprecise science like culture in relation to corporate governance, is that it can become weaponised and could add dramatically to director liability – a wonderful weapon for 'anti-everything' activists. Not only that, it is confusing for directors in terms of their duties and responsibilities.

Oh for the good old days when our primary duty was simply to grow shareholder value.

Jeremy Sammut of the Centre for Independent Studies points out that Corporate Social Responsibility (CSR) has become an industry in its own right, a specialist field of business management consuming ever greater hours of boardroom attention. He says that professionalisation of CSR comes at a great cost. Well-meaning sentiments come enshrined in rigid practices that suppress spontaneous order, the life blood of successful business.

Is it any wonder we complain about lack of productivity growth in Australia and a plateauing of wages and living standards? Latest estimates of the cost of red tape in Australia is $176 billion a year, now Australia's biggest industry, and growing daily.

I am pleased to see that the final edition of the ASX Corporate Governance Principles and Recommendations rejected much of the social engineering hype contained in the first draft. It no longer refers to 'a social Licence to operate'. I thought if I heard that once more I would go mad. Surely all directors worth their salt would take into account the social environment in which they operate: the law, the needs of customers, the workforce, the environment, the community, the regulatory regime; how do you operate in the best interests of shareholders if you don't? In my view we don't need to be lectured by social engineers to meet this fundamental responsibility.

Now there may be people in the audience with a different view point, and I accept and respect that. But while we may have a different view on some of the directions we are travelling, I agree that we must continue to look at new ways of doing things. It is getting harder and harder to provide the skills necessary to navigate companies through tomorrow, because increasingly we don't know what tomorrow brings.

My daughter, who is a leadership academic at QUT, tells me that when preparing people for leadership roles these days, focus is more on Emotional Intelligence (EQ) and relationship skills, as opposed to the basic organisational management skills of yesterday. As a Director in this era of constant learning, you need to be comfortable with ambiguity and at ease with constant change.

A brave new world.

So to conclude. As Directors, and I accept this, we have to deal with the world as it exists, not as we want it to be. There are so many more forces to deal with these days, many of them vague and invisible – sexual harassment, bullying, discrimination, diversity, sustainability (no, nothing to do with remaining solvent), climate change, social and environmental activists banging on about ESG, and the list goes on – and you need to be equipped to face up to these challenges.

But the main advice, and best protection, in this confused world, is do what's right – Integrity with a capital I. Respect the primacy of shareholders, and stick to the Director's golden rule, the fiduciary duty – act honestly, in good faith and to the best of your ability. It's not that hard.

My secondary advice is to be prepared to argue your case, don't roll over and get into virtue signalling. It doesn't help. Be proud of what you do and sing your song. Use every opportunity to promote the value you bring to society as a successful enterprise – the wealth you create and what this wealth means to everyone – better living standards, better health care, better social underpinnings, even better protection of the environment. And the jobs you create, both direct and indirect, the taxes you pay – and not just company tax but royalties and payroll tax to the states, and income tax paid by employees, and the services all these taxes deliver, and the dividends distributed to the Mums and Dads in the super funds of Australia (that's who own BHP and the big banks, not that nasty 'big end of town'), and the payments you make for consumables and how this bolsters a range of micro economies.

And finally, and I know this is currently controversial, but I believe there is no place for corporates in the political world. Leave that to the politicians, they have all the skills necessary to stuff it up on their own. It aggravates me when certain corporates appropriate the status of their company to push the social justice causes of the day, foisting them onto employees and unsuspecting customers alike. How do those Boards know it accords with the views of their shareholders? And is it consistent with their duty to act for a proper purpose, in good faith and in the best interest of the company? And the money companies spend on these social frolics is not their money to play with, it is shareholder money.

As someone said, 'Go woke, go broke!' For those who aren't into post modernism, 'woke' is a new word of African American derivation meaning a heightened awareness of issues relating to social and racial justice.

If you must get into the political arena, stick to your knitting, argue for good economic policy, policy settings that are good for business, good for productivity growth and help expand the economy. This helps everyone, not just business. There seems to be so much silence in these areas today.'

Since that speech the governance environment has deteriorated further. New whistle blower legislation has substantially increased personal liability for directors and officers. Further, APRA has advised that banks and insurance companies will be put through tough new, institutionally focused, climate change stress tests. Not to be outdone ASIC has announced that it would be escalating its climate change policeman role by targeting companies that fail to tell shareholders and customers about climate change risks affecting their business.

For the record I personally don't believe that business is at any increased risk from climate change per se, but they sure as hell are at risk from climate change policy and related regulatory intrusion.

I worry how young directors can accommodate this when they

are not yet comfortable with traditional duties and responsibilities. A good example is Westpac. The directors were right across their woke responsibilities, parading their progressive social justice credentials at every opportunity, big on diversity and inclusiveness and climate change and asylum seekers. All they forgot to be big on was their basic compliance and legal obligations, and responsibility to shareholders! As *The Economist* (quoted in *The Australian* 28 December 2019) said, it is more fun to outline your vision for humanity than for increasing EBITA margins.

Not long ago there was a group of we 'stale, pale and male' company directors shooting the breeze as it were, most with long and meritorious director backgrounds, and each one of us, without exception, expressed the opinion that we were thankful our director careers were coming to an end, instead of just commencing, in view of the uncertain and liability challenges ahead, and in view of the intrusion of social justice forces into corporate governance. I think that is sad. Are we inadvertently hollowing out the gene pool of experienced and competent directors? Is that good for society, and the economy? It will certainly provide more opportunities for younger aspiring directors, and women. But should we be bequeathing them such a regulatory and risky minefield?

Can you imagine how left-wing social activists, emboldened by the warm inner glow of confected virtue, and their animosity towards modern market economies, will seize on this new suite of proclamations delivered from on high, and weaponise them to harass, intimidate and blackmail boards, and sue directors, ultimately to debilitate the sector which creates so much of the wealth and prosperity that we so cherish (and they all luxuriate in).

The specific area where it is already impacting is with insurance premiums. Companies are finding it difficult to access directors and officers (D&O) liability insurance, and to the extent that it is still available there are multiple exclusions that almost render it worthless. The premiums have increased dramatically, by as much as 250% over the last seven years (the Global Insurance Market report revealed the cost of taking out directors' and officers' liability insurance or financial services professional indemnity insurance (PI) doubled in 2019) almost taking the insurance out of the reach of many small companies. Much of this increase has of course been driven by the increasing frequency of class actions. But the escalating imposition by regulators of new and expanded fiduciary duties provides the oxygen for the class action zealots that are stalking Australian corporate life. One slogan is 'fight for fair': what this really means is fight for a fair bit of money!

The spiralling cost for directors and executives to protect themselves against class actions has generated what Marsh has called 'a perfect storm: greater risk, higher premiums, lesser coverage, increased retentions and lower limits'.

For the record I am fundamentally opposed to class actions. It is an American disease imported into this country. In Australia we have always abided by the classical philosophy that shit happens, get on with life. When something goes wrong why is it obligatory to find someone to blame and then sue them? It is not the button that ordinary Australians reach for, but now we have imported litigation funders and greedy lawyers running the show. And it can be quite perverse, as in the case of a shareholder class action suing the company, i.e., suing themselves. You know the only people that will make money out of this.

I am taken by the fact that ASIC, usually so quick to find new areas to regulate, has vacated this field. A law unto themselves, litigation funders demanding a 300% return on their investment. I learned about one case where workers suing their employer walked away without a cent despite a $5 million judgment in their favour – $2 million to the litigation funder, and the rest to the plaintiff law firm and administrators. Access to justice indeed.

Law firm Herbert Smith Freehills (not a class action firm) provided a stakeholder briefing on class actions that uncovered some staggering statistics. It showed that the average distribution of settlement proceeds paid to victims had decreased from 59 per cent of damages awarded in 2016 to just 39 per cent in 2019, whilst at the same time the fees paid to law firms increased by 11 per cent. The litigation funder's commission increased also, from 15 per cent to almost a quarter. It is estimated that the super profits of litigation funders are 17 times larger than those that might be achieved by investing in ASX 200 shares.

There are reports that Australian companies are not proceeding with investments, not because of normal risk, the risk of doing business, but because of the risk of class action should things not work out as promoted. I feel profoundly uncomfortable calling for more regulation, but we don't need regulation; simply take away the right of litigation lawyers and funders (no pay no fee) to operate in Australia. Chase all the ambulance chasers to countries that need them.

Back to insurance. It is not just D&O premiums which are escalating wildly. Property insurance is also increasing exponentially. And will continue to do so as insurance companies need to take into account not only the actuarial liabilities on their balance sheet, but the threat by the regulators to hold them accountable for not taking account of the climate change stresses to which they are theoretically exposed.

One of the great problems of contemporary politics is the notion that the government can solve every problem: legislate or regulate, the answer to everything. I can remember Prime Minister Julia Gillard incessantly boasting about the volume of legislation that her minority Government had passed, as evidence that it was getting on with the business of governing. The questions we might reasonably pose are, who asked for all those pieces of legislation; have they made society better; and has each piece delivered more benefits than costs?

Who regulates the regulators? We should remember that lurking inside every regulation is the universal law of unintended consequences.

No one is saying that we don't need to ensure banks and other financial service providers are regulated in the public interest. But agencies created to address a perceived problem seem to possess a biological need to expand and increase their remit way beyond their original mission. As if a financial services company doesn't have enough oversight, the Australian Prudential Regulation Authority (APRA), Australian Securities & Investment Commission (ASIC), Australian Competition & Consumer Commission (ACCC), the ASX, the Banking Ombudsman, Australian Transactions Reports and Analysis Centre (AUSTRAC), and the Australian Taxation Office (ATO) are all riding shotgun over the industry. We hardly need each of them expanding their mission and in the process multiplying red tape and gobbling more taxpayer and shareholder money.

Let me give you an example to which I was a peripherally involved bystander. In 2014 Aquis Australia, a business controlled by the Hong Kong based Fung family proposing to build a mega resort, including a casino, in Cairns, launched a takeover bid for the Reef Casino in Cairns (of which I was a Director, but that is not relevant to this anecdote). The Australian Competition and Consumer Commission (ACCC) launched an investigation into concerns about potential reduced competition in the casino sector in Cairns. I am serious; reduced competition in the casino sector in the provincial city of Cairns.

At the time, motivated only by my commitment to good governance, I issued a media release which said in part:

> I believe this intervention to be a gross abuse of process. For goodness sake, who has been calling for more competition in the casino industry in Cairns? Where has been the competition during the last twenty years when there was only one casino? If they have so much time and nothing to do, why don't they also do an analysis of the lack of casino competition in Mt Isa where there are no casinos?
>
> Mr DeLacy said the Queensland Government was well equipped and well experienced in issuing casino licences and dealing with all the issues raised by the ACCC. 'That is where the responsibility lie. We can well do without this mindless duplication.'
>
> Mr DeLacy said the ACCC obviously had too many resources at its disposal if it chooses to be involved in make-work-schemes like this. If the Federal Government wants some advice about their budget repair task I can give them some – wind back these unelected statutory bodies like the ACCC who are so obviously over-stepping their mandate.'

Is there a better example of Government agencies out of control? Maybe. On the same issue, after the take-over offer was announced to the stock exchange, ASIC required both Aquis and the

Reef Casino (which has a very small free float, and in a stock exchange sense is a very minor player) to provide details of all meetings between the parties and other relevant bodies, and when each person who had knowledge of the offer became aware of it, probably costing more than a million dollars worth of corporate time, and maybe as much again for ASIC. The alternative would have been to engage a 7th grade school student who could have checked and advised that as there was no movement in the share price prior to the announcement, there was no issue of insider trading to worry about.

4

Philosophical Hot Spots

In the last few decades there has been a massive cultural evolution in the Western world, underscored by a mindset highly critical of the society in which we live, which sees only the bad and ignores the good. It is supported by a range of ideological carcinomas, some newly minted, and others given a new lease of life in a grand post-modern reinvention. I thought I might use this section to discuss these emerging philosophical hotspots, as they will help illuminate my cultural and political evolvement in recent years.

THE OVER-REACH SOCIETY

I walk around Brisbane all the time these days – meetings, coffees, shopping, and the forlorn need to keep fit. I keep observing people, very judgmental: their expressions and what they could possibly mean, their dress, their addiction to devices, their street manners. Some fashion-house decided some years ago that a frayed knee on a pair of jeans (distressed denims) could be seen to be cool, lived-in and care-free, not smart and over-dressed and up-yourself. So cool, so how to be cooler – a tear in each knee. So how to be cooler still, more tears… It's called OVER-REACH. Now some jeans look like they have been through a chaff cutter; so cheap looking, but high-end fashion, and oh so trendy.

The same with short shorts, in the Brisbane sub-tropical summertime, shorter and shorter until … referred to in Brisbane as the labia majora look (proving that not all bogans are illiterate)! My question always is, 'What do their mothers think?' Do their mothers matter any more?

And tattoos. Once upon a time a small colourful embellishment of the skin, perhaps a symbol of rebellion, was cool. Then of course two tattoos were cooler, until the whole body was a quivering kaleidoscope of colour. OVER-REACH, but cooler and cooler. My word, there will be some ugly seventy-year-olds in fifty years' time!

My point is that our society is suffering from a disease called OVER-REACH, and it is not confined to physical ornamentation. Harvey Weinstein was outed as a predatory harasser utilising his position of power and influence to further his lascivious desires. The #MeToo movement exploded out of the blocks. It had broad public support.

But it burst into over-reach territory in the blink of an eye. Millions of women with agendas jumped on board, sexual harassment (poorly defined) became the cry. Many men were tried in the media and the court of public opinion with no presumption of innocence; just widespread acceptance that the man has done something awfully wrong leading to a collective pile-on, public shaming, summary rejection of apologies, and eventually career ending punishment. There was even a demand that journalists abstain from using the word 'alleged' when reporting a woman's claims of harassment, even historical harassment. Surely we can pay appropriate respect to the claims without trashing the rule of law.

An allegation does not a victim make!

Inevitably it became a political tool, the most outstanding case being the use of the #MeToo zeitgeist by Democrats and political activists in the US to oppose the nomination of conservative Brett Kavanaugh to the American Supreme Court. Kavanaugh was accused by a woman, with no corroboration, of sexual harassment thirty-five years earlier when, wait for it, they were in high school; she was 15 and he was 17.

While the movement is still raging it is in danger of losing the mainstream because of the over-reach. There are many women out there who have sons, and husbands, and vex how these loved ones are going to negotiate the rocky shoals of the #MeToo tsunami, the new rules of engagement, the insecurities associated with roles, the potential social disaster or reputational death so easily delivered. As Bettina Arndt said in her Book *#MenToo*: 'Most ordinary women are fed up with the male bashing that has come to dominate the public agenda.'

Men are being turned off, especially the notion that all men are rapists. Many male executives are now reluctant to relate one on one with females, to offer comfort and support, whether working, travelling, mentoring ... And surely that is not good for society in general. But the worst outcome, as the over-reach and over-use discredits the movement and turns it into a women verses men contest, serial predators use it as a cover.

Though it is largely beyond the scope of this memoir, the Black Lives Matter movement suffers from the same disease: over-reach, stoking the fires of racism to overcome racism. Hysterical activists are the greatest dead-weight an otherwise noble cause can have.

On this subject I think it is worth commenting on the counter-productive political consequences of in-your-face protesting. I have said before that revolutions end up eating their own children. My experience in this regard goes back a long way. I learned my lesson during the street marches of the Bjelke-Petersen era. Earlier I made the point that I was out door-knocking as a dutiful aspiring political candidate, while the streets of Brisbane were colonised by protesters full of self-righteous fury. I was shocked to observe that it was turning Mr and Mrs Average off, not seducing them with the merit of the cause. And the proof was in the pudding. Sir Joh, a superficially mediocre leader, served more than seven terms and nineteen years as Premier of Queensland, ably assisted, dare I say, by well-meaning opponents who became intoxicated by a cause, to their own detriment.

The #MeToo tsunami, as discussed earlier in this chapter, has suffered from the same disease, over-reach. And Black Lives Matter (and the associated cancel culture) is becoming counter-productive too. I hate to say it, but the reconciliation overtures of Indigenous Australians, i.e., Constitutional Recognition, and the Voice to Parliament, are in my view now in danger of being killed by the self-defeating exuberance of the Black Lives Matter protests who unfairly stain the motives of all Australians, to the extent that the potential referendum also looks to be a dead duck, killed by friendly fire.

Climate Change alarmism and Extinction Rebellion are destined to go the same way.

During the Same Sex Marriage plebiscite in 2017 I spoke to a number of people who admitted that they voted against the proposal, not because they fundamentally opposed it, but they resented the bullying tone and the name-calling of its advocates. The Australian philosophy is generally to live-and-let-live, which can manifest itself as, I have nothing against it, but if you try to shove it down my neck you can go jump.

IDENTITY POLITICS

Karl Marx was the true father of identity politics. In his view people were not individuals but members of a class. Wherever Marxism was practised, without exception, the concept of class emerged, then class enemy, then a collective guilt. If you were a member of the wrong class you were guilty.

The Labor Party was therefore a logical manifestation of group identity, representing the working class. Although the Party, formed after the great shearers' strike of 1891, aimed to pursue the interests of the working class largely through the democratic process – except it seems to be OK these days for trade unions to break what they term unjust laws, or for groups to ignore democratic verdicts and glue themselves to a public road. There was a strong adversarial element to it; the class war language of 'them and us' predominated. Many ALP members were of course disciples of Marx (some still are), though it takes a special kind of wilful blindness to ignore the gruesome manifestations of Marxism wherever it has been practised around the globe.

Martin Luther-King made what seemed to be the ultimate demolition of identity politics. In his epochal speech in 1963 he said: 'I have a dream that my four little children will one day live in a nation where they will not be judged by the colour of their skin, but by the content of their character.' This was a revolutionary concept, embraced I thought by the left everywhere. We weren't members of a group. We were members of the human race.

Mind you in the post-modern world which we now seem to be inhabiting, a sentiment like this could easily be labelled micro-aggression because it seemed to be rejecting the prevailing identity zeitgeist, and sadly Martin Luther-King would likely be cancelled today!

From that time on great progress was made (in the Western world, though my focus is Australia) to address, to ameliorate, and greatly eliminate many of the 'isms' and 'phobias' that so blighted society over the ages: racism, sexism, homophobia, xenophobia …

Universal liberalism, based on respect for each person regardless of identity, is where I thought we were going.

Then I stumbled on a new insight. Some people see racism almost as a systemic virus: it floats in the air, it is here, it is there and it is everywhere. So you don't need racists to have racism, you don't need bigots to have bigotry, you don't need oppressors to have oppression. In these cases of course the arguments of the aggrieved are unfalsifiable, not susceptible to objective challenge.

Decent people everywhere vehemently oppose racism. Of course Indigenous Australians still struggle to share equally in the benefits society has to offer. But that is not racism. Most mainstream Australians fret about this and wish they could rectify it.

Moving on. Women occupy a vital and expanding role in both our workforce and society, and virtually all of the in-built discriminations of the past no longer exist. You wouldn't know this however if you listened to the so-called progressive elite and feminist activists who promote the identity politics of discrimination; this despite the unremitting music of crashing glass ceilings.

Same-sex marriage has been legalised and gay people no longer need to hide their gayness (in the West that is, but not in many other countries – countries which never seem to attract the ire of social justice warriors in the West). And so the list goes on.

Do we celebrate these wonderful advances? Have we walked away from seeing people as a member of a group instead of as individuals? No we do the opposite. Despite Martin Luther King's liberating proclamation in 1963, we are not 'free at last!' We seem more determined than ever to put people into identity prisons based on race, ethnicity, gender, sexuality, class… Australia's notorious white Australia policy was abolished in 1967 (more than fifty years ago). It had become clear that judging human beings by their skin colour was out of step with contemporary thinking.

This is part of the over-reach that so infects modern society. And it is fast developing into a cancer. People in an identity grouping become prisoners, sentenced to a life of grievance, blame-shifting, non-performance, unhappiness, emotional anger, and even hatred. Once you can absolve yourself of personal responsibility, once it is always someone else's fault, or the fault of history, there is a loss of agency, no way out. There is only misery. The challenge for us all in Australia is to reaffirm our commitment to a universal liberalism whose principles, policies and ways of life are genuinely colour blind, and recognise no identity grouping.

'We don't do personal responsibility,' said black civil rights lawyer Candace Owens, commenting during the race riots in the USA, 'we just blame white people!'

I should take a moment to explain 'liberal', or 'liberalism', as it is very confusing. From this point on I will mostly be using the word 'liberal' in terms of the classic 'Lliberalism' of the Enlightenment – a framework based on liberty, individual responsibility, limited government, freedom of speech, equality before the law, consent of the governed and so on. However, uniquely in Australia, 'Liberal' denotes the conservative side of the two party political system, contrasting this to its dominant use around the world, meaning progressive, i.e., the Left, i.e., Social Democrats, i.e., left-wing. Surely made to confuse.

WHITE PRIVILEGE

The privilege of life is enormous. The odds of even being here as the individuals we are, as determined by ancestral couplings going back millennia, and the conception free-for-alls, is one in a trillion to begin with. And on top of that, to be living in the best place in the world at the best time in history.

I count my blessings. But as I do I hear voices, turning to shrieks at times, to count your privilege instead, white male privilege that is, or as they malign us these days, stale, pale and male (old white men), the tyrannical patriarchy which it seems is responsible for the imperialist, racist, sexist, homophobic, transphobic, hegemonic, cis-supremacist, climate denialist world that we now inhabit.

So, am I privileged? Well in terms of physical gender, certainly so: it is much easier for a man to pee, and much simpler to dress. And as Titania McGrath says in her brilliant satire on wokeism, 'There are perks with being male – they rarely have to queue for toilets and they are statistically less likely to fall pregnant.'

But the sixty-four dollar question is, would I have ended up in what I regard as a good space presently had I been born a female, or a person of colour? The answer is, probably not. Many of the roles I have filled, especially a couple of generations ago, were expected to be filled by white males. But at the same time we should not underestimate the primacy of attitude in making progress through life.

The more pertinent question therefore is, would I have been in this good space if I had spent my life howling about the dud hand I had been dealt and searching for someone to blame? The answer of course is self-evident.

This constant refrain of white male privilege can be a bit tiresome, especially the obligatory guilt associated with it. Also the underlying contentions that this so-called privilege is un-earned, and responsible for the failure of others to prosper. Many of the people I see occupying the higher stations in life these days come from working class backgrounds. Most people that get to the top do it through hard work and application. And attitude. Not because of intrinsic privilege. And I hate to say it, most people (not all) who end up on struggle street do so because of their own personal shortcomings, not because privileged oppressors got in their way.

I understand that some people see privilege in a much more generic sense, the all-pervasive white domination that theoretically prevents others from realising their destiny. This is another construct of the culture wars so overwhelming Western society today.

I was amused recently to read that Chelsea Clinton finished college and got a job at NBC that paid US$900,000 per year. In the meantime her mum Hilary flies around the country speaking out against white privilege.

This makes the obvious point, that in imputing privilege, we see it in others, more so than in ourselves. That being as it is, I still formally reject the notion that what I got out of life was unearned, or not fully earned. And I reject the notion that I have a privileged attitude that prevents others from being active participants in modern Western society. But the opportunities that present themselves have to be grasped, not sneered at, and the bad times accepted with the good. I had to elbow my way into the opportunities as they emerged in life, none were preordained, some were not attractive, and some were tough. And as I reflect, there were always people, at every turn in the road, who were stronger, or faster, or smarter or more talented than I was, yet … Is that privilege, or attitude?

There are many white people out there struggling unmercifully to grind out a life. They must be wondering where all this white privilege is.

We can't do much about our maleness, or our whiteness – apart of course from beating ourselves up because of it, something I am unlikely to do. So the question is, how does 'calling out' this so-called privilege help?

How does railing against confected oppressors help? As I said elsewhere, human dignity and fulfilment come from earned success, not wallowing in victimhood. Manufactured hatred of the so-called privileged just leads to an ugly life. My advice: climb out of that deep trench teeming with grievances like tormented serpents and have a go, meet the challenges, accept the vicissitudes, lighten up, enjoy life, love your loved ones, laugh a lot and make the most of this wonderful world we live in.

RACISM – stamping it out makes it worse.

The Indigenous community of Yarrabah, just south-east of Cairns, was part of my State electorate of Cairns which I represented for fifteen rears. I was very close to many of the residents, and I thought Alf Neal, an elder, one of the true gentlemen of the world.

I was good friends with Indigenous identity Clarrie Grogan, from Mona Mona Mission near Kuranda, but a member of the Ewamian People, and a State boxing champion, as was his brother Harry. Clarrie loved driving bush and was my unofficial campaign manager (and bodyguard) when I stood for the electorate of Barron River on both occasions, bearing in mind Barron River took in Mareeba to the west of Cairns and Port Douglas and the Cape Tribulation area to the north. Clarrie's sister Esme Hudson was very supportive of our branch (from memory I think she was a member for a time). Esme's son David Hudson was a famed Indigenous entertainer and Didgeridoo player, and was one of those instrumental in establishing the renowned Tjapukai Aboriginal Cultural Park just outside of Cairns.

I was also quite close to the O'Shane's. Militant unionist and rough-hewed Irishman Tiger (Patrick) O'Shane married Kuku Yalanji woman Gladys. Their daughter Pat O'Shane became an aboriginal activist, as well as being the first female aboriginal barrister, first female aboriginal magistrate, and first female aboriginal NSW departmental head. Tiger lived down the road from me for quite some years after his wife died. His sons Danny and Terry were also up front in agitating the aboriginal cause.

I also was friends with Pat O'Shane's first husband, school teacher and aboriginal activist Mick Miller who for many years campaigned for greater social justice, land rights and improved opportunities for aboriginal people.

Back to Yarrabah. The message I took away from there was that Indigenous communities need real work opportunities for a critical mass of the population, for two reasons: (i) the culture of work needs to be learned, and absorbed, and shared, through doing, and through realising the financial and life-fulfilling benefits, and (ii) a sharing society, such as is the traditional aboriginal way, what's mine is yours kind of culture, where the few in the workforce share their earnings with community, even sharing in the costs of the brother's addiction, soon erodes the work ethic.

In this context it is time that large mining and agricultural enterprises stepped up to the plate, as Twiggy Forrest proposed doing in Western Australia, and commit to employing critical masses of Indigenous workers, in partnership with Commonwealth Government agencies training them to be work-ready.

I was chairman of a consortium aiming to establish a large-scale irrigated agricultural project in Cape York Peninsula (see p. 155). We had committed to employing at least 20% indigenous workers, approximately 200 when in full operation. In this context it would have been a life-saving breakthrough for a number of aboriginal communities on Cape York Peninsula, and contributed enormously to the objective of 'closing the gap'.

However the growing notion that Indigenous Australians are essentially a separate race, as epitomised by the term first nation peoples, who should be funded at great expense to live in places where there are no viable jobs, where supplying basic services is very costly and where alcohol, cigarettes and drugs are the only antidote to degradation, boredom and despair, doesn't bode well for substantial improvement in the future.

The Labor Party, and people who identify with the left, claim to have a more sympathetic attitude to Indigenous disadvantage and Indigenous causes generally. I was 100 percent on board with this predisposition. But as time went by I began to recognise that although the sentiments could not be faulted, the policy positions adopted by the party and the left intelligentsia generally were counter productive and producing negative outcomes.

The original inhabitants of Australia were dispossessed of their land and way of life by British colonists. No intelligent Australian of whatever extraction would dispute that assertion. Nevertheless, it is grossly dishonest to pass judgement according to current standards and values on events of two and a half centuries ago. Had Captain Cook not claimed Australia for George III, then French, Dutch or other explorers would most certainly have claimed it for their own less benevolent empires. And in my view, supported by much literature, it is a gross sham to pretend that the arrival of British settlement and Western civilisation on these shores heralded the destruction of a pre-existing Garden of Eden.

Aboriginal leader Noel Pearson, employing his vintage oratorical exuberance, accused the ABC, 'the miserable racist national broadcaster' of being racist by engaging in the 'soft bigotry of low expectations'. He argues strongly that notions of entrenched victimhood hinder, rather than help, Indigenous people. It fosters a culture of low expectations, and robs people of a sense that they can change their lives for better or worse. The ABC was outraged; they are the least racist (most woke) of all institutions, and most sympathetic to left wing causes. But that was Noel's point. He runs educational programs on Cape York Peninsula for Indigenous students and his strongest message is that you must take responsibility for your own actions, your own progress in life. Yet there is this ever escalating voice arguing that this disadvantage is because they have been colonised, dispossessed, invaded, victimised, discriminated against … It is always someone else's fault, a state of mind that is seriously at odds with the notion of self-improvement.

The more racism recedes as a factor in modern society the more the left activists see it everywhere. They demand ever more recognition of their plight, more concessions, more gestures, more punishment of the oppressors.

I read somewhere that if you deny you are racist it obviously proves you are a racist. Of course if you admit to being racist then of course you are racist. It's a tough world out there!

As Frank Furedi pointed out in *The Australian* (10 March 2019):

> From the standpoint of identity advocates, the role assigned to Australians is to apologise and continue to apologise for the misdeeds of their ancestors centuries ago.

The sixty-four dollar question is: does it help?

Let us look at the way the body politic in Australia has recognised, and responded to, Indigenous disadvantage over the last fifty years. I said above that mainstream Australians are aware of the disadvantage suffered by Indigenous Australians and would do whatever it takes to overcome this.

According to a 2017 Productivity Commission report, total direct government expenditure on Indigenous Australians in 2015-16 was $33.4 billion. This represents $44,886 per capita for Indigenous Australians, compared to $22,356 for non-Indigenous. Ordinary Australians do care. They would move heaven and earth to remove this disadvantage, but it is an issue so frustratingly impervious to solution.

An extraordinary range of other actions also points to the goodwill of mainstream Australians and their support of reconciliation.

The referendum in 1967. The first great breakthrough, overwhelmingly carried by Australian voters (one of the few successful referenda in Australian history), which effectively recognised Aborigines as Australian citizens for the first time, and delivered all the benefits that came with citizenship.

Aboriginal and Torres Strait Islander Commission (ATSIC) was established by the Hawke Labor Government in 1990. It was a representative body through which Aboriginal and Torres Strait Islanders were formally involved in the processes of government affecting their lives.

Mabo High Court decision in 1992. This breakthrough recognised native title in Australia for the first time.

The Native Title Act 1993 quickly followed. It enabled Aboriginal and Torres Strait Islanders (ATSI) to make an application to the High Court to have their native title recognised under Australian law.

The Stolen Generation report, emblematic of the bleeding heart orgy which consumed Australia at this time. The Human Rights and Equal Opportunity Commission conducted an inquiry into the separation of ATSI children from their families – a gut wrenching read but with little concession that although misguided, many of the separations were well intentioned.

1991, **reconciliation walk** (250,000 walkers) across the Harbour Bridge.

The Redfern speech. PM Paul Keating in 1992 acknowledged the impact white settlement, with its attendant death and destruction, had on indigenous people, culture and society.

Parliamentary apology. PM Kevin Rudd, not to be outdone, in

2008 delivered a long demanded apology to the stolen generation, recognising the decades of mistreatment of Indigenous Australians.

The Racial Discrimination Act making discrimination on the basis of race unlawful was passed in 1975.

Section 18C added in 1995 took it a step further, making an action unlawful if it was likely to offend, insult, humiliate or intimidate. Together with the formation of a Human Rights Commission to police the Act.

A new national curriculum for school years K-10 mandates that students study 'the contribution of Aboriginal and Torres Strait Islander people to the Australian nation, the significance of Dreaming and the perspectives and meaning in dreaming stories' (nothing incidentally in the curriculum about the contribution of Western civilisation or Judeo-Christian values).

The University of Western Sydney has a policy that 'Perspectives of Aboriginal and Torres Strait Islander Australians must take primacy in any discussion about Australian nationhood, national identity and democracy.'

Welcome to Country ceremonies. Virtually every formal public presentation in Australia today commences by recognising aboriginal land and paying respects to Elders past, present and emerging. And very often, a special ceremony to kick things off.

The aboriginal flag was officially proclaimed Flag of Australia status in 1995, and flies over most Government buildings.

Not to mention the endless hand wringing in political circles about the lack of progress in 'closing the gap'.

We now have a **National Apology day** on 13 February, **Close the Gap day** on 19 March, **Harmony Day** on 21 March, **National Sorry Day** on 26 May, **Reconciliation Week** 27 May to 4 June, **Mabo Day** 3 June, **NAIDOC week** (July), **National Aboriginal Children's Day** on 4 August, **International Day of Worlds' Indigenous people** on 9 August, **Indigenous Literacy Day** 5 September.

To show respect to indigenous culture we now have **Indigenous NRL and AFL rounds** in the national competitions.

The words to our national anthem **Advance Australia Fair** have been changed from 'young and free' to 'one and free' in order to be more inclusive.

And **Coon Cheese** – lonely and lost on the supermarket shelves.

There are still further demands on the table.

First Nation's Voice. In accordance with the Uluru Statement from the Heart, a First Nation's Voice is proposed to be enshrined in the constitution, a Makarrata Commission for truth-telling established, and Indigenous recognition in the constitution.

Australia Day. Another symbolic step it seems is to change the date of Australia Day – or to re-name it Survival Day, or Invasion Day.

And so the list goes on. Don't you think it is about time the extraordinary reservoir of goodwill reflected in these gestures and reforms over the years was acknowledged? How do we appease the unappeasable? How much reconciliation is enough?

The sixty-four dollar question is, have they helped? Judging from the ever-increasing activism (and not only from Indigenous voices but increasingly from the broader self-loathing left establishment) we would be justified in coming to the conclusion that they have not advanced the cause of Indigenous Australians one iota; that all these reconciliation initiatives weren't worth the paper they were written on. Or worse still, in trying to stamp out racism we are making it worse. So the logical question to ask is what is the point of further concessions, further gestures, further acknowledgements?

It seems for some people it is not progress and reconciliation they want, it is the intoxication of the battle and the warm glow of victimhood. Race activist Nayuka Gorie showed her appreciation for all of these reconciliation concessions by proclaiming on ABC *Q&A* in November 2019, 'We've tried for 230 plus years to appeal to colonisers' morality which doesn't seem to exist.' 'Let's burn stuff,' she went on to urge (gee don't you like 'our ABC?' In order to provide balance and demonstrate fidelity to its charter, *Q&A* also included on the four person panel anti-ageism female activist Ashton Applewhite, militant feminist Mona Eltahawy and feminist Jess Hill – all advocating or defending violence against white males. It was moderated by ABC left-wing personality Wendy Harmer, charged it seems with ensuring that the left message was not corrupted!)

Further improvement in the lot of our Indigenous brothers and sisters will forever elude us if we continue to entrench the notion that it is the membership of the group that determines a person's progress, or lack of progress, in life, and not one's own efforts and sense of responsibility.

I have heard aboriginal leader Noel Pearson describe the dole as 'passive welfare' or 'sit-down money' – money to do nothing. One of the consequences of this, in the absence of real job opportunities, is that Indigenous communities around Australia are now plagued by chronic unemployment, welfare, alcohol dependency, child abuse and dysfunctional families.

But instead of focusing on this, and the notion that human dignity comes from earned success, the activists keep emoting the so-called black armband view of history. But name a culture on Earth that hasn't got some shameful chapters in its past? Australia much less than most. We can't change history. But it is counter-productive to blame history for every vicissitude in life. The solution is in the here and now, and involves a massive change in attitude, a targeted look at welfare, some tough love, education, and real economic development leading to real jobs in the communities – the dignity of work and a role in modern society. And the opportunity to feel good about life.

As an aside let me ask who was the saddest victim of the Queensland University of Technology imbroglio when a number of students were abominably treated by the Human Rights Commission? No, not the students, but the original claimant, poor Cindy Prior, a victim of resentful and confused identity politics. As they say, if you spend your whole life seeking grievances you will surely find them.

As for the Australian Human Rights Commission: can it point to one person it made happier over the years, happiness like that which comes from love, or success, or achievement, or helping others, or laughing at things that are funny (even politically incorrect things), or laughing at yourself ... No, we have a taxpayer funded body with a nihilistic world view, which spends its days soliciting complaints from Australians about how racist we are. Its whole purpose, it seems, is designed to entrench victimhood and resentment; and if this was indeed the organisation's mission, it has been an extraordinarily successful institution.

But in reality it is another breathtaking example of well-intended government policy intervention turning to slush on the vine.

But back to the pathway for Aboriginal advancement. As Jacinta Price (30 November 2018) recently pointed out, Aboriginal activists campaigned for decades for full rights as citizens. Now they have them they should also accept the responsibilities that come with citizenship.

Aboriginal people must adapt; sure, be proud and celebrate, and promote, your heritage, and the dream time, but don't become a prisoner of it. I know it is controversial to say so but Australia is now a Western civilisation, and a very successful one, and the only road to fulfilment, for every citizen, is to be part of that society, not standing outside throwing stones at it. Martin Luther-King never played the victim card. He inspired his people to be the best they could be. Of course we can always have a better society, but that is a challenge for each one of us. But please focus on now, not yesterday.

I can hear the screams of racist, white privilege; regrettably that is the way of much debate these days. The fact is I was not brought up to be racist. I would argue that my parent's identification with left ideology and concern for the oppressed (what better symbol of the failings of capitalism than the plight of Aboriginal people in this country) rubbed off on me.

I have always had a great deal of sympathy for the Aboriginal cause, though I confess a big weakness for practical outcomes and little tolerance for the current overreach, the plethora of gestures and symbols which in the end make no difference, the blame and grievance culture, and the counter-productive embrace of the shackles of identity politics. The irony couldn't be greater. The so-called left progressives today determined to negate the progressive clarion call of Martin Luther King all those years ago.

SEXISM – the default setting

I lived a large part of my adult life in a household of females, a wife, three daughters and the cat. Because of this historical gender reality I am amused these days at the widespread disapproval directed at Alpha Males. Dare I say it, our household would have ceased to function without a constant injection of a bit of toxic masculinity. 'Dad there is a toad in the pool!' 'Dad there is a dead rat at the front door!' 'Dad there is a big frond on the driveway!' 'Dad the gutter is full of leaves!' 'Dad there is a snake in the laundry!'

My wife was largely what is referred to as a home-maker. She did spend quite a deal of time in the paid workforce (and four years effectively running the Railway Newsagency in Cairns) but she still saw herself largely as a home-maker, proud to be so, and pleased to be the pillar of unconditional support for all members of the family no matter where their aspirations took them. The point I am making is everybody to their own, no choice is morally superior to any other. Her three daughters all became consummate professionals. The two daughters with family are also proud mothers, an accomplishment of equal value.

In 2014 I donated a kidney to my wife. It was a successful procedure and she enjoyed four more years of enhanced lifestyle without the burden of dialysis. People often said that we were lucky to have the appropriate compatibilities. My stock answer always was that you had to be compatible to be married for fifty years! She passed away in 2018 (after 56 years of marriage) from an unrelated illness, though no doubt expedited by the compromised immune system she had to manage as a result of the transplant.

I miss her very much.

The Women's Liberation Movement was active in Cairns during my early political days, the 1970s. They mounted a campaign to establish a women's shelter (titled Ruth's Shelter after one of the founders), an initiative almost before its time, led by a small group of women of great character and drive. My eldest daughter, who had a good singing voice, used to sing Helen Reddy's 'I am woman' at all of the supporting events, an empowering song if ever there was one.

Regrettably it seems the women's liberation experiment in our family has run its course as all of the grandchildren and great-grandchildren (seven so far) are males; you can't keep the buggers from re-asserting the patriarchy!

There is no culture, nation, race on earth that hasn't treated women badly at some stage in its past, cast them as second class citizens, or chattels, with no sense of equality. Some nations still do it today. One explanation is that it was a biological thing. Men were bigger and stronger because of the Darwinian self-selection theory that they needed to be bigger and stronger and more aggressive in order to win the race for a mate. It seemed to apply not just to humans, but all species, almost without exception. In the late twentieth century, when survival of the fittest was no longer the determinant of human relationships, feminism stepped up to the mark to address these ingrained inequalities.

It is widely accepted that there were a number of waves of feminism. The first wave focused on fundamental legal rights: the right to vote (the flag bearer), to divorce, equal guardianship over children, equal property rights. It took a long time, but eventually these rights were achieved, entrenched, and largely accepted by all and sundry.

The second wave of feminism took off in the 1950s, underpinned by access to birth control, and which moved on from basic rights to all of the lifestyle rights of a modern society: equal access to education, the right to pursue a chosen career, equal pay, maternity leave, childcare support, reproductive rights, and the safety of women inside marriage. The aim was to allow women an equal shot in the journey of life, comparable to men.

But it took a while. In the 1960s women were still not allowed in the public bar of a hotel (unless they were on the other side serving the men). Merle Thornton, mother of actor Sigrid Thornton, together with Rosalie Bogner, famously chained themselves to the public bar at the Regatta Hotel in Brisbane in March 1965. It became a pivotal moment in the women's liberation movement Australia-wide (though I wonder about the rationale of a well organised and executed protest aimed at obtaining the privilege of fronting a public bar with the proletariat).

Thornton also led a successful campaign for the removal of the marriage bar in the Commonwealth and State Public Services (women had to cease their employment when they married). The end of the marriage bar was legislated in 1966.

The principle of equal pay for equal work was recognised in the Universal Declaration of Human Rights in 1948. In Australia, the principle of equal pay for equal work was sanctioned by the Conciliation and Arbitration Commission in 1969. Nearly fifty years later it is rare, but not unheard of, for women to be paid a lower base wage than men doing the same job. This was collaborated in a report commissioned by the Australian Government in 2016 which found longer interruptions in work-life for women, and industry and occupational segregation were primarily responsible for the pay gap. (Note the practice of women making different career choices than men is now called 'occupational segregation', drawing it into one of those interlocking circles of oppression, and somehow making it sexist).

There is arguably some progress still to be made. But it is hardly the end of the world if some women make a choice to enter lower paid occupations or respond to a biological need for parenting (I know I am getting into dangerous territory here – maybe micro-aggression!)

The question is, have the gender activists sheathed their knives now that basic legal and lifestyle rights have been largely achieved, and widely accepted by the broader community? Of course many of them have. But others have taken out the sword instead. It's the same old story, sexism, as with racism, the more it recedes as a factor in society the more the activists see it everywhere.

Gender politics seems to have morphed into identity politics; women are one of the minorities (not sure how they work that out!) and prevented from blossoming because of the insidious nature of male privilege, and the power that comes from that privilege. As Douglas Murray says in *The Madness of Crowds*, 'if anything ever picked up steam and careered off down the tracks it was feminism over recent decades.' These third wave feminists (sometimes called fourth wave), primarily in the US, all of a sudden saw men as launching a war against women to roll back the progress made by women over the years. A number of very influential books were published by feminists: Susan Faludi, *Backlash: The undeclared war against American women*, and Marilyn French, *The War against Women*. These third wave feminists saw this subterranean war everywhere. It was all in the eyes of the beholder however as most of us war-mongering males were blind to it. Of course these movements are fed these days by that sewer now called social media, and hashtaggery. 'All men are trash' became a popular hashtag in the US. It seems third wave feminism had turned on men. Another popular hashtag was 'Kill all men.' The #MeToo movement, as I point out in the chapter Over-Reach (p. 172), further nurtured this sentiment that men were the enemy.

One wonders how this vulgar misandry promotes the women's cause such as it is, and how it would have affected the initial movements for suffrage had it been in vogue then. Marilyn French takes up the cause of male violence. She says that every time women make an advance, men can be found mustering all their forces to defeat the challenge. 'All male violence toward women is part of a concerted campaign that includes beatings, imprisonment, mutilation, torture, starvation, rape and murder'. Bloody hell, what world does she live in? And she is talking about Western countries, not the Taliban!

One wonders, when the concept of male privilege is discussed, have they taken into account that men are three times more likely to commit suicide than women, get killed in a dangerous occupation, be sacrificed in a war, or experience homelessness?

But wait, there is some sympathy for men. The American Psychological Association claimed that 40 years of research showed that traditional masculinity, marked by stoicism, competitiveness, dominance and aggression, is undermining men's well-being. They want us all to be snowflakes. How will we ever retain the Rugby League State of Origin if this gets a head of steam?

But Australia is not much better. The Australian school curriculum presents traditional male characteristics such as fortitude, courage, physical strength and mateship as negatives.

Now we see it has seeped into the armed forces. In the same week America let us know they'd lose to China in a Pacific war, the Australian Defence Force is sending our troops to 'gender sensitive, gender inclusive and gender responsive' training (one wonders what kind of battle the armed forces are being prepared for?)

Now it is not for one moment that I think most women are disciples of this nonsense. However it is just amazing how it developed a head of steam. Cries of sexism have in many instances now become the default setting for some women whenever things don't go their way, much more so today than when real discrimination and real sexism were the determining factors in progress through life.

In the US tennis open in 2018, Serena Williams was beaten by Japanese rising star Naomi Osaka, and she put on a terrible turn, abusing the umpire, calling him a cheat, smashing her racquet and screaming sexism. HUH, sexism! Serena Williams just happens to be the greatest beneficiary of sexism in the history of sport. She is allowed to play in a women's only competition (men not welcome), earning tens of millions of dollars per annum. If she had to play in a truly non-sexist competition, an open competition, including the likes of Roger Federer, Rafael Nadal and Novak Djokovic, she wouldn't be smashing an expensive racquet because she may not be able to afford a new one.

Not that I am advocating this. I support the current (sexist) arrangements. Are they under threat from transgenderism?

Like female runner Alex Blake who took part in the Queensland University of Technology (QUT) Classic Fun Run in April 2019. It was an open event and she was first female home. However when she learned that the first three place getters, all males, shared the $3,000 in prize money, it was blatant sexism! 'In 2019 I rarely feel discriminated against as a female, especially in running. However, today I did. The place getters in the male race all took home money, the women got nothing,' Blake said in a Facebook post. But it wasn't a male race, it was an open race. What Ms Blake really wanted was a sexist race, where she only had to compete against the same sex. QUT quickly caved in and Ms Blake was suitably appeased, remunerated, and reassured in her peculiar understanding of sexism.

South Australian High School teacher and union delegate Regina Wilson posted the following on the Australian Education Union's Facebook page in November 2018:

> I am going to try to ensure that the next generation of voters in my classroom don't vote Liberal, without being political of course, as I won't tell my students what to think, but I will teach them how to be critical thinkers who question those in power and especially those who seek to keep the status quo for the rich, upper classes and refuse to acknowledge the rest of us.'

Outrageous don't you think? Yet when the social media dam burst it was all because of sexism, not an egregious abuse of professional responsibility.

I sometimes wonder what these campaigns, fingering sexism and discrimination, are designed to achieve. I can remember one prominent female company director advising aspiring female directors not to pour the water, 'because men will expect you to do it all the time.' Wouldn't that be terrible if you were cast in the role of a woman? Imagine spending the rest of your directorial life being stereotyped as a woman. I really don't get it: if you want to pour the water pour the water, if you don't want to, don't. It is only a small cohort of practitioners who see a negative in being a woman.

Julia Banks was the Federal Liberal member for Chisholm, elected in 2016. When Malcolm Turnbull was unceremoniously replaced by Scott Morrison, she left the Liberal Party in a huff and moved to the cross benches. The reason she left was her claim that she had been bullied. You don't have to be a political psychologist to work out what happened: she went through a torrid leadership spill, as did many others, members lobbying for votes, politics at its rawest. My view is that if you see that as bullying you should be in another game. Then she claimed sexism, and at one stage said that her primary objective was the empowerment of women. Uncorroborated claims of bullying, deserting the party that elected her, and non-specific claims of sexism wouldn't in my mind empower women, either in the eyes of men or women. Or am I getting a bit harsh?

When I was on the national Board of the AICD I had a view on gender equality which didn't exactly coincide with that of my colleagues. At that time there was a concerted movement for greater gender diversity focusing on ASX 200 Boards, with a target of at least 30% female. While I am a great believer in diversity on boards, all types of diversity (diversity of skills, of work experience, of qualification, of personality type as well as gender), my view was that we were not social engineers; our mission was to improve governance. Of course if we could do that by increasing female representation, then OK. As it turned out this was easy because there were many intelligent and qualified female directors standing at the entrance door. Accessing this pool would add to the depth of governance firepower. In summary I was not against more women on boards, it is just that it had to be done for the right reasons consistent with our charter.

Mind you there was another factor of which we had to be aware: if we didn't move fast enough then a busybody government could introduce quotas which in my view would be in no one's interest, whether women, men or governance.

Just in case some readers may have jumped to the conclusion that I am marooned in a sea of misogyny, I rush to defend myself. I sincerely believe I only ever judge a person by the content of their character. I am a supporter of gender diversity. But as usual I am always committed to practical outcomes and consistent principles. I make the point here that for four years I was an AICD 200 mentor to aspiring female directors, something I enjoyed very much – and sometimes I thought that the mentees had so much talent they should have been mentoring me!

And just to drive home this point a little further, I was succeeded as the Member for Cairns by Desley Boyle, I was succeeded as President of the Queensland Council of the AICD by Sally Pitkin, and of course I was Chairman of Macarthur Coal when we appointed Nicole Hollows as Managing Director; all in all, a very poor record for a misogynist.

And I do have three daughters!

And my favourite all-time singer is Ella Fitzgerald!

So to conclude, let women be women in all of their feminine complexity, and men be men in all of their masculine complexity.

There is one area of gender relations that troubles me, indeed troubles a lot of people, and that is what seems to be an epidemic of violence against women, especially domestic violence, so much in the news these days. Has it deteriorated to the extent it seems, or is it a product of increased focus and media attention – cell phones and rugby league? I simply don't understand it. What sort of society are we turning into?

I am sure it wasn't like this in my day. It seems it was a different society then, more respect for women, more discipline, fidelity to the family and to society generally, fewer welfare dependent families, fewer single mothers and teen pregnancies. The institutions of society played a major role in the inculcation of values – institutions like the church, so influential then, so marginalised now. Even I, the product of an atheist family, had to attend church at Townsville Grammar School. And those timeless passages from the bible had meaning: 'Do unto others as you would have them do unto you.'

The narrative of heaven and hell had real meaning too. And the marriage vows – these days very often not seen as an expression of mutual love and consent, but as a construct of the patriarchy.

I can remember years ago, I was chatting with an older cousin of mine Ronnie Clarke (incidentally Grandfather of Cowboy's hard man Scott Bolton). I was about 12 and he 16, and he was giving me some cousinly advice: 'You never hit a woman, that is something a man never does,' he said with such sincerity and feeling that it has stuck in my mind for seventy years.

I also often think of those wonderful love songs of the 1950s, the golden age of music: Ella Fitzgerald, Bing Crosby, Frank Sinatra, Nat King Cole, Doris Day and so on, and always singing songs of everlasting love. Compare that to the rap songs that so absorb young people today, the messages they leave, and where it leads them. And pornography largely demeaning to women, aided and abetted by social media, has exploded onto the scene.

I am not saying for one moment that there was no domestic violence in those days, but unless community mores conspired to keep it out of sight (which I think they did to a certain extent), it was nothing like the scourge it appears to be today. Is civilisation going forward or backward?

In summary, it is not hard to understand why there is a deficit of discipline and respect in society these days. There is a crisis in values out there, and we are paying the price, as are many vulnerable women and their children.

I also make the point that those progressives that complain loudest about the patriarchy, about domestic violence, about the oppression of women, about harassment, have led the way in discrediting the institutions of modern Western society. Many engage in a sneering put-down of religion, and Christianity in particular, and therefore undermine the value system it once nurtured.

Rape is rape, no argument there, a crime that goes back into antiquity, no excuses. Harassment is a different subject, not nearly as black and white, nevertheless, unacceptable in the modern value construct, and men need to understand this, even decent men without lascivious intentions. It can be compounded when inept advances are made in the context of so-called workplace dominance syndrome. Boy/girl relationships are destined for a major rewrite going into the future. Let's hope they don't make the relationships obsolete!

5

DIVERGING FROM THE FAITH

I thought it might be useful at this stage to analyse the increasing estrangement I have felt from the ALP in recent years. It is part of that timeless debate: is the Labor Party leaving me, or am I leaving the Labor Party; a story of values and the policy settings to deliver those values. Who has deviated from the chosen path?

It is appropriate also at this time (before I get into negative territory) to recognise that there are many wonderful people in the ALP, people I respect, and people who have honourable intentions. So sometimes when I lament changing values or counterproductive policies and attitudes I might be referring to the left generally, and more so the so-called progressive left or green left, not necessarily the ALP *per se*.

As I said before, when I left politics I closed the door behind me, closed it on that echo chamber which conveniently reaffirms prejudices, so essential for keeping the faith and being a political practitioner. I started to see policies through a different lens, but not I am quick to say, different values. I believe I have never changed values, but certainly at times, changed in my mind the policy prescriptions necessary to realise those values; or at times I came to the conclusion that the policy settings the left championed were inimical to realising its own values, or at best just empty slogans.

The ALP started to lose me during the Rudd and Gillard (RGR) governments. It wasn't just their incompetence, though that was manifest. Can you remember Kevin Rudd's grocery watch and fuel watch just after he was elected? I remember saying to my wife, 'I can't believe this. That's the stunt you do in Opposition. You don't set up things in Government which will have no effect, but will gradually attract to yourself all of the latent resentment associated with the issue.' But it soon became clear that Rudd was not about fixing things, he was about announcing them, king of the announcables. Bob Hawke (I hate to include him in this pantheon) did it too, but he wasn't afflicted with the disease to the same extent Kevin was – 'By 1990 no Australian child will live in poverty!'

In the beginning I may have been able to accommodate this incompetence with a bit of ideological filtering. After all most other governments were hardly heroic models of competence. But it continued to add up.

Firstly the rapid transition from budget surplus to deficit worried me greatly, it always does, it is a hang-up from which I can't escape. This debt affliction is not confined only to Labor, but they seem always to get the gold medal.

Running up debt like there is no tomorrow is a cardinal sin in my view, asking our children and grandchildren to fund our lifestyles. We are stealing their childhood. I might conscript Greta Thunberg to this one as the young are entitled to cry, 'How dare you!' Of course this applied at both a state and federal level – the loss of the Triple A rating, and the uncontrolled spending and expansion of debt, under Labor's watch in Queensland, has been hard for me to digest.

Edmund Burke's timeless truism, more than 200 years ago, 'Society is indeed a contract. It is a partnership ... not only between those who are living, but between those who are living, those who are dead, and those who are to be born.'

I can remember all of the progressive media, the apologists for the left and the big spenders, the ABC, the *Guardian* and the Fairfax papers defending this rapid deterioration in fiscal position by pointing out Debt-to-GDP is worse in many other countries, especially countries in southern Europe like Greece. Whoopee, what a measure of accomplishment. That's like saying that although our cricket team lost the World Cup, Bangladesh did worse!

Labor (and the left generally) seems to have developed an addiction to debt, as though it is good (an alternative to that horrible austerity I presume).

Mind you this attitude to debt and spending is not necessarily an electoral liability. Generally the public doesn't penalise governments for overspending, in fact they welcome it. They don't see government as a guardian of taxpayer funds, but rather as an entity that distributes taxpayer funds.

The following truisms underpin public spending.

- We used to thank previous generations for the prosperity they have bequeathed us. Now the table has turned: we must thank future generations for bequeathing us today's lifestyle!
- Hardly an election goes by without the Labor Party accusing the Coalition parties of preparing to slash expenditure. In other words it is not over-spending that is the mortal sin, it is not spending enough (of other people's money).
- Election campaigning is never about saving money, it is always competition to see who can spend the most, i.e., deliver the most goodies.
- When governments don't support a cherished proposal they are labelled lousy, never prudent.
- What does it do to our democratic system when the voting public realise they can vote themselves largesse from the public purse?
- Debt and deficit are sadly no longer issues in election campaigns.
- As I have said previously, debt doesn't give you more money to spend, it just brings the spending forward, bequeathing the austerity to future generations.
- Remember, all spending is ultimately at the expense of other spending: 'Is this the most cost effective spending?' should be the eternal anxiety.
- And I must continually re-emphasise the point: spending other people's money is hardly a measure of generosity.
- Nothing is free; who pays is the eternal question.

- The spenders and the spoilers live in the same body. Those that want to spend big are invariably those who do their very best to stifle the wealth creation which would underwrite the spending. Think Greens!
- Prudent tax payers should be rewarded, not penalised.
- One of the iron laws of life is that there is always a day of reckoning.
- What goes up must come down.
- It is easy to give money to the undeserving, but it is hard to take it away from them.
- If it seems too good to be true, it probably is (example following).

There is now a new and beguiling justification for financing deficits, a radical departure from Economics 101, called Modern Monetary Theory (MMT): a sovereign government can create as much money as it likes, so long as the money is denominated in its own currency, without backing it with assets (gold, silver, etc), without having to borrow (issue bonds), and without taxing its citizens. The left, especially in the US (but no doubt now infecting the Australian left), have jumped on this: money for nothing, wealth without end, and no end to the charity you can lavish on a grateful electorate.

I am doubly concerned about this theory, especially the prospect that governments feel they can print money, and this 'debt' does not have to be repaid. With the onset of the coronavirus (almost outside of the remit of this book) governments feel they have had little choice, after summarily inflicting great privation on the economy chasing health outcomes, but to increase debt, stimulate the economy and find answers for rapidly increasing unemployment. In other words, 'whatever it takes', with little acknowledgement of the trials and tribulations ahead, dramatically reducing the budget headroom for future shocks, or how these measures largely rule out productive micro economic reforms in the future. Adopt the mug theory to suit the moment.

I don't quite understand all components of Modern Management Theory. But as I said above there will always be a day of reckoning.

Money that has purchasing value, can't come from nowhere, and ultimately must be repaid. Who repays it is the essence.

I have re-named the MMT the Venezuela Monetary Theory (VMT), where people are now eating their own pets, and burning their currency to keep warm.

Some call it the magic pudding theory of government finance.

Or I could call it the Zimbabwe Monetary Theory. In 2008 the Zimbabwe trillion dollar note was worth US40 cents.

Ah, how it takes a slab of socialism for the underlying truths to emerge.

There is no doubt that there is a considerable gulf between the ALP and myself when it comes to attitudes to debt and public spending. It seems to be getting worse with the advent of MMT. I therefore have to admit it is me who has deviated from left orthodoxy in this regard (though I would hope the Labor Party doesn't take pride in the fact that its orthodoxy is debt worship).

The next assault on my relationship with the ALP was the anti-business rhetoric which flowed daily from the Federal Government during the Rudd/Gillard era. Federal Treasurer Wayne Swan could not open his mouth without attacking the private sector by invoking the class war and the politics of envy. He saw business as the enemy and made no secret of the fact. It is hard to know if he genuinely believed in this philosophical misadventure, or whether it was a conveniently concocted narrative designed to rally the deluded faithful.

I know the Labor Party emerged from the trade union movement and its adversarial mind-set, workers versus the bosses as it were, or more classically Marxist, the proletariat versus the bourgeoise, which Marx saw as the titanic struggle which would end in the triumph of the righteous. You know where it really ended! History forcibly demonstrates that the triumph of the righteous can only be delivered by a truncheon wielded by a totalitarian state.

Many (but not all) ALP members are genuinely hostile towards business. Profit and private sector are dirty words. In their minds business is on one side and they are on the other – this is the class war. They see only the worst excesses of business (because obviously they are looking for the worst). Perhaps this is another example of confirmation bias, all inhabiting the same narrow silo, reinforcing and exaggerating widely held beliefs. It is not based on fact. I spent over twenty years heavily involved in business, on a whole range of fronts. And I seldom, if ever, came across this alleged greed, this alleged anti-social anti-worker mindset. There is some of course, humans are humans, and when it occurs no one supports it.

When discrepancies in administration do occur in the private sector, nine times out of ten it is by mistake; try interpreting some of the complex awards and the sometimes multiplicity of industrial awards that some small businesses have to deal with (sometimes over 200 permutations), while deploying the scarcest of resources. If Woolworths and Coles can fall foul over the detail with the resources they have access to, imagine the challenge for the local café? The Restaurant Industry Award has 23,500 words and is very complex; probably meaning most restaurants will be breaking the law sooner or later, in one way or another.

My advice, focus on the real indiscretions, and if valid call them out, but don't extrapolate wildly from there.

I thought times had changed in the Labor Party too. Bob Hawke did not seek to alienate or demonise business, or promote the essence of the class war. He co-opted business into the prices-and-incomes accord with the unions. Keating cut company tax from 49% to 33%. Then Hawke and Keating introduced a range of business friendly, free-market, micro-economic reforms which set Australia on the path of continuing growth and prosperity, which of course benefitted workers as much as business (as they knew it would). How different this is to Labor in 2019, which is determined to see business as the enemy in a world divided into good and evil. Treasurer Swan would have seen the accord as a pact with the devil.

In respect of the class war, I think it timely to face a breath-taking truth, it doesn't exist anymore, except it seems in the minds of some obtuse trade unionists (the present ACTU leadership comes to mind) and Labor politicians who have never been out in the real world. As I said above, not many people have sat around more board-room tables than I have over the last twenty-five years. Yet I never heard an anti-worker sentiment promulgated. The IR discussion was always about the three R's: how to recruit, retain and remunerate the work-force, not screw them. On top of this, class consciousness is increasingly an alien concept to most workers these days, apart from the rapidly diminishing cohort of the heavily unionised. After all everyone now plays at the same golf course!

As I said earlier, many of the captains of industry now come from working class backgrounds, totally bereft of class-war hang-ups. And as I lamented in the chapter on corporate governance, a large swath of corporate leaders are joining the woke mob, hardly the refuge of class war soldiers. But one thing is certain, if you categorise all business, all employers, as the enemy, as a mob of crooks, then don't expect any of them to vote for you, even old Labor voters.

I'll therefore leave it to you to decide whether the anti-business narrative was true blue Labor, or political expedience. Did it reinvigorate electoral support from the so-called working class lost by the Party's flirtation with progressive green left causes, surely its major justification?

A bigger question, and this is important to me: what was this policy of division doing to the communal fabric of our nation, pitting class against class, employee against employer, and poisoning the image of business. The old truism: you cannot further the brotherhood of man by inciting class hatred. Bob Hawke had moved on many years ago in this respect too, when he said, 'Australia can no longer afford to go down the path of confrontation and fragmentation which has embittered so many aspects of the political life.'

From a personal point of view, where did it leave me, immersed in business, believing that a strong and growing economy was in the best interests of everyone, including the worker, and particularly those on the lower rungs of the income ladder. Being in the corporate world did not diminish my desire for a fair society and equality of opportunity. It was just the strong belief that Labor's prescription for a fairer society: industrial relations rigidity, high penalty rates, anti-business, anti-bank, high tax, anti-investment and anti-aspiration policies, would achieve the opposite.

It's not that Labor afficionados are always on the wrong horse. They universally see 'jobs' as fundamental to both a functioning economy and a fairer social system, and the objective of full employment is enshrined in their platform. Many of the new Left however do not understand how an economy works, and that many of their social and environmental interventions destroy jobs and standards of living, especially for those people they purport to represent. In Australia the workers lose their jobs, not their chains.

As Friedrich Hayek, famed Austrian-British economist and philosopher said, 'If socialists understood economics they wouldn't be socialists.'

I was amused recently to see in the ALP policy platform the following: 'Entrepreneurs and innovators from around the world should be encouraged and invited to come to Australia to see their ideas developed, deployed and commercialised.' So romantic and well meaning, almost brings a tear to your eye. One might ask how these innovators will be encouraged: by globally uncompetitive corporate taxes, increasingly rigid and inflexible work practices such as the re-invigorated proposal for industry wide bargaining, energy policies leading to ever increasing costs and deteriorating reliability, and an ever growing miasma of green and red tape. Good luck. So sugary, so motherhood, so meaningless, so devoid of practical policy pathways. It is not what you say that counts, it is what you do.

As an aside, isn't it funny how protagonists can capture neat metaphors to encapsulate their ideological position. The left belittle the advocates of growth as the answer to inequality by describing it as 'the trickle down theory of economics.' Those who see increasing growth and prosperity as in the best interests of all participants (as I do) claim that 'a rising tide lifts all boats.'

Mind you, for the record, there has never been a formal intellectual trickle down theory found or proposed in economic literature, voluminous as it is; it is a nice debating point conjured up by those who are implacably opposed to basic rational economics. As Thomas Sowell says in his essay *Trickle Down Theory and Tax Cuts for the Rich*, 2012, it is the classic case of arguing against a caricature instead of confronting the argument actually made.

There is no doubt in my mind that progressive policies, especially those that have led to some of the highest energy prices in the world (despite our abundant natural resources), trade union intransigence, which in many cases has moved well beyond wages and conditions and into management prerogatives, planted the seeds of our rapid manufacturing decline, ironically at the expense of the blue collar worker they were theoretically designed to assist. This was nowhere more obvious than in the car industry. One might ask where is Holden today, but be careful you blame the right miscreants for its disappearance (see op-ed below).

In 2012, depressed by where we were heading, I wrote an op-ed for *The Australian*, a satire, with my tongue planted firmly in my cheek, on: A strategy to de-industrialise Australia.

'A clean green economy – how we are winning the war' (Keith DeLacy *The Australian*, 2012):

> Ford is going, Gove Alumina is going, now Holden … we've still got Toyota, Qantas, SPC Ardmona, but the pace is hotting up. It has been easier than we could have imagined.
>
> We knew we were on a winner when we had two parties, the Greens and the ALP, chanting the mantra – 'a clean green economy'. We expected it of the Greens, but we couldn't believe our ears when the Labor Party started. They used to be the party of blue collar workers, and as we all know, there is no place for blue collar workers in a clean green economy.
>
> We held our breath when Paul Howes, the national secretary of the Australian Workers Union (AWU) and very close to the Labor Party, one of the so-called faceless men, said he wouldn't support a carbon tax if a single blue collar job was lost. The AWU is one of those unions that has actually stood up for their workers in the past, unlike some other unions best left unnamed, so this could constitute a problem.

Still we were confident we were on a winner. You see most union officials these days don't come from the factory floor, they are educated in the green fields of academia, and only come to the union as a stepping stone to a career in parliament. So it was unlikely they would rock the boat by sticking up for workers. And so it proved.

When we started this campaign for a clean green economy we knew we had two lethal weapons. If we were to get rid of the brown parts of the economy like manufacturing, it had to be via energy prices and labour costs.

Australia has a plentiful supply of cheap coal, much of it located close to population centres. We therefore had some of the cheapest base load power in the world, a crucial factor for competitive manufacturing. We needed to tackle this front on.

We love hung parliaments, it makes life so much easier. We insisted, in secret of course, that a carbon tax be the price of stable Government. She fell for it like a dream, never saw it coming really. The carbon tax served two purposes, it pushed up the price of energy of course, but perhaps more importantly, it took the spotlight off our other schemes, which are even more important in increasing electricity prices.

The Renewable Energy Target (RET) mandates that 20% of energy must come from renewables by 2020. Battalions of magisterial windmills now grace our hillsides, and rows of photovoltaic cells glisten in the sun. Really makes no impact on total global emissions (the blessed wind won't blow when you want it and the sun won't shine in the night, so it all has to be backed up) but it meets our objective of greatly increasing the cost of electricity – set to cost Australian consumers $1.6 billion per year by 2020.

The one we really like is the Feed-in tariff. Over the last decade State Governments around Australia, mostly Labor, introduced fixed tariffs for excess electricity fed back into the grid from roof top solar panels. Some of these tariffs, as high as 60c per kilowatt hour, were up to ten times the cost of coal generated power. Some recalcitrant Liberal governments have started reducing the tariffs but the original premium schemes have been grand-fathered till at least 2024 – so they will have a large impact on electricity prices for a long time yet – long enough for us to achieve our goal.

What we especially like about the feed-in tariffs is that it is not costing our own people in the leafy suburbs – in fact they are making a quid out of it. Not only do they get these inflated prices for the solar power they generate, very often when the grid doesn't need it, but they also get generous taxpayer subsidies for the installation of solar panels. The poor of course don't get any of this because they can't afford the panels, or they live in rented accommodation. It is the classic case of the poor subsidising the rich.

You would think someone would make an issue out of this. However the people with a voice are ones who are gaming the system. Nearly makes you giggle really – remember the days when the ALP looked after the poor!

The cumulative effect of these three schemes has been to more than double the price of electricity in Australia. Now a lot of people think it is all about reducing global warming. Gee how lucky are we that no one ever asks, like the French revolutionaries, what the sacrifice is for? The fact is if we achieved our goal in Australia of reducing emissions by 5% by 2020 it is estimated it could reduce projected global temperature increases by 0.0007C by 2050 – that's less than one thousandth of a degree! But even that won't happen because at the same time China is increasing emissions each year by more than our total.

The ABC of course is on our side so they won't be asking difficult questions. Don't you just love it when they do a story on emissions of carbon dioxide, a colourless, odourless gas, and they highlight boilers belching steam. It's a classic con, but oh so effective.

But we are not a one trick pony.

There are a number of large brown industries in Australia that not only depend on cheap power to survive, they are very vulnerable to uncompetitive work practices. In order to achieve our goal of a green economy, we therefore select those that have strongly unionised workforces – aviation, car making, refining and smelting, food processing and so on.

Look at Qantas. It used to be Government owned so it is very heavily unionised. And it is operating in an extraordinarily competitive international market, so selecting it is a no brainer. Though there is one downside – if we close Qantas down it will make it more difficult to travel to our international conferences to save the world? But sometimes even we have to make sacrifices for the greater good.

We were very close to a major victory in October last year with a brilliantly engineered industrial campaign. Steve Purvinas from the Aircraft Engineers Union even warned passengers against flying Qantas, the company that employed him. We respect such commitment to the cause but I wish he wouldn't be so frank and honest – someone might wake up to our real game.

Bloody Alan Joyce stuffed it up by grounding the whole fleet. I can remember the days when the Irish were on our side! But we live to fight another day.

You should have a look at Holden's Enterprise Agreement (EA) negotiated with the unions. Holden workers are getting about twice the award in terms of base rate of pay, but when you add in loadings, penalties, allowances and hardship payments it is three times the award and multiples of our global competitors.

But it is not the actual wage rates that are winning the war, it is the work practices. Under the EA Holden has very little control over its own business. Even to employ a casual for an hour they have to get permission from the union. Half of the people working for Holden aren't building cars – they are supervisors (it seems there is one team leader, who is not allowed to touch the plant, for every six workers), Occupational Work and Safety officers, union delegates and what have you. Union delegates get ten paid days a year for union training, and we would be highly surprised if they came back from these sessions with a plan to improve workforce productivity!

Our biggest obstacle in closing down the car industry has been bloody Governments. They keep piling subsidies in. I was really upset when earlier this year Julia announced a strategic co-investment of $275 million. I was upset about the language too. It is just a bloody tax payer subsidy, yet strategic co-investment sounds so grand. She's on to us, control the language and you control the debate we always say!

And it is not only Julia. What about Kevin bloody 'I don't want to be Prime Minister of a country that doesn't make things' Rudd? He's gone now, but blokes like him can be very dangerous as there is be no limit on how much tax payer's money they are prepared to waste.

But even then we were still confident, for two reasons. Firstly Kevin was usually only concerned with the announcement, not the outcome. And secondly, we were confident that no matter how much money Governments threw at the car industry we could soak it up in labor costs and prevent it going into more competitive product.

You may well ask, why would workers conspire in this plot, when it means they eventually engineer themselves out of a job? It's simple, just blame the Government – you have to have a bogey-man. And of course convince them that the employer is a long standing enemy who has to be defeated for the greater good!.

And in respect of the union organisers, well when the plants close and the jobs are gone, we simply make them members of parliament.

When we achieve our goal of a clean green economy, we will be a lot poorer as a country, there will be fewer jobs, and less revenue to pay pensions and healthcare. And, as is always the case, the people at the bottom will be the ones that suffer most.

But hey, how can you put a price on the warm inner glow?

So in this respect I believe it is the ALP that has deviated from the chosen path, throwing in its lot with the Greens, with the progressive elites, with the anti-wealth brigade, and their mantra of a clean green economy, all at the expense of the blue collar worker and the poor. As I have said a million times before there is no place for Hi-Vis shirts in a clean green economy. And high energy prices, an unavoidable consequence of the mindless pursuit of renewables (proof in jurisdictions around the world, the perfect correlation between the uptake of renewables and the high price of electricity), impact the poor most of all, and blue collar jobs in manufacturing, once rusted-on constituents of the ALP.

Do we need a manufacturing industry in Australia? I think we do. It creates wealth, it diversifies our economy, it diversifies our supply chain, creates good jobs and dignity for those who are disinclined to pursue the university rat race, and it re-vitalises the TAFE, apprenticeship and trade environments which used to be so central to our culture. And don't believe that nonsense that our internal market is too small to sustain a competitive manufacturing industry. There are many things we can do, especially value-adding our resources and agricultural outputs. For instance, gas is much more than an energy source; it is an extraordinarily valuable feedstock, and we are locking it up. We just have to be efficient, creative and competitive that's all. And don't underestimate the value of 'Buy Australian', strengthening daily as a brand.

Twenty years ago, manufacturing made up 12 per cent of our economy, today it is barely 5 per cent. It seems we put our foot on its throat at every sign of life. As discussed in the op-ed above, our determination to increase energy costs through quixotic attempts at climate control, an industrial relations system that is inflexible, expensive and combative, red tape like you wouldn't believe, all conspire to kill it off. On top of this, corporate and personal taxes that are internationally uncompetitive, a host of non-productive social-engineering add-ons in the HR domain that prevent half the workforce from getting their hands dirty (note particularly the Diversity and Inclusion (D&I) industry and its surging growth in the woke world we inhabit), and now a de-industrialisation agenda by the green energy merchants of despair.

Unlike many in the Labor Party I am terrified if I hear talk about emissions reductions in Australia: all it means to me is more manufacturing going off-shore, emissions, jobs and wealth exported to other countries who nod their heads and silently say thank you. All for no discernible beneficial effect on the climate. The apostles of renewable energy often boast that it creates jobs. It does, in China!

You would think that trade unions would do all in their power to facilitate manufacturing, in other words, keep it in Australia. Yet when they get a foothold they so often do everything they can to make the enterprise uncompetitive and drive it off shore, with excessively high wage costs and anti-productivity interventions into management. No one is saying that we should have third-world pay and conditions, but we should aim for productivity and innovative supremacy, and work together, employers and employees. The people that employ you are not your enemy. Why can't unions pursue and promote productivity linked wage increases. After all we all stand to benefit. Keep the jobs in Australia.

As Labor luminary Peter Walsh once noted, unions have 'a policy of putting the interests of those with jobs ahead of those without jobs.' Not all unions I might add, but too many of them.

Under a new agreement between Multiplex and four unions including the CFMEU, Queen's Wharf employees in Brisbane will be able to stop work when the temperature reaches 28C and humidity is 75% or higher three hours or more from the start of a shift. Some people call it the snowflake award, especially refugees from the tropics like me!

New details of the Queen's Wharf agreement (the 3.6 billion casino and integrated resort on the north bank of the Brisbane River) have emerged since its approval by the Fair Work Commission, including estimates by employers that traffic controllers (Lolly-pop operators) will earn $194,302 a year if they work 10 hours overtime a week – on top of the standard 36-hour week.

Industry figures said the four-year deal was based on the CFMEU's Queensland pattern agreement 'but with steroids'. Employees can earn $7,800 in productivity payments on top of a $20,800 site allowance (in the CBD mind you, overlooking the Brisbane river!), 10 days paid family violence leave, 26 rostered days off and 12 per cent superannuation.

Casual workers will receive a 40% pay loading if they are refused permanency after six weeks under the deal, which includes previously disclosed pay rises of 5 per cent each year. Industry figures estimate carpenters working 46 hours a week will earn about $240,000 a year.

Can you imagine anywhere else in the world receiving pay and conditions like this? They massively increase the cost (and therefore reduce the stock) of Australian infrastructure, crushing productivity and eventually boosting automation leading to job losses – so different to the contribution of health and essential service workers so wholesomely praised during the fire emergency. Do we all live in the same country? Is there such a thing as consideration of the national well-being?

I am sure the MUA runs a similar racket on our wharves, which are so vital to our trade performance.

I need to stress I am not against good wages. That is the Australian ethos. But the only way wages can be sustained and increased, economy wide and over time, is by maintaining, and increasing, productivity. They can't simply be seized by industrial action, or imposed by Government, or grown in the back garden.

Why can't trade unions be part of this push for increasing productivity, join with their employers in a common cause which is in everybody's best interest, instead of seeing their employers, those providing their jobs, as the enemy? There is a better world out there.

I recently received a copy of a petition from a Labor Senator (as you do), blaming the current Federal Coalition Government for the lack of manufacturing in regional Australia and challenging them to get it going again. I was tempted to write back to the effect that I presume this means Labor will support lower company taxes, cheaper electricity by reverting back to fossil fuels, a much more flexible industrial relations regime, and a massive regulatory clean out at both State and Federal levels. Or are you just shouting and singing and demanding the government delivers, while opposing the policy settings that might actually allow it to deliver?

Whilst it is nothing to do with manufacturing *per se*, a recent incident further makes my point. I travelled (prior to Covid-19) from Brisbane to Sydney to attend an AICD national conference, termed the Australian Governance Summit. I was surprised when I attempted to access Virgin's premium entry facility in Brisbane only to be told it is now closed on week-ends. I arrived in Sydney at 7pm and booked into the Rendezvous Hotel on Quay Street. As I had had little lunch and no dinner I attempted to order room service only to be told that the restaurant did not open on weekends any more.

Well congratulations all of you penalty-rate warriors. We now have hundreds, if not thousands, of workers who were getting $20 an hour now getting nothing. And, more importantly, not getting skills. As I have always said, the best pathway to a good job is a job. The outcome, more people on the scrap heap, while those advocates of excessive penalty rates soak in the warm inner glow of wage justice. For the record I count 2½ times on public holidays as excessive and definitely job destroying. Time and a half on Saturdays is tolerable, though the rationale for penalty rates has virtually disappeared from our cultural milieu. When I was young Sunday was a holy day – no shops, no pub, no industry – the only people working was the priest and the local dairy farmer!

If we keep working at it we might be able to get some of these people out of work and onto welfare for life!

For the record I am not against a minimum wage either. But it has to be set with a full understanding of the balance between meeting the essentials of life, not the luxuries. The minimum wage in America is up to 50 percent below Australia's, but I am not advocating that.

You will note that all of these negative, productivity killing, employment destroying influences are left enabled. So where do I go when I say I support a manufacturing revival?

LABOR AND ITS EXISTENTIAL THREAT

In this context I believe the ALP is facing an existential crisis (I pinched that term from Extinction Rebellion!). Labor these days courts two constituencies: the traditional blue collar, socially conservative working class in the suburbs, and the so-called green left, cosmopolitan, progressive elites in the inner city.

So-called progressives have appropriated to themselves the relatively positive title of 'progressives', theoretically because they claim to support social progress and reform. People of the right see this as a gross misnomer given the role of so-called progressives in impeding economic progress and wealth creation through environmental, social and activist interventions.

In my early days local branches used to be dominated by old tradie types, wearing singlets or flannelette shirts, attracted by union solidarity and redistributive policies. But even then the local branch had its share of bleeding hearts and crazies. I can remember Tony McGrady, the State Labor Member for Mt Isa, saying, 'You go to a branch meeting and when it is finished you step out into the real world!'

Peter Walsh, finance Minister in the Hawke/Keating Governments, took it further:

> Labor has become an instrument of the tertiary educated establishment, prepared to sacrifice blue collar jobs and opportunities to appease bourgeois left and middle class trendoids in the gentrified suburbs of Sydney and Melbourne.

Gee, and that was thirty years ago!

If that was the case in the 1980s then it is a great deal more so now. Branch meetings are dominated by largely younger, white collar, save-the-world activists, big into political correctness, identity politics and grievance exploitation, sprouting compassion, fairness, equality, climate alarmisn – sprouting them but with not a clue as how to achieve them.

In this sense it is germane to look at the changing composition of Labor's parliamentary team over the years. When I was elected to parliament (1983), and that wasn't so long ago, most of our team graduated from a job in the real world: tradesmen mostly but from a variety of occupations largely of the blue collar type. It is so different now, with the majority of Labor members coming from what we call the political class (unions, operatives working for the Party, for ministers, for members of parliament or for trade unions) or Labor aligned lawyers. Under the Gillard Government at one stage there seemed to be only one cabinet minister who did not come from the political class, and he was a rock star!

As a consequence there was not much experience in coping with the vicissitudes of the real world, not much street wisdom as it were, and certainly not many blistered hands. Is it any wonder that well-meaning members of parliament would surrender to the prevailing group-think which often is at odds with the ethos of the suburban working class.

I admit this political class syndrome is not confined to the ALP. At times it is hard to find a real-world denizen in the whole parliament – though to be fair the Liberal Party do have more refugees from business, and the National Party more farming types.

Over the years most people see unions projecting a negative image and having far too much influence in Labor Party affairs and policies. This is hard to argue against, and has led to continuing calls from within, and from media commentators, for more democracy in the Party. But be careful, more democracy means more left populism. Strange to admit it but I have a view that over the years the Labor Party has been moderated somewhat by the role of the much despised faceless ones, the unions, the factional heavyweights, for using their institutional numbers to inject some common sense and pragmatism into party affairs and policy deliberations, protecting the party from itself as it were. Allow the progressive left its way, and the old working class people will head for the hills, and Labor will become an unelectable rabble. Off-shore socialists like Bernie Sanders and Jeremy Corbyn, both products of ever increasing party democracy, are evidence of this.

My older brother Ian, who has been a card carrying member of the ALP for 65 years, said to me one day, 'the Socialist Left is always looking at new ways to lose elections, and going to heaven!' And he admitted he was guilty of this sin when he was a long-haired, bearded, headband wearing, counter culture ALP State election candidate in the early 1970s; no chance of winning but peddling furiously on the highway to heaven!

However I am not sure the union theory above retains currency these days. Unionists now make up a very much smaller percentage of the total work force (reducing from over 50% in 1976 to 14% now) though they are so much richer today due to their association with Industry Super Funds and nefarious deals they are able to negotiate with some larger gullible corporates. With their militancy and millions as it were, they seem more interested in power and personal advancement rather than agitating to deliver genuine long term benefits to the working class.

I can't believe the way the union movement has rolled over at the prospect of net zero emissions by 2050, a policy designed to eliminate manufacturing, mining and blue collar jobs into perpetuity.

Because of their left leanings and the inevitable left echo chambers to which they migrate, they are losing their working class roots and becoming increasingly vulnerable to woke causes. The spectre of blue collar unions meekly acquiescing in the ALP anti-coal mining bias during the 2019 Federal Election left me flabbergasted (I appreciate there were a few half-hearted protests from some Queensland reps, largely insignificant, and to no avail).

But the existential challenge remains, and it is difficult to see its resolution. The more the Party cosies up to the progressives, as they feel they must to counter the Green threat in the cities, and which is increasingly being forced on them by the rise of progressive ideologues within the Party, the more they alienate their blue collar constituency. Alternatively the more the Party cuddles up to the old working class (by supporting coal mining for example), the more they haemorrhage votes to the Greens, and lose their progressive backers, especially in the media. This was never more obvious than in the 2019 Federal Election, with the Labor leader saying different things to different audiences at the expense of his authenticity.

I have a view that the Democrats in America have virtually ceded the working class to their Republican opponents and are working on a coalition of alienated minority groups to construct an electoral majority, the final manifestation of identity politics. Mind you this realignment is underwritten by massive media support, turning the old convictions on their head. Hence their dive into the politically correct grievance pool. But in my opinion that is not an option for the Labor Party, because Australia is a much less fractured society, without the volume of bitter and alienated identity blocks that so dominate and divide US cultural and political affairs these days.

But we in Australia are working on it!

And my, how the Democrats in the US have turned sharply left. In a free enterprise country like America, the home of capitalism, widespread support for the economy-busting so-called Green New Deal by influential figures in the Democratic Party, beggars the imagination. With the Alt-Right and Trump on the other side isn't there a sensible centre of enormous proportions somewhere in the land of the free? Does politics have to be so divisive, and so ugly?

But the existential threat goes further than this; Labor's reason-for-being is under siege. Perhaps the Party has become a victim of its own success. Labor has traditionally been the party of social justice, a fair go, looking after the losers, welfare, wages-and-conditions justice, equal opportunity…

But the fact of life is these policy positions have all largely been achieved. Nobody is fighting about them any more, except at the edges. Unionism is facilitated, awards and state supervised enterprise bargaining agreements (EBAs) protect pay rates, and legislation (such as unfair dismissal laws) ensures that employees have fundamental rights. We have a universal, and generous, pension scheme for the elderly and the disabled, we have a comprehensive safety net for those who are unemployed or lost, and one of the most progressive income tax systems in the world. In 2015/16 the top one per cent of taxpayers paid almost 17% of total income tax, and the top 25% paid 67%. Forty percent of Australian households paid no net income tax (i.e., they received more in cash transfer payments than they paid in tax). This taxation progressivity is further boosted by means-testing of welfare, with its rapid phasing out as income increases. Medicare for all, free public hospitals, free public schooling, highly subsidised pharmaceuticals, and a tertiary education scheme which ensures all income levels have access to tertiary education.

And few of these are really up for sale. Perhaps we have a lot less to argue about in Australian politics than we know. Yet the tribalism of modern politics is so manifest, so obvious from some of the breathless hyperbole and vitriolic name-calling that characterises modern political warfare; still nothing like America though.

When I ask Labor people what they stand for, how they differentiate themselves from the Libs, all I get in response is fine sounding virtuous slogans like social justice, equality of opportunity, higher wages for working people, usually followed by a tirade of fabricated insults about the motives of their opponents, mostly nonsensical allegations. But in summary, no clear, or enhanced, pathway to a better world.

Many people now claim the Liberal Party is a centre-left party, supporting virtually all of the above. Does that leave any room for the Labor Party? Is this a reflection on Labor or the Libs?

How do you remain electorally relevant when your *raison d'être* has been used up? There are three options. Firstly, you can become more extreme on the fundamentals, on the policy prescriptions you have always worked on, push the lever to over-reach, join the American Democrats as it were; and articulate and exaggerate grievances that don't really exist.

Secondly, you can throw in your lot with the post-modern progressive elite. They provide a new dimension to the political game, a modernised ideology, a belief that by breaking down the established order they can create something better. They assert that our traditional system of liberal democracy is broken (maybe the no-hopers have too much say), national sovereignty is contrary to the human rights of non-citizens like asylum seekers, a self-hating conception of Western civilisation which they believe has been responsible for the sins of the world (racism, slavery, inequality, colonialism, white privilege, and so on), our economic systems don't deliver fairness, environmental destruction is leading to extinction and despair.... and so the list goes on. A whole panoply of new reasons to fight the good fight, to re-create the heroic campaigns of the past.

The trouble is that many of the people who promote these progressive causes have nothing more than a patronising, sneering contempt for working class people and their culture. In the real, competitive world of politics, therefore, there doesn't seem room for both: as progressivism marches in, old working class cultural conservatism marches out.

Thirdly you can get into identity politics. The Labor Party should be good at this as their class-based philosophy constituted the original identity politics. There are plenty of 'oppressed' identity groups out there: women, blacks, gays, trans, dairy cows, caged hens ... all with particular grievances. It doesn't take much these days to articulate these grievances. Then overlay intersectionality when oppressions multiply. And bingo, you have a cause, or causes, and a moral superiority for life. But this approach has the same shortcomings as the one above. There are not enough broken-hearted identity groups in Australia to construct a majority (unless the caged hens get a vote!).

Of course there is a fourth way forward: forget the national interest and the ideological differences, just attack the other buggers, accuse them of policy deviations they don't subscribe to, attribute nasty motivations to them, and criticise everything they do (sound familiar?). It is so easy to construct an opposing narrative, and indeed feel good about it. I consistently say good public policy is counterintuitive, so it is easy to lay punches on your opponent's policy, even if it is good policy. But is this in the national interest?

Of course this predisposition is not confined to one side of politics.

I also acknowledge that many Labor supporters have strongly and genuinely held views about the motivations and policy goals of their opponents, views taken straight out of their ideological box, a construct dare I say not necessarily reflective of the real world. Read their talking points: their opponents are positively evil and heartless! In this context it is easy to understand why they see the genuine need, in the national interest, to oppose them at every turn in the road.

I will discuss the relevance and attraction of socialism in the context of 'reason-for-being' in the next chapter.

Re the second option above: as I said, a lot of Labor voters are attracted to this new critique of Western society because it puts meaning back into their crusade. But how does it sit with the suburban mainstream? Does the ALP have to make a choice? The ideological divisions seem so irreconcilable. Most of the fashionable dogma of the progressive elite is anathema to the old working class, to regional and suburban voters – agendas like political correctness, open borders, climate alarmism, identity politics, affirmative action, multiculturalism, environmental activism and so on. On the other hand the progressive elite sees the blue collar rejection of this agenda (which the Progressives believe is founded on moral imperatives like compassion and fairness) as boganism, or worse still as bigotry, hate, racism and ignorance – a basket of deplorables as Hillary would say!

Affirmative action, in my view, has also had a major impact on the make-up (as was intended), attitudes and policy evolvement of the ALP, firmly at the expense of the old working class, or the so-called forgotten people in the ALP. Generally women recruited to the ALP under the banner of inclusiveness and affirmative action were middle class, white collar, educated women with professional backgrounds, not the less educated, homemaker, or shop-floor women; and it also rapidly diluted the influence, and speeded up the alienation, of the old, traditional blue collar (male) working class in the suburbs.

Maybe we need affirmative action for blue collar workers in the ALP!

In my view it is amusing, and somewhat perplexing, to see Labor people throwing in their lot with the educated elites. Labor has spent its whole existence fighting the elites, the bourgeoise; it was its *raison d'être*.

It is probably worth mentioning once again, as one of the existential threats already played out: the long-gone but once powerful role played by the Catholic Church in the Labor party; the Irish Catholic working class as it were, opposed to the English owners of capital. It is hard these days for people to comprehend this influence. I often re-visit it because I grew up with it. As I outlined in an earlier chapter, the Labor Party exercised power in Queensland for forty years, underpinned by the AWU and the Catholic Church. This of course broke down in an alarming way during the sectarian split in the 1950s when the estranged DLP (the QLP in Queensland) conspired not so much to win government but to keep Labor out – which they did very successfully for a long period of time. Long held allegiances faded and hollowed out the ALP, fuelled by the ugly split, the gradual end of sectarianism, and all accelerated by the progressive left's disdain for Christianity in general, and Catholicism in particular. Finally the unthinkable: a practising Catholic in Tony Abbott elected as Liberal PM in 2013, something unimagined decades ago.

The Pope still talks the language of the social engineering left, but nobody is listening any more.

One consolation for Labor is that the Liberals have their own existential threat (can any of us thrive without an existential threat?). Many Liberal traditional blue-rinse seats in the inner city are slipping away too, into the clutches of green independents. This constituency of course has little time for old, union based, blue collar Labor. They are old Liberal voters (sometimes sacrilegiously referred to as doctors' wives) but susceptible to environmental (climate change), compassion (asylum seeker) and politically correct identity politics. Tony Abbott's high wealth electorate of Warringah, formally true blue, voting conservative for 97 years from its inception in 1922 until it fell to left independent Zali Steggal in 2019, is a conspicuous example.

This constitutes a minefield for the Liberals, and is manifesting itself into an eternal battle between the so-called progressives (moderates, small L liberals) and the Conservatives in the Coalition. Very similar in fact to the juxtaposition of the inner-city progressives and the suburban working class do for the ALP. To defend these inner-city seats the Liberals can be tempted to drift from their conservative base, a tendency intensified by Party cognoscenti spending too much time in the bubble, prisoners of twitter, ingesting the group think, alienated from their true constituency in the suburbs and regions. Those quiet but socially conservative Australians can then easily be purloined by populist right parties such as One-Nation (to a much greater extent by Trump in the USA). It represents a quandary similar to the quandary progressive intrusions hold for the Labor Party.

The other consolation for the left is that it reigns supreme in the so-called culture wars. This cultural supremacy has been facilitated by the gradual decline of traditions in society: decline in respect for authority, and respect for institutions like the church, like parliament, marriage, the family, the community, the school, the nation … Conservatives tend to be the party of tradition, and as the traditional institutions lose their influence Liberal hegemony is eroded. This decline is also a result of a creeping complacency, and an appalling lack of understanding of the history and values that have delivered us to where we are today as a society.

To take this a bit further, it is a result of a determined assault on these values by a self-loathing progressive elite, and I regret to say, an abdication of duty by those who should be defending liberal democracy, our society and the values underpinning it.

As Paul Kelly wrote in *The Australian*, 20 May 2017):

> In Australia, progressive ideology has a grip on many of the formative institutions that shape the nation's values: the university sector, the public education sector stretching into the school curriculum, the ABC as the most influential media outlet, the trade union movement with its deep pockets, campaigning armies and links to Industry super funds, the public sector professionals and decision makers, the extensive and media savvy lobbies on the environment, climate

change, welfare, the charitable and not-for-profit sector, and the creative arts, writing, film, stage. When in the last twenty years have you seen a creative event that did other than promote progressive values?

Ah yes indeed, when did you last see a right-wing utterance seeping out of Hollywood? And my, how the Left elite in Hollywood use the Oscars to lecture we plebeians about all the woke issues of the day. I wonder why they think they have the moral authority or special expertise to embark on these sanctimonious crusades of moral virtue. As someone said, bring back the silent movie stars!

Antonio Gramsci, the Italian Communist, considered the world's most important and influential Marxist theorist since Marx himself, popularised the revolutionary theory of 'the long march through the institutions.' He believed that the only way for Marxists to achieve their revolutionary ideals would be to destroy the foundations of Judeo-Christian Western culture altogether.

I'm not into conspiracy theories of that magnitude but you would have to say the long march has largely happened anyway, with the left owning most of the institutions in society. And where is the Liberal Party's countervailing cultural power? Well it's hard to find. Business these days mostly chooses to be officially neutral, both in terms of advocacy and political donations. I noted BHP and Origin Energy urging their representative bodies not to criticise the Greens, so help me God!

Yet this represents one of the great transitions in cultural warfare in recent times: the Left has become the establishment, and in many cases the money and influence and media and aura of morality has followed them (look at the Tech giants in the US). Strange times, so different from the way I grew up when the establishment was staunchly conservative.

There are some business organisations which advocate public policy reforms supporting business, and defending business against escalating government intrusion and spiralling compliance costs; but they don't campaign with anything like the same intensity and party particular vehemence as left organisations such as the trade unions,

GetUp, the Australian Conservation Foundation, Greenpeace, and the like.

It seems the conservatives in Australia have waved the white flag in the culture wars. They will of course come to regret this as they see academia, the education sector more broadly , the public broadcaster, much of the mainstream media, the public service, all dive into the progressive pond.

However this cultural superiority is not as advantageous in an electoral sense as you might expect. It can be a massive turn-off to a large section, if not a majority, of the population, as Hillary Clinton found out in the US. Labor's drift towards progressive ideology is anathema to those Australians who are not directly politically engaged, who don't make much noise, who don't contribute conspicuously to political debate, who don't even respond to opinion polls frankly and honestly, sometimes called mainstream Australians, or I guess, Scott Morrison's quiet Australians, many of them old Labor voters (Labor's forgotten people).

I came across a missive recently from the Chief Minister of the ACT, canvassing political donations by boasting about his achievement of *Labor causes*:

> We are not the biggest jurisdiction in Australia, but here in the ACT, we've proudly led the nation on many important Labor causes over the last two decades:
>
> 1st to elect a majority woman parliament in 2016.
>
> 1st to fully protect a woman's right to choose in 2002.
>
> 1st to reach 100% renewable energy.
>
> 1st to welcome refugees by making the whole ACT a refugee welcome zone in 2015.
>
> 1st to legislate for civil unions in 2006 and marriage equality in 2013.
>
> 1st to elect a LGBITQ+ head of government (that's me).

Well, good on him. They are his values and he is entitled to be proud of them. And I acknowledge he rules in the public service citadel of the ACT, an economy and comfortable lifestyle effectively underwritten by taxpayers in the rest of Australia who don't get a vote in ACT elections, a world so remote from the battling class from which the Labor Party emerged. But '*Labor causes*', excuse me. I would say 'causes of the cosmopolitan Progressive Elite writ large!'

And I can't help pointing out with respect to the third, virtue-signalling dot point: The fact is 95% of Canberra's power comes from the east coast electricity grid, 80% of which is powered by coal and gas. Their claim to be 100% renewable is apparently based on the fact they have invested in intermittent renewable energy projects elsewhere, presumably none of which they are able to use, and none of which provide 24 hour power. Turn off the coal and it will be a shivery night in the nation's capital!

Question: If my super fund invests in a renewable energy company, a company that cannot supply energy 24 hours a day, does that mean I'm carbon neutral and can beat my breast and pretend I am saving the world?

The more Labor stands for inner city lefties, the green left, the more it loses its old blue collar constituency. I'm not saying that all members of the ALP embrace this progressive, politically correct infatuation – why would they, after all it has virtually killed off the larrikin and legendary sense of working class humour. You can't tell a decent joke any more, or indulge those evocative Australian metaphors that added such colour to our speech. Our insecurities are *all bunched up like a galloping rat*, or should that be, *all bunched up like a dog rooting a cricket ball!*

Not sure if this is relevant, but I can't help myself. Harry Truman, the wartime President of America, when asked by General MacArthur to define political correctness, said it holds forth the proposition that it is entirely possible to pick up a piece of shit by the clean end! Gee and I thought PC was a post-modern innovation!

The Labor Party, or at least much of the Left, is leaving me as it falls under the spell of this rush to post modernism; and the politics of the clean end!

There is one other cultural/political advantage enjoyed by the Labor Party which probably deserves a mention, and that is the predisposition of Australians to support higher levels of government spending, and accept the notion that governments can solve every problem. The ALP thrives in this environment. You can make much more political progress in Australia by calling for more government, more spending, more resources, after all that is what governments are for. Have you ever seen a royal commission, or special inquiry, or coroner's report recommend other than an urgent injection of funds? I know opinion polls consistently show that the conservatives are considered better economic managers, a not inconsiderable advantage. But I never cease to be amazed at the regular calls from a million lobby groups, for government to increase spending here, and there, and everywhere, and not to wind it back here, or there, or over there. Take our money and spend it better is the prevailing orthodoxy. And the ALP is much more comfortable in this eco-system than the so-called conservatives.

As is evidenced by the above, in many areas I have gradually drifted away from Labor orthodoxy. The question remains, as I posed before, who has changed? Has the party left me or have I left the party? I maintain (and I have said this a number of times) that my values haven't changed, but I have certainly changed some of the policy prescriptions necessary to realise those values. I think there is also the factor of new insights. For instance when I first started my own muddled policy constructions, socialism's utopian promise was very persuasive. As can be seen from the next chapter on socialism, how wrong can you be? But this is part of growing up, of being honest and open-minded, and not hiding reality in group-think echo chambers. If this process has alienated me from my past then so be it

But the Labor Party has changed too. It no longer has a policy suite capable of realising its founding values. This is what leads to all of that envy politics and class war nonsense so irrelevant to today's policy needs. In the meantime Labor largely has a policy manifesto full of empty slogans, but with no transformative roadmap. What it proposes very often will deliver the exact converse of its intention.

Immediately following I have focused on some of these areas where I have big trouble endorsing Labor Party orthodoxy today.

SOCIALISM – utopian promise, dystopian record

There is one area where I have very definitely deviated from ALP orthodoxy, and that is in respect of socialism. It took on a new dimension for me once I got out of the group-think of the echo chamber. The Labor Party still has a socialist objective in its official constitution:

> The Australian Labor Party is a democratic socialist party and has the objective of the democratic socialisation of industry, production, distribution and exchange, to the extent necessary to eliminate exploitation and other anti-social features in these fields.

Now I know this has been there since 1921, and has had a number of ameliorating qualifications appended; and many ALP members don't take it seriously as it is just a utopian something, keeping the faith, inherited from a purer past. But the question needs to seriously be asked, why is such an anachronism still there? It is a worry that there are still members of the ALP who believe in socialism, who defend this objective and would fight to retain it, as though they are bringing Heaven down to Earth. One wonders if these people have read any history at all – which they haven't of course. That is the nature of ideological posturing, stick to the confirmation bias, don't open your mind to anything that challenges it.

As I said before, I climbed out of the echo chamber when I left politics in 1998. Gee when you examine the history of socialism with eyes wide open it sobers your ideological passion, and it starkly poses the question of why be even mildly associated with it. As Michael Novak is reputed to have said, 'the evils of socialism have to be explained afresh to each generation, over and over again.'

It is times like this that I think of my dear parents, socialists until they died. They must be looking at me from up there with tears in their eyes. To be fair they never really had the same opportunity as I've had to re-assess the legacy of socialist experiments worldwide.

Khrushchev's secret speech in 1956 to a closed session of the 20th congress of the Communist Party of the Soviet Union, denouncing the atrocities of Stalin and the cult of personality, and exposing the evils of Communist Russia, never really became a public document till 1989.

Aleksandr Solzhenitsyn's graphic account of life in the Soviet State, *The Gulag Archipelago,* was not published till 1973. Solzhenitsyn is one of the literary greats of the twentieth century; in fact many people say that *The Gulag* is the most important literary work of the twentieth century. The abridged edition sold 30 million copies. It should be compulsory reading for all those millennials who, reportedly, think that socialism is superior to democracy. In many circles Solzhenitsyn made it positively shameful to defend not just the Soviet state but the very system of thought that led to the state being what it was.

When Marxist historian Eugene Genovese was asked how he could remain a communist when the horrors of the socialist experiment had been laid bare in the *Gulag Archipelago* and *The Black Book of Communism,* he replied, 'We believed that if the workers' paradise was going to happen, one generation would have to be sacrificed.' How romantic, what a paradise. If this is the mind set of the flag carriers then heaven help us.

Socialism has never worked anywhere, never delivered on its utopian promise, it has always, without exception, done the opposite. It has been directly responsible for killing more people in the twentieth century than have been killed in all the wars of history, a doctrine of tyranny, mass murder, and human suffering on a vast scale.

A total of twenty-five countries worldwide have fully embraced socialism, all without exception ending as unmitigated disasters, not just social and political failures, but economic failures as well. As an example on re-unification the per capita GDP of socialist East Germany was just one-third that of capitalist West Germany.

So one wonders why is it still acceptable to preserve a socialist objective in the ALP constitution, to admire the works of Marx, to accept the Marxist diagnosis of the hypothetical evils of the free market, democratic West? Why can we still divert our eyes from the truth? In my view it is unpardonable historical ignorance.

According to the *Black Book of Communism,* twenty-five million people died in Stalin's Soviet Union because of internal repression, gulags and pogroms. In 1989 the Soviet historian Roy Medvedev was a little more moderate. He estimated that about 20 million died as a result of the labour camps, forced collectivisation, famine, and executions. Another 20 million were victims of imprisonment, exile, and forced relocation.

70 million dead in Mao's China, and not just dead but brutally dead.

And what better example of how socialist utopians turn into dystopian monsters. Mao Zedong's *One Hundred Flowers* campaign – *Let a hundred flowers bloom and a hundred schools of thought contend*, in the late 50s, prior to the Communist Party's final takeover, was designed to promote the flourishing of the arts, the progress of science, freedom of speech and invitations to intellectuals to critique the new Communist regime.

This benign beginning quickly led to the first phase of the revolution proper, when Mao sought to destroy the property-owning class (and the people who indulged in the criticism under the one hundred flowers campaign), by killing at least one landlord in every village via public execution. Hundreds of thousands were shot, buried alive, dismembered, and otherwise tortured to death in the early years of the regime.

Then came (i) *The Great Leap forward* in 1958, the collectivisation of agriculture, the transition of the economy into pure communism, and the massive famines as a consequence – 45 million dead, life expectancy reduced by twenty years; and (ii) *The Great Proletarian Cultural Revolution* (1966-76) when Mao unleashed the Red Guards to purge the bourgeois remnants of traditional society, the intellectuals, and those who resisted the grand utopian experiment, with unspeakable cruelty – 25 million dead. The Cultural Revolution was a war against the 'Four Olds': old ideas, old culture, old customs and old habits, involving the wanton destruction of Buddhist temples and statues (not unlike the cancel culture of the *Black Lives Matter* lobby so cluttering the philosophical debate today).

It is said that Mao Zedong, in one act in 1976, did more than any other person in the whole of history to alleviate poverty and violence – by dying!

As an aside, you would wonder why so many intellectuals in the West support socialism when they are usually the first ones eliminated as society makes its transition from freedom to socialist nirvana.

The Cambodian killing fields take the cake. Pol Pot is now remembered as a mass murderer, but he was first and foremost a socialist. He studied on a scholarship in France, joined the Communist Party there and soaked in Marxist philosophy. When he led the Khmer Rouge to victory in the Cambodian civil war there was much celebration and joy. Not for long. Virtually the whole population of the capital Phnom Penh was rounded up and herded into the countryside onto communal farms in the name of the socialist agrarian utopia, with private property abolished. Anyone who objected, or anyone thought to be an intellectual, or educated, or wore glasses, was eliminated. In just four years Pol Pot's totalitarian regime is estimated to have claimed more than two million lives (out of a population of less than seven million), from executions, torture, starvation, disease or overwork. At one stage they ran out of bullets and took to clubbing class enemies to death.

One of the killing fields, Choeung Ek, an hour's drive from Phnom Penh, has up to 20,000 bodies buried in a single mass grave. In the centre of Choeung Ek is a giant tree called 'the Killing Tree'. It is said that the Khmer Rouge bashed the heads of children against the tree to save ammunition; and to prevent them from growing up and avenging their parents' executions.

These are just the most obvious examples of the inevitable decay of society under socialism. But there aren't exceptions, it is always the same: Cuba, North Korea, Ethiopia, Zimbabwe, North Korea, Venezuela ... After the Korean war in 1953 the Communist North went its totalitarian and collectivist ways under three generations (so far) of Stalinist overlords, while South Korea opted for open markets and free trade. Now it is estimated the South Koreans are, on average, three inches taller and live eleven years longer than their cousins in the North.

There are now reportedly three hundred execution centres in North Korea. No wonder a lot of people have very short life spans.

Venezuela was one of the wealthiest countries in South America. It had the richest oil reserves in the world (greater than Saudi Arabia), and in the 1950s was ranked fourth in the world on a per capita income basis. How can you stuff that up? Easy. Give it to Castro-loving socialist Hugo Chavez. It took him a while to destroy this once vibrant economy because of the endless flow of oil money. But he did it: nationalised the means of production, including the oil industry, and then the inevitable introduction of price and currency controls, then the shortages, and then the black markets, then the secret police, then the state violence, then the queues and the hunger … a pattern followed in socialist experiments worldwide. Economic catastrophe ensued, hyperinflation (one million percent in 2018), mountains of debt, catastrophic food shortages and a general humanitarian crisis.

Venezuela now ranks 179 in world per capita income and some estimates are that four million people have fled Venezuela – to anywhere that is not Venezuela. No wonder President Trump was building a wall.

Some blame Chavez for this collapse. Some blame Maduro, his successor. Some blame the earlier socialist leaders who began the nationalisation programs. But blame the game not the player. Socialism always ends up here.

In the meantime Maria Gabriela Chavez, Hugo Chavez's daughter, is reportedly Venezuela's wealthiest person, worth more than US$4 billion, most of it secreted away in foreign bank accounts. It proves again the point, socialists are not against money, they just think the wrong people have it!

Glen Reynolds said ('Don't be a sucker for Socialism', May 2016), 'under capitalism, rich people become powerful. But under socialism powerful people become rich'.

The question needs to be asked: why does the same thing happen over and over in socialist regimes? Five-year plans repeated again and again, collectivisation of agriculture, nationalisation of industry, the concentration of power into the hands of a few lead inevitably to economic collapse, repression, and large-scale killing. It has happened according to script wherever socialism has been tried. Socialism always and everywhere begins with humanistic promises and ends in barbarism. Human nature and socialism simply do not mix.

Prominent Austrian/English economist Friedrich Hayek wrote in 1982:

> The mere idea that a planning authority could ever possess the information necessary to run the economy is a somewhat comic fiction. What prices ought to be can never be determined without competitive markets.

Indeed. Can you imagine our present-day, over-bloated, creaking bureaucracy making all the calls to construct and manage our economy, without markets and prices guidance, when they can't even fire-proof a national park.

Socialism is contrary to human nature, that is why it always fails. We are not all equal, in motivation, in desires, in intellect, in ability, in needs. As Michael Shermer, publisher of *Sceptic* argued in 2018:

> Utopias are especially vulnerable when a social theory based on collective ownership, communal work, authoritarian rule and command-and-control economics collides with our natural born desire for autonomy, individual freedom and choice.

How many utopian dreamers have turned into dystopian murderers?

Paul Keating put the case for the socialistic instinct when he said, channelling his mentor Jack Lang, 'In a two horse race always back self-interest, at least you know it is trying.' Dirty capitalist principles rule the world, the gospel of envy!

I can remember reading the book *Mr China* by Tim Clissold, who was recounting his experiences in China as it opened up to the West under Deng Xiaoping. He was wanting to check into the hotel but the receptionist kept saying there were no rooms left. This was obviously not the case as there was no one moving about. He later discovered that the business, state-owned, the staff paid a salary by the Central Communist Party in Beijing, unrelated to the profitability or throughput of the hotel saw another guest meaning more work, more hassle, but no change in pay. The dead hand of socialism.

Western socialism's defence

The grim story above is of course not universally accepted. The left must have an ideological response.

We are socialists, not communists.

Really? What is the difference? Both involve a command economy where governments make the decisions about the allocation of resources, socialisation of industry production distribution and exchange (yes, straight out of the ALP manifesto), price and production controls, and ultimately state violence to enforce policies that are fundamentally contrary to human nature. If there is a difference, it is that communism is a more pure form of the ideology. Marx described socialism as a pit-stop on the glorious road to communism.

For those who like to think that there is a meaningful distinction between communism and socialism, they should remember that USSR stood for the Union of Soviet Socialist Republics. Whatever Lenin and Stalin thought they were doing, they agreed they were engaged in a *socialist* enterprise.

We are democratic socialists.

Democracy is not a bulwark against authoritarian collective rule. Many socialist regimes started off with elections – Zimbabwe, Cuba, Venezuela, Angola. Even North Korea calls itself the Democratic People's Republic of Korea. It is not how it starts that counts, it is how it finishes, with the need to empower the collective at the expense of the individual, totally inconsistent with true democratic principles.

Right wing totalitarianism, i.e., fascism, is just as bad..

That's true. But be careful how you differentiate them. Adolf Hitler claimed to be a socialist, and of course he was leader of the National Socialist Workers Party, more commonly reduced to its German acronym, the Nazi Party. In 1920 Hitler presented the Nazi Party with a twenty-five point plan for national socialism, most of which could proudly be featured in any decent Bolshevik publication, especially the defining principle: 'The good of the community before the good of the individual.'

True, he didn't expropriate private property, but industries were privately owned in name only. State control was so complete, and price and production controls so extensive, it amounted to de-facto state ownership. It is true that Hitler overlaid his socialism with a racial animus (hatred of the Jews), a messianic nationalism, and an extreme glorification of the Aryan race, but does that make it any less socialist? It is convenient these days to smother reality by using terms left-wing and right-wing. In this context I don't know what right-wing means, but in Germany it was certainly not capitalism. The Nazi elevation of the state above the individual made it a lot closer to socialism than capitalism. Sure Germany was totalitarian; but so was the Soviet Union, China, Cambodia, Zimbabwe, Cuba …

The socialism we support is not Stalin's model but the Scandinavian one.

Yes the Scandinavian one, the final refuge of Western apologists of socialism, sometimes called Nordophilia. The uncomfortable reality is Scandinavian countries aren't socialist. In fact they are at least as capitalist in their economic system as the US. They have stock exchanges of long-standing tradition that trade capital goods and services, they believe strongly in open markets, free trade and private enterprise, virtually all of the means of production are in private hands, private property is protected by legislation, they have among the lowest corporate tax rates in the world. Resources are allocated by the market, not government or community planning. How capitalist can you be?

During the 2016 US Democratic Primaries Bernie Sanders was extolling the virtues of the socialist economies of Scandinavia. Denmark's Prime Minister chided Sanders and asked him to stop insulting his country as 'socialist'.

They are certainly not socialist, but it is true they are welfarists. They have a comprehensive cradle-to-the-grave welfare state, much admired by people the world over who like free stuff, but it is important to remember that this welfare state is funded by their capitalist economy and massive middle-class taxes: a Value Added Tax (VAT) of 25% on everything including food, 100% car tax (a tax of $30,000 on a car worth $30,000), and a top marginal income tax rate of 60% kicking in at less than $70,000 pa (no special taxes on the rich – they are too few and too important to the economy).

The Nordic people have an enviable, cohesive and insular culture, i.e., very few cultural outsiders dipping their hand in the welfare jar. They accept exorbitant middle-class taxes like this in the cause of the welfare state. Australians surely wouldn't.

Most self-proclaimed socialists in the West don't know what socialism really means, and have little comprehension of its dark underbelly. They know only its utopian promises. And they are usually welfarists, and thus are entitled to conscript the Scandinavian example to promote this policy ideal, but they should also be honest enough to spell out the way the Nordics flog the middle-class to achieve it, and of course credit the capitalist economy for underwriting it.

In summary, there is widespread historical ignorance in the ALP of the depredations of socialism, which makes it difficult for the ALP to clean up the constitution, and the policy excursions in that direction. Ironically, however, were the ALP to accept the ugly historical failures of socialism and purge the ALP playbook of socialist rhetoric, this would create its own conundrum. Socialism, with its utopian, though greatly misguided, vision is, for many people, part of the ALP's reason-for-being. As mentioned earlier, the ALP's reason-for-being is already compromised by national success in delivering our social justice underpinnings. How many reason-for-beings can a party jettison and remain airborne?

Because of my understandings of the evils of socialism and its unmitigated gruesome global record, as presented in this chapter, I find it difficult to retain affinity with a party that eulogises it, or even flirts with it. I confess this represents a major psychological departure from my inherited world-view, and obviously makes me the policy deviant.

'Dear Mum and Dad. I am really sorry. Can I ask your forgiveness. I now know I should never have climbed out of that echo chamber.

The world outside is too confused, and doesn't remain true to the old certainties. It was so safe and secure in there!'

'Dear Labor Party ...

PRODUCTIVITY – everyone benefits

There is really no theoretical argument to make against the widespread, economy-wide benefits of improving productivity, as I have explained earlier on. And there is no argument against the benefits that accrue to wage earners and the less well-off (I am counting benefits to these two groups as a proxy for delivering on the Labor Party's traditional mission – the reason we donned the uniform in the first place).

I reject the notion, which I have sometimes heard, that increasing productivity leads to less job satisfaction. This is based on the notion that job satisfaction comes from bludging on the job. But the fact is that the engaged worker, those workers who feel they make a difference, are always the happiest, most fulfilled and most productive. Dare I say it, those promoting the union line, who see their employer as the enemy, are generally the least happy and fulfilled in their workplace.

Regrettably, it is my strong observation that the ALP has put all the tools for improving productivity back into the tool box and closed the lid. They now seem to be apostles of productivity destroying policies: higher taxes, trade union inflexibility, high energy prices, wage add-ons that stifle employment creation, government intervention that increases red tape, a welfare policy that subdues the work ethic, and a general support for trade protectionism.

UNEMPLOYMENT – most solutions make it worse

I accept that the Labor Party doesn't like unemployment any more than anyone else. The Party consistently espouses the virtues of high employment, as do all other parties. But as I have made clear in the paragraph above, most ALP policies stifle employment creation. Further, the ALP is consistently stymied somewhat by an ill-advised commitment to the public sector. The fact of economic life is that the public service does not create wealth, it consumes wealth, and therefore ultimately costs jobs in the real world. The notion that increasing public service numbers reduces unemployment is simply wrong. For every job created in the public sector up to three are lost in aggregate in the real economy. Currently, of the 13 million jobs in Australia there are 2 million in the bureaucracy (federal, state and local). Many of these jobs are vital, but many are not, and just add mindlessly to budgets and regulatory inertia. Well over 80% of all jobs in Australia are in the private sector, yet many on the left see this sector as the enemy.

This is a defining difference between the left and right in Australia: Labor sees the solution to all issues via government and the public sector, whether the policy challenge is reducing unemployment, stimulating the economy, promoting manufacturing, or whatever. The alternative, which I advocate, is more supply-side intervention, stimulating the private sector to chase the same objectives: making it less costly and more attractive to do things, to invest and create wealth and jobs, to accelerate real wage growth. On this issue therefore, it is me that has drifted away from the faith.

I guess there is another issue: a well-fed public service helps generate a significant voting bloc, not unimportant in this polarised political world we inhabit. And there is an ever pressing need to keep the unions on board, so they don't withdraw their considerable largesse.

Because it is the *modus operandi* of the ALP, some of its members seemed to go perilously close, during the 2019 Federal election, in their campaign against stagnant wages, to advocating legislative or regulatory intervention. Gee you get into dangerous territory when you espouse wage and income controls. It's been tried a million times before, usually with the same ugly end (see *Socialism*, p. 226); hardly the model for a market economy like Australia in the 21st century I would have thought.

The eternal message I try to get across: get the settings right and let it happen. The more governments try to legislate it, or subsidise it, or do it themselves, or pick the winners, the worse it gets. But this policy approach goes against the emerging zeitgeist I am sorry to admit.

BIG GOVERNMENT – the modern scourge

There is a tendency these days to ask governments to solve all of our problems, the theoretical aim of course being to create a better society. The public keeps demanding it. To add to this, many politicians seem very eager to champion new causes and invoke government, while bathed in a warm inner glow in that eternal quest for a perfect society, to save the world as it were. Except, as I've argued incessantly, government involvement seldom leads to solutions, and usually leads to sclerosis, stagnation and red tape.

This is mainly a disease of the left. The article of faith (though poorly practised) of conservatives is small government, underwritten by the principles of individual liberty and personal responsibility.

I admit some interventions are necessary, building standards for instance. But most simply lead to bigger government, an ever expanding and increasingly moribund bureaucracy, higher taxes, more red tape and declining economic output. The link between red tape and economic stagnation is clear. Cutting red tape therefore allows for increased business activity, more jobs and higher wages.

Big government is the scourge of modern society. I admire people, they mostly come from the left, whose standout mission is to improve the world, but I wish they would do it at home in the tranquillity of their own boudoir, and leave the rest of us, and the economy, alone. We would all be so much better off, wealthier and less troubled.

HIGH TAXES – trickle down theory

The Labor Party is wedded to the notion of high taxes. I doubt even their disciples would dispute this. If we can put a positive spin on it, they see higher taxes as a means of redistributing the wealth of society and rectifying disadvantage, in other words, creating a fairer society. However there are two downsides. Taxes simply appropriate part of someone else's earned income – which cannot usually be done with impunity. If the state takes (an increasing) share of a taxpayer's earned income it quickly erodes the incentive for that person (or company) to earn that income in the first place. This leads, either consciously, or subliminally, to less aspiration, less effort, less productivity, less overall revenue to the state, and a less prosperous society. In other words it is not a zero sum game.

Internationally uncompetitive corporate taxes do the same thing – they send investment off shore. Good public policy should always be highly cognisant of its incentivisation properties, and high personal and company taxes should be judged on this criterion (analysed further later on).

Wouldn't it be wonderful if we could all see tax for what it is: other people's money appropriated by government? As Thomas Sowell said, 'What is your fair share of what someone else has worked for?'

Or as Churchill said, 'There is nothing a government can give you that it hasn't taken from you in the first place.' (Though I guess this isn't so if they take it off someone else to give to you!)

Secondly, this attitude to taxes quickly morphs into a punitive mind-set, so amply demonstrated in the class-war rhetoric personified by phrases like 'the big-end of town' (so liberally thrown around by the Labor Party during the last Federal Election) leading to the impression that the main reason taxes are being increased is because the bastards deserve it. In these circumstances it has migrated away from a policy aimed at a fairer society.

THE WELFARE PRISON – the end of opportunity

As I will make clear later on, tax and welfare policies should always be guided by the incentives they generate. Now I know it is difficult to have an intelligent discussion on welfare without being accused of demonising welfare recipients, but here we go. Let me say at first, no one is really opposed to the notion of a safety net, a system designed to give a leg up to people who have lost their jobs or who are down on their luck. That reflects a modern civilised society. But there is an ever present danger of making them a prisoner of the welfare system, a fate we shouldn't wish on anyone.

According to Ian Harper, the inaugural Chairman of the Australian Fair Pay Commission, unemployment is the chief cause of relative poverty and social exclusion in Australia. Joblessness is not just an economic problem, it is a profound social and spiritual problem. Work not only provides an income, but it provides dignity, a sense of purpose and ultimately all of the other benefits of life – social, housing, family and the list goes on. Sometimes the solutions look mean, but the alternative, sentencing people to a life of welfare, is the meanest trick of all.

Children growing up in a single parent welfare family have the odds stacked against them: harder yards at school because of less support at home, no role model in the work-force to promote a work habit, values development compromised and so the list goes on. And the corollary, the child grows up unemployed, alienated from society; not the only people who commit crimes, but I am sure over-represented.

What we need in Australia is a much more comprehensive profiling (including family history) of welfare recipients and incarcerated persons. We can't address the problem of recidivism and anti-social behaviour unless we understand its causes. As they say, what gets measured gets managed. I know this will stimulate cries of stigmatising dole bludgers, but I am calling for the opposite: a non-discriminatory, objective understanding of society's shortcomings so that we can lead to practical solutions.

Higher welfare payments, well intentioned as they always are, create a disincentive to migrate away from welfare (I am not suggesting penury – there is a right amount which I don't have the data or the expertise to determine – one which preserves personal dignity but does not turn into a negative incentive. It must be determined by data and expertise, not vote-chasing politicians or lobby groups).

Research shows that there is high upward mobility from low paid work into better work. The longer individuals have been unemployed, the longer they will be unemployed. This is how unemployment becomes entrenched.

I support the cashless welfare card. We owe the unemployed a safety net, the essentials of life, not a lifestyle. We shouldn't be paying for their alcohol, gambling and cigarettes, crippling their well-being and entrenching the welfare culture. This is not demonising anyone, it is providing the necessities of life until such time as people can move into a more rewarding lifestyle.

Family Tax Benefit (child allowance) also provides an incentive to have children, particularly for low income groups. This is not all bad, of course, as it is consistent with Peter Costello's plea to increase the national birthrate in Australia's interest. However it can create its own problems if it adds to the welfare culture.

It is a fact that welfare people have more children than more financially secure middle class people. Having children requires an enormous reservoir of human capital – financial, emotional and time. In a perfect society potential parents would take this into account, but in the welfare world, incentivised by the dole and child allowances, many don't. The difficult question is how do we provide necessary support for expanding families without creating incentives for people to have children they are not fully equipped to have? A very difficult challenge, and one I will leave as a challenge, rather than as a solution.

The problem with the ALP (and most of the welfare lobby) is that they seem to love welfare recipients so much they seem determined to keep them there. Could this be another voting bloc?

It seems we diverge again!

ENERGY PRICES – the abysmal failure

I know I carry on about the increasing cost, unreliability and impracticability of the renewable power regimen being foisted upon us by apostles of the left.

Wind and solar energy, because of higher costs, less density and lower efficiency, account for only a few percent of total global energy use, despite billions and billions of dollars poured into them as subsidies over the last thirty years. Fossil fuels, because of their lower costs, higher density and higher efficiency, account for around

85%. Substituting low-density, intermittent energy sources like wind and solar for high-density, constant energy sources like fossil fuels would be catastrophic for the world's economy and the world's poor. It would simultaneously raise the cost and reduce the reliability and availability of energy (and this is without taking into account the huge costs of subsidies and mandates borne by the tax-payer rather than the consumer). This, in turn, would raise the cost of all other goods and services, since all require energy to produce, to transport and to retail. It would slow the rise of the poor out of poverty. It would threaten to return millions of others to poverty.

Coal is the cheapest source of energy in the world: the good Lord has spent three million years storing and concentrating it for us. For the foreseeable future, wind and solar energy cannot effectively replace fossil fuel and/or nuclear energy. It follows that reducing fossil fuel use means reducing economic development and condemning poor societies to remain poor. How can anybody justify that?

One thing I can say with certainty: the cost of climate change policy to humanity will be thousands of times more expensive than climate change itself.

The Labor Party used to be the party of the coal miner, the shearer, the cane-cutter, the blue collar worker, the tradie and the less well-off. In other words it was the workers' party, opposed to the elites and the establishment. But it seems many members have thrown in their lot with the elites, the virtue peddlers, the bed wetters, all at the expense of their own. Who would have believed that the left would have become part of the establishment, once its *bête noir*? I appreciate the concern some people have about what they see as the galloping menace of climate change (though I don't share it); but look at it realistically. What can Australia do anyway, apart from exporting all of our industry and jobs to those countries who are more concerned about increasing living standards and looking after their people, than indulging quixotic pursuits?

Where is the Labor Party of old, home of the anti-elite, no nonsense, grounded, practical realists? Heaven forbid that they are swimming with the green progressives in the warm waters of virtue? If they are, then they are swimming swiftly away from their traditional support base. And, of course, from me!

There is one piece of good news however: it seems Australia is well placed this year to comprehensively win the international Wally Award for energy policy. We produce less than 1.3% of global emissions (China's emissions are more than twenty times Australia's, and growing exponentially). We are on track to meet our Paris commitment to reduce emissions by 26-28% on 2005 levels by 2030 despite Australia having among the fastest population growth rates globally (how many other nations can so boast, even among the urgers?) We underwrite the fastest global per-capita increase in intermittent, inefficient and expensive renewable energy. At the same time we are sitting on three hundred years of thermal coal; we have the largest uranium reserves in the world; and we are the world's largest exporter of Liquid Natural Gas (LNG). We export our fossil fuels to other countries to make them rich while we purchase solar panels and wind turbines from China to feed our delusions, creating jobs and wealth over there at our expense.

It will be an award well won, daylight second, and it seems well on the way to establishing a Wally dynasty!

EDUCATION – the Snow Flake factory

I have reservations about education too, with leftist fads taking it over, to education's detriment, and leading to Australia's sub-standard and badly deteriorating performance in international mathematics, science and literacy tests. And associated with this is what seems to be a deliberate assault on our Western values.

Joan Kirner, former Victorian Labor Premier and Education Minister declared in 2008: 'Education has to be re-shaped so it is part of the socialist struggle for equality, participation and social change, rather than an instrument of the capitalist system.'

According to Dr Gregory Martin, former lecturer in the School of Education and Professional Studies at Griffith University, 'A major task for Leftist activist academics is ... to connect education with community struggles for social justice.'

In her address to her union's conference in 2005, the Australian Education Union president Pat Byrne openly boasted about the ideological bias that dominates the school system. As she put it: 'We have succeeded in influencing curriculum development in schools, education departments and universities. The conservatives have a lot of work to do to undo the progressive curriculum.'

Grant Banfield, a lecturer in education at Flinders University in South Australia, says his research is 'informed by commitments to social justice and human emancipation'. In particular, as his biographical note goes on to say, 'his work is directed towards the application of Bhaskarian Critical Realism and Marxist social theory to an emancipatory sociology of education' – whatever that means!

There were nine Sydney University professors and another five faculty types who pledged allegiance to Extinction Rebellion in September 2019. As an aside, one wonders why they expect continued state funding when their objective is to subvert democratic principles, civil law and classical Western values. Western civilisation, in the view of many on the left (should I say far left?), was a bastion of imperialism and racism, and students should be devoted to learning about those shortcomings, rather than about the glories of our achievements or philosophy. Isn't it sad if the focus of universities (and schools) is to breed a hatred of our own society?

I could quote many more examples of leftist educators promoting ideology at the expense of scholarship in our education system. It seems no matter what the subject discipline, it has to be subsumed into the narrative of privilege and oppression, of class, race and gender. Any notion of objective truth goes out the window.

I do make the point that I have been a supporter of the humanities over the years, as many of the great scholars of history are both products and progenitors of this discipline. I do have an arts degree after all, mostly populated by humanity disciplines. It is just that there is a movement, not quite universal yet, but mushrooming wildly, to require intellectual submission to a range of left-wing political ideals and make the study of the humanities a vehicle for the trashing of our national heritage and our national image. It is hard to understand why an Australian curriculum can be so unsympathetic to the early European settlers who, let's face it, created the most sought-after society on Earth; and, dare I say, and contrary to contemporary opinion, one which now boasts an Aboriginal population more than twice as large as it was in 1788.

Instead of concentrating on the fundamentals of Western philosophy, science, mathematics, technology, literature and art that should underpin our education system and that constitute being educated and job ready, in the fullest sense, the curriculum now argues Indigenous 'cultures, knowledge and experiences are fundamental to Australia's social, economic and cultural well-being.' Say that again! All I can say is our young people are paying a heavy price for the unnecessary educational diversions of the past three decades.

Another good example of the rejection of the tenets of Western civilisation in our education system was the widespread refusal of a cross section of universities to accept the freely available offer of the Ramsay Centre course in Western civilisation (see above) which the Unis claim is little more than a conservative project aimed at glorifying straight white European male supremacy. My, what a mis-characterisation of those great philosophers and scholars, who opened up a window to the world, our history and our intellectual evolution, on the left and right; Adam Smith and Karl Marx were hardly singing from the same hymn sheet. Yet it seems that the same universities have no problem in hosting Confucius Institutes sponsored by the Chinese Government, i.e., the Chinese Communist Party. There are fourteen such Institutes at universities in Australia.

But it is not just in the university sector that this virus has taken root, it has to be fed from somewhere. As I said in the chapter on racism, non-tertiary teachers, under the so-called Melbourne declaration in 2008 (re-confirmed by the Northern Territory Declaration in 2019) have been required to overlay all their work with the three mandated cross-curriculum priorities of (i) Aboriginal and Torres Strait Islander histories and culture; (ii) Asia and Australia's engagement with it; and (iii) sustainability. No mention of the role of Western civilisation in delivering the prosperity and freedoms that potentially allow us to enjoy a sophisticated educational menu. The question remains: do we want a world class education system or is the object to reshape the world? Should we be indoctrinating our children at such a vulnerable age, or should we be giving them the educational tools to objectively analyse the world and develop their own ideological predispositions as they mature?

The other fad which has crept into our curriculum is the postmodern concept of so-called child-centred learning. Students increasingly are not being judged on the basis of merit, or the pursuit of excellence. Assessments have no clear consequences for success or failure. All students are equal, all deserve success, no one is better than anyone else, it's all about personal well-being; all fine sounding sure, but going nowhere in an educational sense, or in a resilience sense. How can they graduate with the toughness to deal with the vicissitudes of an uncertain world when they have been quarantined in safe spaces, protected by trigger points, rescued by therapy sessions, and shielded from contrary opinion. With the Australian (and global) economy entering difficult and unchartered waters, we are doing our best to produce a generation of snowflakes!

We have self-described Marxists authoring gender-fluidity programs for our schools, local councils are refusing to celebrate Australia Day, and Human Rights Commissions are censoring free speech. One could be forgiven once again for thinking that the inmates have taken over the asylum.

At the same time there has been an insidious rise of identity politics in schools, dividing society into identity groupings divorced from individual merit and character. In my view this country needs to accept that a person's race, gender and sexuality are irrelevant to their worth. What counts is having a go. We have all of these curriculum experts claiming the new approach has served the test of time, yet we keep spending more and more money on education while mental illness increases and we slip alarmingly down the PISA scale (Program for International Student Assessment), i.e., measured educational performance. Is that what we want as a nation: a dumbed down curriculum, delivering a dumbed down education, producing second rate performers, all costing more and more.

In 2016-17 $57.8 billion was spent on education by all levels of government. This was an increase from $36.4 billion in the nine years since Gonski one. An extra $18.6 billion has been committed across four years for Gonski two.

All of these leftist inspired obsessions leave me cold. I am sure many ALP members and supporters, especially the traditional blue collar types, feel the same, and I am sure also do a majority of parents. Let's give away this leftist indoctrination and get back to basics, let parents be involved and consulted. More local autonomy, more discipline, more common sense, more teacher/student appraisal, and a more competitive and productive Australia.

With respect to education, it seems it is the Labor Party which is diverging from the orthodoxy. This wasn't the Labor I knew. I find it difficult to believe that the Labor Party could pay homage to so many policy excursions that self-evidently don't deliver Labor values. In fact they deliver the opposite. I have tried to highlight these in this section, Diverging from the Faith, and of course I don't expect that this will be accepted by the party; although I suspect, in fact I know, many old-fashioned Labor people, and those non-university educated masses that live in the suburbs and regions, are feeling a similar alienation.

It seems the trend these days is to surrender to friendly bubbles where facts have been replaced by feelings. I said earlier that when I retired from the political hurly-burly I climbed out of the echo chamber, that sanctuary of group-think and confirmation bias. My divergence was no doubt the result of the multiplicity of career pathways I followed in life, orthodoxy busting pathways; so hard to stick to the collective faith in these circumstances.

FREEDOM OF SPEECH – the Left changes sides

When I joined the Labor Party it owned freedom of speech. I can remember the furore in the sixties over *Lady Chatterley's Lover*, a novel by English author D. H. Lawrence, full of explicit descriptions of sex, and its use of then-unprintable four letter words, but a classic in the sense it was written by a master literary practitioner and its primary aim was literary merit, not pornography. Though printed much earlier, it was not published openly in the United Kingdom until 1960 and was fiercely opposed by the conservative establishment. It was the subject of a watershed obscenity trial against the publisher Penguin Books. Penguin won the case, and quickly sold three million copies. It was banned in Australia (and other Western countries) and became the subject of a massive free speech campaign led by the left.

They didn't even want us to read *Playboy*, which we interpreted as the puritanical conservative establishment telling the rest of us how to live. As H. L. Mencken said, 'Puritanism, the haunting fear that someone, somewhere, may be happy.' *Peyton Place*, *Portnoy's Complaint* and many others suddenly were considered to be pornography. The opposing free speech campaign was part of the left counterculture which was so in vogue in those days. I was of course only peripherally involved as I was living in Papua New Guinea, but I was nodding my head furiously in agreement.

I'm still not sure to this day whether we were genuine advocates of free speech, or whether we just liked the *Playboy* centre-fold!

My memory, imperfect as it is, seems to remember that student unions, left protest groups, and Bohemian cults generally, were the spear throwers for free speech, both on campus and in the community generally. But it seems so different these days. There has been a massive movement away from free speech, debate, and the contest of ideas. The modus operandi these days seems to be to kill debate, de-platform or de-legitimise (mostly by ad hominem or character assaults) those with a contrary opinion, who stray into wrong-think. This of course ties in neatly with the seismic emergence of identity politics and political correctness. Anything that is said or published which is contrary to the accepted wisdom, or the zeitgeist, is quickly dubbed hate speech and needs to be removed, shut down, and the perpetrators punished. And this shut-down is powered by social media, the ugly manifestation of post modern communications, full of insults and vitriol, a medium it seems designed to bring out the worst in people under the shelter of group-think and anonymity.

The question needs to be asked, as I chart my political journey, does this work both ways, or is it the preserve of one side. The answer seems to be obvious. Those people who oppose free speech and intellectual debate these days tend to be participants in the identity politics maelstrom, and this is surely the left. This is borne out by the many instances of de-platforming and ugly demonstrations – always against the right. It is most prevalent in universities, those so-called bastions of intellectual inquiry and academic freedom. Bettina Arndt was de-platformed for the temerity of suggesting that claims of a so-called rape culture on uni campuses were over-blown.

As I write, a right-wing think-tank has been refused a stall at the Queensland University of Technology (QUT) market week 2020 because, according to the Student Guild, 'your values do not align with our values'. This at a university, mind you, where the contest of ideas should be paramount. And the weak-kneed response by administrators to these (and there are many more than I have cited) can only be interpreted as tacit support.

As I write it has happened again (emerging events are writing my

Keith DeLacy has been Patron of Cairns Amateurs Racing Club for twelve years – pictured here with two previous chairmen, Ross Moller (dec) and Michael Delaney

book for me). The Student Union (MSA) at Monash University has rejected an application from Generation Liberty for a stall at Orientation Week at Monash. 'Regretfully we must decline your booking application on the basis of our terms and conditions. Generation Liberty's positions on issues such as climate change do not align with MSA's.' The left has migrated from being the primary defender of free speech to its mortal enemy. And it seems that migration has been facilitated by the knowledge that the left has won the culture wars; they make the rules now – like it or lump it.

Isn't that outrageous? It is not about whether you agree or disagree with the various ideological positions, it is about free speech, the fundamental sub-structure of a liberal democracy; and also of course the sub-structure of a university system committed to free intellectual inquiry.

What about the extraordinary university resistance around the country to the proposed Ramsay Centre offer to fund a course in Western civilisation. Western civilisation, mind you, of which we are a product, not all glory of course, but the home of the industrial revolution, the Reformation, the Enlightenment, the Magna Carta, exquisite practitioners of the creative arts, of towering philosophers (certainly not propaganda as they represent an extraordinary diversity of philosophical views) like Socrates, Plato, Rousseau, Voltaire, John Stuart-Mill, Kant, Thomas Aquinas, Edmund Bourke, Adam Smith, Karl Marx. Such a mind-altering, enlightening and exciting opportunity. But seen as right-wing, as an instrument of the patriarchy and the oppressors, glorifying all the ills of past society such as colonialism and imperialism, slavery, the oppression of minorities and all of those evils I have mentioned before.

I know this is not a Labor Party thing, but it is the left run wild.

Whitlam's *Anti-Discrimination Act 1975* was a bit problematical because it erected impediments to free speech, but a grudging okay. Section 18C, however, added by the Keating Government in 1995 took it a step further, making an action unlawful if it was likely to offend, insult, humiliate or intimidate. There are justifiable legal restrictions on free speech (defamation, not to incite violence, etc). But we get into dangerous turf when we make it unlawful to offend someone, because offence is very much in the eye of the beholder, and can easily be misused, gamed or weaponised; and backed by a Human Rights Commission to ensure it is.

The Australian Human Rights Commission (AHRC) is another of those unaccountable, agenda laden, territorial driven NGOs with a nihilistic world view, stoking grievance at every opportunity, and soliciting complaints from Australians about how racist this country supposedly is. And if we need proof that this whole edifice is inimical to free speech, consider Gillian Triggs, the former boss of the AHRC, theoretically entrusted to defend fundamental freedoms, when she scolded Australia as a country where 'Sadly, you can say what you like around the kitchen table at home' – emblematic of the fact that the default setting of the AHRC is to stifle human rights, not defend them.

It is beyond dispute that this assault on free speech and freedom of expression is the nuclear warhead of the warriors of identity politics, i.e., the progressive left. Because of this it has further nurtured my estrangement from the left.

CLIMATE CHANGE – the great delusion

I'm sorry, but in my eyes this is the greatest exercise in collective insanity in the annals of the human race, a monomaniacal obsession unmatched in history. I frankly can't understand how grown men and women could believe cattle emissions to be a threat to human existence on planet earth, or that by changing light bulbs we can change the weather. Does hubris have no limits? To think we humans are the primary controllers of climate, in the face of cosmic forces like the sun, the planets, the moon, the seas, the tides … Future generations will look back at us and laugh.

As Bruce Bunker argues in *The Mythology of Global Warming*:

> There has always been plenty of data to support the idea that natural variations in climate are a normal thing, and that only the biggest egos on Earth could believe that our activities could influence the weather.

But it does indeed fit in with a human need to be tormented by Armageddon.

In 2016, feeling quite strongly about it, and remembering my personal progression through all of the iterations of Armageddon throughout human history, I was stimulated to put pen to the following op-ed, 'AFS – Apocalypse Fatigue Syndrome' (2016):

> As an inherently impressionable person I have been dealing with the coming apocalypse all my life. It started with the bible. The Book of Revelation in the New Testament vividly warned of impending doom, and many of the Hebrew prophets forecast the apocalypse.
>
> Pope Sylvester II, at the beginning of the millennium year 1000, predicted the Millennium Apocalypse, the end of the world. Riots occurred throughout Europe and pilgrims headed to Jerusalem seeking salvation.
>
> And the Apocalypse was always associated with sin, it was deserved. 'And these will go away to eternal punishment, but the righteous into eternal life' (Matthew 25:40). If I had been thinking sinful thoughts, I trembled at night, fearing the fires of hell.
>
> Thomas Malthus wrote an Essay on *The Principle of Population* in 1798 and became the pre-eminent father of doom. Unchecked population growth would lead to inevitable catastrophe – population growth was exponential while the growth in food supply was arithmetical.
>
> We were impressionable kids, we grew up with Malthusianism, waiting for doomsday. It was a compelling argument. Yet more than 200 years later, despite exponential population growth, the world is so much wealthier and better fed. The Malthusian apocalypse was no better than Pope Sylvester's.
>
> Paul Erhlich became a cult figure in the 1970s. Malthus' inability to deliver on his population apocalypse proved no deterrence to Erhlich. He wrote *The Population Bomb* in 1968 forecasting that 'sometime between 1970 and 1985 the world

will undergo vast famines, hundreds of millions of people are going to starve to death.'

Yet while he was prophesying doom and gloom the green revolution (nothing to do with Bob Brown) was dramatically changing global food production. The number of people in acute poverty decreased from 40% of the world population to just 10%. Calorie intake per person increased by one third.

He became the Father of misanthropy and alarmism. In a 1971 speech he said, 'If I were a gambler, I would take even money England will not exist in the year 2000.'

In fact he was a gambler. In a celebrated wager with Julian Simon he bet the average price of 10 commodities (selected by Ehrlich) would dramatically increase over the next 10 years pointing to mass shortages. The prices reduced by 30%, rendering Ehrlich's doomsday thesis a joke.

Ronald Bailey said Erhlich was 'an irrepressible doomster who, as far as I can tell has never been right in any of his forecasts of imminent catastrophe'. But he knew no shame. He is still around prognosticating doom. But is anybody listening?

The Club of Rome, a group of world leaders, celebratory scientists and industrialists met in Rome in 1972 and published *The Limits to Growth*, banging on about overpopulation and resource depletion. They said exponential use could exhaust known world supplies of zinc gold tin copper oil and natural gas by 1992 and cause a collapse in civilisation in the early 21st century.

If only they were a bit right, a resource rich nation like Australia could get much better prices for our raw materials today – a resources boom that goes on forever! Like all prognosticators of terminal doom they were dead wrong. But they became a very influential group, and some of their scary solutions on curbing population and economic growth were enough to make one wake up in a cold sweat.

It was inevitable that the United Nations would jump on the bandwagon, who could resist such an opportunity to save the world and bathe in the virtue? In their Agenda 21 summit in Rio in 1992 they said, 'Humanity stands at a defining moment in history. We are confronted with a perpetuation of disparities within and between nations, a worsening of poverty, ill-health and illiteracy, and a continued deterioration of the ecosystems on which we depend for our well-being.' Notwithstanding the fact that the following decade saw the sharpest decrease in poverty, hunger, ill health and illiteracy in human history.

It was around this time that I came to realise that there was a great dividend in alarmism, we seem to lap up darkness and reject the light. Good news is no news. The media megaphone is at the disposal of any activist who can forecast Armageddon. And the beauty is that the forecast doesn't have to be right. There is no comeuppance.

The last straw for me was Y2K, not long after I had moved into the corporate world – a calendar change at the turn of the millennium that spooked fears of the end of the world. I thought who could believe this nonsense? But the frenzy became overpowering. *Time Magazine* staff set up a generator-powered 'war room' in the basement of the Time/Life building in New York filled with computers and equipment ready to produce the magazine in the face of a catastrophic breakdown of electricity and communications.

2000 came and went without a whimper, apart from extinguishing billions of dollars worldwide on the impossible scare. My impressionability was finally extinguished also.

The UN Agenda 21 inevitably morphed into the global warming scare.

Global warming? As a tropical boy who couldn't stand the cold I had been terrified in the 1970s at the prospect of an ice age. In a 1975 article 'The Cooling World', (in language eerily similar to the warming alarmism of today) *Newsweek* warned that the changes 'may portend a drastic decline in food production'. *Time Magazine* ran a front page story, 'If present trends continue, the world will be eleven degrees colder in the year 2000. This is about twice what it would take to put us into an ice age.'

Now Global warming! Please forgive me but I have surrendered the faith.

Climate change, potentially the greatest apocalypse of them all – we were all going to fry and the cardinal sin was human emissions of CO_2. The United Nations Environment Program predicted in 2005 that global warming would create 50 million climate refugees by 2010.

And all the talk is of scientific consensus. Well I know one area where consensus has been overwhelming: 100% of IPCC predictive climate models have grossly exaggerated observed global temperatures over the last 25 years. The bloody climate just won't obey the models.

The high priest of global warming Al Gore predicted in December 2008 that 'the entire North Polar ice cap will be gone in five years'. Arctic sea ice area was 12.5 million sq kms in December 2008 and, would you believe, 12.5 million sq kms five years later in December 2013.

The ABC reported in 2005 that our own worthy apostle Professor Tim Flannery, then Climate Change Commissioner, predicted that the ongoing drought could leave Sydney's dams dry in just two years. The prediction missed by 2.5 million megalitres. In fact more than 10 years later he was still out by 2.5 million megalitres.

The *Canberra Times* ran a headline story on 26 September 1988 quoting the Environmental Affairs Director from the Maldives, Mr Hussein Shihab, saying that the rise in sea level is threatening to completely cover this Indian Ocean nation of 1196 small islands within the next thirty years. In 2018, thirty years later, you still had to run out and dive into the ocean to get wet, as has been the case for hundreds of years!

I could go on forever. Maybe one day one of these horsemen of the apocalypse will reach the finishing post, but I won't be backing it. I have a chronic case of AFS (Apocalypse Fatigue Syndrome).

I recently asked one believer how he could justify the avalanche of predictions of doom which never eventuated. He replied that all predictions came with the caveat 'providing all things remain the same'. I see, what they predicted was wrong so the prediction doesn't apply!

We are frightening the children, and in these impressionable times this could lead to gross anxiety and psychotic disorders, yet there seems to be no let-up, no sense of guilt. Surely children should be allowed to grow up with a modicum of innocence, without this burden, and soak in the prospect of a wonderful future. But I guess we weren't allowed either, we were always tormented by the biblical fires of hell. It seems this is the way of the world. Still sad to see youngsters like Greta Thunberg lost and angry in the fires of rebellion.

I share the widely held view that CAGW (Catastrophic Anthropogenic Global Warming) is not a scientific construct at all; it is more a quasi religion aimed at meeting the psychological and spiritual needs of its adherents, especially those who may have discarded their traditional spiritual faiths. God has been replaced by nature, the new religion sometimes called Apocalyptic Environmentalism.

As they say, if you believe in nothing you'll believe in anything.

Stephen Pinker characterised the global warming establishment in his book *Enlightenment Now* 'as a community of like-minded brethren, a catechism of sacred beliefs, a well populated demonology and a beatific confidence in the righteousness of their cause.' They believe they are ordained with a divine purpose, that purpose being to save mankind from self-destruction.

If you oppose the 'consensus' you are not wrong, you are evil. You are not guilty of just having an alternative viewpoint, you are guilty of spreading misinformation. And they call you names like 'climate denier' (echoes of the Holocaust) rendering all debate superfluous.

Sure the world has been warming since the end of the Little Ice Age. But nothing catastrophic or unprecedented that I can see: one degree centigrade in 150 years, big deal. And the warming has practically petered out this century. To use a scientific term, the *null hy-*

pothesis says that the world has been warming from 'natural causes' since the Little Ice Age which ended more than 150 years ago. This hypothesis has never been falsified.

The world is so much more liveable also because of that one degree of extra temperature, especially in the cold countries in the northern hemisphere which suffered greatly during the Little Ice Age. They now have a more equitable climate and extended growing seasons. We all know that warmth and moisture have always been good for mankind. It is cold that kills: records show seventeen times more people currently die from the cold than the heat.

And the planet is so much greener too, because of the increased CO_2 in the atmosphere. NASA's Vegetation Index Data shows that the globe has greened 10% so far this century. In the last twenty-five years maize yields worldwide have increased by around 80%, rice by around 65%, wheat by around 70% and barley by 65% – not all because of CO_2 in the atmosphere of course, but it sure doesn't sound like the end of the world. Greta, get a life!

And this will continue. As has happened during the last century there will continue to be large advances in science, technology, income and living standards, dwarfing the effects of changes in climate.

The point also needs to be made that rapidly increasing agricultural production has equally been underwritten by fossil fuels, their energy and transportation networks.

The scientific method demands that theories be tested by empirical observation. By that test, the predictive models are clearly wrong. And more importantly, the models' errors are not random but clearly biased, consistently forecasting well above observed temperature values. They therefore provide no rational basis to forecast dangerous human-induced global warming, or indeed justify all of the extraordinarily expensive public policies aimed at moderating these increases.

Ceres Researches, a team of Irish and US based researchers, point out that 55% of all global expenditure on energy in years 2011-2018 was spent on solar and wind energy (US$2,000 billion). Despite this, wind and solar energy still produced only 3% of world energy consumption in 2018 while fossil fuels (oil, gas and coal) produced 85% between them. Imagine the cost of transitioning to 100% renewables.

In summary, so far all 'scientific' predictions have failed, life has survived happily with much higher CO_2 levels in the past: the worst ice age in our planet's history occurred when CO_2 levels were twenty times as high as they are now. The medieval warm period a thousand years ago was much warmer than today (as it was during the Roman Warm Period 2,000 years ago and both of the so-called Holocene Optima) long before human industries were emitting CO_2, comprehensively invalidating the hypothesis that CO_2 emissions are the primary cause of warming

Those who claim that Green House Gases (GHG) are causing dangerous global warming have the burden of proving their case – not with allegations, shonky computer models, headlines or mob rule – but rather with solid, irrefutable evidence; which they can't do. To the extent that there appeared to be any correlation between temperature increases and GHG emissions in the final quarter of the twentieth century, it has now evaporated – bloody climate won't respect the models! As Thomas Huxley said, 'The great tragedy of science is the slaying of a beautiful hypothesis by an ugly fact.'

Or as one famous scientist said, 'science progresses, one funeral at a time!'

As I said, all of the so-called predictive models have grossly over estimated observed warming. You would think if the data didn't support the models the scientists would be required to change the models, and the pet assumptions that go into those models. What a novel scientific concept that would be. Instead of that they keep trying to change the data by fake news articles, so-called homogenisation of temperature records, or by jumping on a single event and extrapolating wildly from there.

Extreme events. The data shows absolutely that there has been no increase overall, either in frequency, duration or intensity, whether we are talking about hurricanes, cyclones, tornados, heat events, droughts, bushfires or what have you. Check the data, a quantitative analysis, it doesn't lie; it beats all of the scaremongering and hyperventilation in the world.

Danish economist Bjørn Lomborg notes that deaths from climate-related events (floods, droughts, storms, wildfire and extreme temperatures) have reduced by 90 per cent since the 1920s despite the global population tripling since then. Likewise, damages due to all forms of extreme weather as a share of global GDP have declined over the last three decades. Even the IPCC (Intergovernmental Panel on Climate Change) said there has been 'no significant observed trends in global tropical cyclone frequency over the past century.'

In Australia we went ballistic during the bushfires in the summer of 2019-20 when thirty-four people sadly lost their lives. Climate change they all screamed, screams amplified by the smoky fires of moral virtue. What they forgot to acknowledge was that we have had up to a dozen bushfire events of such frightening intensity in the last 100 years, whether you measure them in acres burnt, human casualties or whatever; this is Australia you know. Eleven years ago in Victoria 173 people were killed in the Black Saturday bush fires, five times the casualty list from 2019-20; 37 years ago in South Australia and Victoria 75 people died; 53 years ago 62 people died in Tasmania; back in 1939 and the 1920s in Victoria; and so it goes back into the 19th century. In 1851 when Australia's population was only a fraction of today's, a dozen people were killed, along with a million sheep and five million hectares burned.

Where was the climate change fingerprint in all of these? Isn't it awful when the facts don't fit the fiction?

The total area burned during the bushfires in 2019 has now been revised down by 25%, as have the number of wildlife deaths – an official admission they got it wrong. Because of the reluctance of authorities to do controlled burns (the environmentalists are still calling the shots), one scientist estimated that there are 10 times more wood fuel in Australian forests than when Europeans arrived.

As Chris Kenny put it in *The Australian* in early 2020:

> I have written about the inanity of the hysterical attempts to blame the bushfires on climate change. To suggest a bush-

fire threat that has bedevilled this country for millennia, has shaped our ecology and will always trouble us can be ameliorated by our climate policies is silly beyond words.

The Amazon Rainforests. Save-the-world French President Emmanuel Macron jumped on the bandwagon when fires in the Amazon received global attention in 2019. He called it an 'international crisis' and said 'Our house is burning.' He was joined by celebrities such as Leonardo DiCaprio. Yet the severity of the fires was actually below average for the last 15 years, and the rate of deforestation in the Amazon has declined by about 70 per cent since 2004, thanks to better forest protection and farmers boosting yields on existing farmlands.

Macron, like many of his colleagues, operates in a shame-free world. He was one of many to use outdated photos, featuring a photo from 1989 in his tweet. Further, far from driving deforestation, according to satellite data from NASA, increased atmospheric carbon dioxide over the past 35 years has caused increased greening and an increase in foliage on trees and other plants.

Sea level rise. The rate is decelerating, not accelerating as the models predicted. More atolls in the South Pacific are gaining area rather than shrinking; not disappearing under the sea as the wild-eyed alarmists were prophesying and hoping.

A delicious aside. According to a fact-check by that doomsday cheer squad at the ABC, the total land area of the Pacific Atoll Tuvalu is growing not shrinking. The ABC cited a peer-reviewed study which used satellite imagery to measure Tuvalu's changing land area over four decades. Between 1971 and 2014, it showed the country grew by more than 73 hectares, or 2.9 per cent. Each period of the study experienced net increases in land area, including the most recent decade. I'm pleased to advise there was no reported self-harm at the National Broadcaster on publication of that fact-check at the time.

The oceans rose some 400 feet during the last 20,000 years, without any help from burning fossil fuels. Perhaps nature itself has something to do with climate change.

And have a look at those week-end ads for wonderful holidays in the Maldives, a truly enchanting and idyllic tropical Indian Ocean setting – despite the fact that it was supposed to have disappeared under the waves by now. In fact to help with the task of ferrying the rapidly increasing number of tourists (1.7 million in 2019) to and from the resort islands the Maldives recently opened four new island airports.

A recent study (Dr Virginia Duvat 2020) found that between 2005 and 2016, 97% of the 186 Maldives island coasts have either grown (59%) or not changed (38%).

I spent more than seventy years in and around Cairns, one of the lowest cities on the Eastern sea-board of Australia, but I never noticed any sea-level rise, nor did anybody else I know, even devoted fishermen with a keen eye for such things; maybe a few unnoticeable millimetres, enough to make a cup of tea.

Barack Obama, ex-Commander-in-Chief of the global warming army seems to have swallowed his sea-level rise alarm, spending US$11.75 million on a seven bedroom, eight bathroom estate with 29.3 waterfront acres, at Martha's Vineyard, a low-lying small island off Massachusetts on America's north east coast. I'm not saying there is an element of hypocrisy there, but less trusting people than I am may be inclined to so suggest this.

But just to be safe let us agree to spend another trillion dollars on intermittent renewables that can't do the job, just to assuage the howling multitudes. World energy demand has been growing by two percent a year for forty years. To simply meet this increased demand using wind power would require a land area greater than the British Isles, piling up, year after year.

The large glaciers. Like those in the Himalayas these have refused to melt as they were supposed to. The ice sheet volumes in Greenland and the Antarctic go up and down, but with no big change overall. It must be so frustrating when you want the world to end.

Polar Bears. Remember that 2017 video of an emaciated and dying polar bear shared by *National Geographic* and three million viewers? The video started with the subtitle: 'This is what climate change looks like.' I wonder how many of those viewers know that since the 1950s, polar bear numbers have increased around 400 per cent? Or how many know of the work of Canadian zoologist, Dr Susan Crockford? According to her 2017 *State of the Polar Bear Report*, polar bear numbers have improved to between 22,000 and 31,000, the highest since becoming protected under international treaty in 1973.

Well what about **the scientific consensus** on CAGW? Well what about it? Is that now part of the scientific method, to claim a consensus? Science is supposed to be a search for truth, and a brake on our willingness to believe nonsense. The much touted 97% statistic has as much scientific relevance as last week's high tide. It is pure nonsense in the first place. Read the way it was constructed, and corrupted. If that is the level of scientific rigour that goes into the theory of anthropogenic climate change then help me God. The science of catastrophic anthropogenic global warming is indeed settled – it is a myth.

As Bruce Bunker goes on to say: '4,000 scientists, including 72 Nobel Prize winners, signed the Heidelberg appeal clearly stating that there is no scientific basis behind man-made global warming. Over thirty-one thousand American scientists signed the Oregon Petition stating that "proposed limits to greenhouse gases would harm the environment, hinder the advance of science and technology, and damage the health and welfare of mankind. There is no convincing evidence that human release of greenhouse gases is causing, or will in the foreseeable future, cause catastrophic heating of the Earth's atmosphere and disruption of the Earth's climate".

49 former NASA (National Aeronautics and Space Administration) scientists wrote an open letter to NASA in 2012 alleging NASA is hyping unsubstantiated and unverified claims that man-emitted carbon dioxide is having a catastrophic impact on climate change. They say it is clear that the science is not settled.

No less than 450 peer reviewed scientific papers were published in 2019 challenging climate change orthodoxy. So much for the 97% consensus. As Dr Peter Ridd, notoriously sacked from James Cook University for questioning the rigour of Great Barrier Reef science, pointed out in 2019, 'Science is advanced by the exercise of intellectual freedom and by the testing of evidence. Facts are not established by consensus.'

Or, as Booker T Washington reminded us, 'A lie doesn't become truth, wrong doesn't become right, and evil doesn't become good, just because it's accepted by a majority.'

To conclude on climate change. If you are a believer (and I appreciate that not everyone sees things as I do) then give up on this delusional and extraordinarily costly determination to solve the problem by reducing CO_2 emissions, in reality a climate change solution looking for a problem.

A much more cost effective solution lies in economic development and growth. This will continue to grow living standards, with the big plus that a rich society will underwrite adaptation and innovation, realistic and practical responses to whatever turns up at the front door.

THE GREAT BARRIER REEF – it's not going anywhere it hasn't been before

The Great Barrier Reef is still there in all its splendour. It goes into a bleaching event every now and then which causes the climate change scaremongers to lurch into alternate paroxysms of glee and outrage. But it continues to exist, indeed thrive. Corals have outlasted the dinosaurs, the mammoths and the sabre-toothed tigers.

The worst thing we ever did as Australians was agree to a World Heritage listing of the Great Barrier Reef. That makes it the property of every two-bob activist organisation in the world, ceaselessly screaming, without scientific validation, that global warming is destroying the reef, and it's all our fault. The damage they do to the image of the Reef far offsets the so-called positive publicity benefits from heritage listing in the first place.

The World Heritage authority keeps classifying the Reef as endangered. But they will never go further than that, otherwise they will miss out on a snorkelling trip to inspect it each year.

Professor Terry Hughes is Director of the Centre of Excellence for Coral Reef Studies at James Cook University. He can't take a deep breath without screaming that the reef is dying, without of course doing anything to fix the problem he has so thunderously articulated. In any case, even if climate change was adversely affecting the reef, it is nonsense that Australia's climate change policies would make a difference (with China increasing emissions equivalent to Australia's total emissions each year). Professor Hughes has successfully convinced most of the world (with the help of Barrack Obama and Greenpeace) that the reef is dead, in the process dramatically damaging our greatest tourism asset in the eyes of the world, and inflicting a great deal of damage on many operators.

Another op-ed, 'The reef is under no threat from fishing shipping or tourism' (2013), was written before the activists appropriated coral bleaching as their *bête noir*, and prompted by a government decision in 2013 to declare a further 1.3 million square kilometres of the Coral Sea as a Marine Protected Area:

> Have we lost our sense of reality in Australia? Who is running the show? Have the inmates really taken over the asylum?
>
> Our reef is under no practical threat from fishing, shipping or tourism. Yet we are proposing a Coral Sea Marine Protected Area (MPA) of 1.3 million square kilometres (about the combined size of France, Germany and Italy). This is in addition to the existing Great Barrier Reef Marine Park and all of the other protected zones. Why? What are we trying to protect, what demonstrated problem are we trying to solve?
>
> We will destroy this great country of ours if we continue to lose touch with reality, if our resources are squandered on grand gestures based not on science but misguided do-goodism. It seems if you can use words like biodiversity and sustainability three times in the one paragraph then you don't need science. I am not a fisher, I don't use the reef. But I have lived my whole life in Cairns, and I fly over it every week, and I am involved in the tourism industry so it is important to me.

Well managed reefs around the world can sustain an average seafood harvest rate of 15,000 kilograms per square kilometre per annum. The average harvest rate for the Great Barrier Reef is 9 kilograms.

Australia has by far the largest per capita fishing zone in the world yet we import two-thirds of our seafood consumption, at an annual cost of $1.7 billion. A quarter of this comes from Thailand, yet their fishery zone is about 1/20th of Australia's, and they have three times the population to feed. Our catch is about half that of New Zealand and about the same as landlocked Poland. Now we are proposing to reduce it more.

Claims of widespread over fishing at our levels of harvest are the height of absurdity. There is absolutely no scientific evidence of threatened marine species, population collapses or impacts on marine biodiversity due to fishing. Almost without exception, away from the coastal and tourist influences, the Great Barrier Reef is pristine, rarely visited and home to the same number of fish species today as at first European settlement, and none are now threatened by it on the GBR.

The Coral Sea, the site for this new MPA is one of the world's prime yellow-fin tuna fishing grounds. The Japanese fishermen used to sustainably catch about 30,000 tonnes per year there, but we stopped that. Meanwhile PNG now licenses Asian fishing companies to fish the same migratory stocks of tuna in their water. They currently catch about 750,000 tonnes per annum. We then import $165 million in canned tuna each year. In other words we protect our fish for Asian fishermen to catch and sell back to us.

Now it seems it will cost tax payers more than $100 million in a ludicrous scheme to compensate fishermen to cease fishing in our healthy under-utilised fisheries so that we can import even more fish from much more heavily exploited resources elsewhere. The result: fewer Australians gainfully employed, less wealth created, a less diversified and resilient economy, further negative impact on our current account, not to mention the massive costs to the taxpayer for compensation and management.

And please spare me the nonsense about the danger posed to the reef by shipping. One cyclone like Yasi causes more reef destruction than if all of the ships that ever sailed the reef crashed into it.

In World War II hundreds of ships were sunk on or around the reefs. And where is the evidence of that today? To the extent that they went down on a reef they are now part of that reef.

The Chinese bulk coal carrier *Shen Neng 1* ran aground on the reef east of Rockhampton in 2010 amid cries of outrage and demands to cease bulk shipping through the reef. But in reality an infinitesimal blip on the vastness of the reef, one which will quickly rectify itself.

In March 2009 the *Pacific Adventurer* was hit by Tropical Cyclone Hamish and spilled 230 tonnes of fuel oil and a large number of fishing containers into Moreton Bay. Premier Anna Bligh called it the worst environmental disaster that Queensland has seen, and a large clean-up effort was mobilised. In February 2010 the Australian Maritime Safety Authority issued its report into the incident. One sentence stands out in my mind: 'The total oil-related mortalities were three dead animals comprising one sea snake, one Little Tern and one Petrel species.' I feel for the snake but hardly another Fukishima!

The boundary of the Great Barrier Reef Marine Park, inexplicably, extends right into Gladstone Harbour, even though the reef is 40 kms away. But this doesn't stop the park being invoked endlessly and shamelessly in the campaign against economic development in the harbour.

Of course we all believe in sustainability and preserving our precious environmental assets. But please base it on good science and good sense. The Great Barrier reef is truly one of the great wonders of the world. But it is a massive self-correcting ecosystem with great powers of renewal. It is under no threat from fishing or tourism or shipping. It seems to me the reef, and particularly our lifestyle and economy, is under more threat from grand and unnecessary gestures.

RENEWABLES – humanity's great folly

In 2016 I wrote another op-ed, 'Solar and wind power simply don't work – not here, not anywhere' (*The Australian*, 22 June 2016)) on the subject of wind and solar. It is a little dated, but it has, in my view stood up to the test of time better than the alarmists and their hysterical exaggerations:

> One policy which seems to have escaped scrutiny during this election campaign is Labor's commitment to increase the Renewable Energy Target to 50 per cent by 2030. I am surprised because it is a proposal that has enormous ramifications for economic growth and living standards, and disproportionate impacts on traditional Labor constituencies.
>
> The problem we have in Australia is when we talk renewable energy we are talking wind and solar only – low value, expensive, unreliable, high capital cost, land hungry, intermittent energy.
>
> According to the Department of Industry and Science wind currently generates 4.1 per cent and solar 2 per cent of Australia's electricity. But even this is highly misleading because it is such low value power. You could close it down tomorrow (which it regularly does by itself) and it would make no difference to supply.
>
> If we talk about total energy, as opposed to just electricity, wind and solar represent 1 per cent of Australia's energy consumption. This despite billions of dollars of investment, subsidies, creative tariffs, mandates, and so on.
>
> Solar and wind simply don't work, not here, not anywhere. The energy supply is not dense enough. The capital cost of consolidating it makes it cost prohibitive. But they are not

only much more expensive because of this terminal disadvantage, they are low value intermittent power sources – every kilowatt has to be backed up by conventional power, dreaded fossil fuels. So we have two capital spends for the same output – one for the renewable and one for the conventional back-up. Are you surprised it is so much more expensive, and inefficient, and always will be?

So wind and solar, from a large scale electricity point of view, are duds. Now I know that will send the urgers into paroxysms of outrage. But have you ever seen an industry that so believed its own propaganda? Note, when they eulogise the future of renewables they point to 100% capacity outputs, or to costly investments, never to the real contribution to supply, especially at low capacity levels.

Let's look overseas where many countries have been destroying their budgets and their economies on this illusion for longer and more comprehensively than we in Australia. The Germans are ruing the day they decided to save the world by converting to solar and wind. Germany has spent US$100bn on solar technology and it represents less than 1 per cent of their electricity supply.

Energy policy has been a disaster. Subsidies are colossal, the energy market is now chaotic, industry is decamping to other jurisdictions, and more than a million homes have had their power cut off.

It is reported electricity prices in Germany, Spain and the UK increased by 78 per cent, 111 per cent and 133 per cent between 2005 and 2014 as they forced additional renewable capacity into their electricity markets. Sunny Spain used to be the poster boy for renewables in Europe – photovoltaic cells and wind turbines stretching on forever. Now they are broke, winding back subsidies, even the feed-in tariffs which were guaranteed for 20 years. But wait, what about the green energy jobs that everybody gushes about? Spain has an unemployment rate of 21 per cent with a youth rate of 45.5 per cent.

Britain is little better. Subsidies are being wound back, and a Department of Energy report points out that in 2013, the number of households in fuel poverty in England was estimated at 2.35 million representing around 10.4 per cent of all households.

It is no better in the US either. States with renewable energy mandates are backtracking faster than Sally Pearson can clear hurdles. Ohio has halved its mandate level (it was 25 per cent by 2025) because of high costs. West Virginia has repealed its mandate because of high costs, and New Mexico has frozen its mandates. Kansas was repealing its mandate which reportedly would save ratepayers $171m, representing $4367 for each household, and so the dismal story goes on. The US Department of Energy has found electricity prices have risen in states with mandates twice as fast as those with no mandate. As of 2013 California was the only state to adopt a feed-in tariff for solar power. It was immediately dubbed a failure by the renewable energy community because it offered only 31 cents per kWh, only five times the rate for conventional base load power.

Ah, but Asian countries are jumping on the bandwagon. Maybe. China built one new coal-fired power plant every week in 2014, and India's coal-powered investment in that same year equalled the total electricity capacity of NSW and Queensland. To summarise – with all of the billions spent worldwide on wind and solar, wind currently represents 1.2 per cent of global consumption of energy, and solar 0.2 per cent.

The good news, it is possible to reduce fossil fuel use in electricity generation – through hydro-electricity and nuclear fuel. Plenty of countries have done it – Canada 60 per cent hydro and 15 per cent nuclear; Sweden 45 per cent hydro and 48 per cent nuclear; Switzerland 54 per cent hydro and 41 per cent nuclear; France 11 per cent hydro and 79 per cent nuclear.

Germany has taken over as one of the leaders in the wind and solar hysteria. However France produces one tenth of the carbon dioxide emissions per unit of electricity as Germany, and pays half as much for its electricity – because it is largely nuclear powered.

But Australia has zero tolerance of these two workable alternatives to fossil fuels (hydro and nuclear). At least we are consistently inconsistent.

So where does that leave us? The cost of electricity in Australia has increased by more than 225% since 2000. On the basis of evidence everywhere we could easily double the price again and get nowhere near the 50 per cent target. What would that mean?

First, it means rapidly disappearing blue collar jobs in high energy industries like manufacturing, car and ship building, smelting and refining, steel making and food processing. There may be still some construction jobs, but they will largely be assembly only, as all of the components will come from those countries more interested in growing the economy and eliminating poverty than stoking the warm inner glow.

Second, rapidly rising electricity prices and the subsequent increase in the cost of living disproportionately affects those at the bottom of the income scale.

Policies like this are OK for the Greens. They can keep their virtue intact because they never have to deliver. As Gough Whitlam once said, 'only the impotent are pure.'

Mainstream parties don't have that luxury. They need to look at the true costs, and benefits, of all policy proposals.

The trouble with the Greens is that they not only oppose the problem, they also oppose the solution. If CO_2 emissions represent the existential threat they consistently proclaim, then surely emissions free, base-load nuclear power is the answer. But no, please stop giving us solutions.

The Green lobby has gone to extreme lengths in America to close down nuclear reactors over the years, leading of course to increased CO_2 emissions as a consequence.

They want to transition to renewables. Wind and solar are intermittent sources of power, and there is a serious limit to the amount that can be absorbed into the system without seriously impacting reliability. Gas is a part answer, but who wants an answer when you can dine out on the problem.

The bottom line in this argument is that renewable energy cannot replace conventional power (read coal/gas) because at the lowest level of supply of sun and wind they deliver no power. To keep the lights on there must be enough conventional power available to meet 100% of demand – a total duplication of the system, or back-up storage prohibitively expensive and impractical. It hasn't impacted greatly so far as there is so much existing coal fired back-up, but when Liddell closes in 2023, take a deep breath and buy a box of matches. And even if we doubled, or quadrupled, wind capacity it would not make an iota of difference when the wind didn't blow.

I see many armchair experts criticising the (now) $10 billion plus. so-called Snowy hydro two scheme; it uses more energy than it produces they claim. Well that's true, it is the role of pumped hydro, to store and provide energy when the intermittent renewables can't. So just add $10 billion to the bill, for no extra overall capacity, and Bob's your uncle! Renewables have effectively destroyed the business plan of coal fired generators, not because they are cheaper. When apologists promote renewables as cheaper they disingenuously omit to include the cost of storage and/or back-up, the massive extra cost of new transmission lines, the on-going subsidies borne by the taxpayer not by the consumer: $30 MWH for the Renewable Energy Target for instance, and the cost of feed-in tariffs, and subsidies on the cost of household solar.

Gas back-up could be a part solution to the intermittency of renewables as it can fire-up at a moment's notice. But no, we don't want a solution, we love the problem. Gas is a dreaded fossil fuel anyway, let's keep it under the ground to power those subterranean life forms down there.

The price of gas fired power is compromised anyway when for much of the time they are amortising capital costs, maintenance, labour, etc, for no return, while the sun and the wind enjoy their benevolent government monopoly.

And we should not forget the reality that coal fired power in Australia is twice as cheap as gas, so gas is not necessarily the best solution to the challenge.

Are we saving the environment? Eliminating fossil fuels would require literally millions of acres, millions of wind turbines, billions of solar panels, and millions if not billions of batteries like the half-ton power sources used in Tesla vehicles. This, in turn, would require a massive worldwide increase in mining for lithium, cobalt, copper, iron, aluminium, and numerous other raw materials. In summary, expanding mining on the scale needed to replace fossil fuels would cause unimaginable harm to the environment, wildlife, and humans (children are actively involved in mining some of these rare earth metals in a number of places around the world).

Of course both wind turbines and solar cells with their short life spans present an epic waste problem, an enormous cost to the environment we know.

According to P. Gosselin (*NoTricksZone*, November 2000):

> Future generations will wonder how dumb their ancestors must have been to opt for a form of energy that blighted the landscape, destroyed ecosystems over vast areas, killed avian wildlife, was an unreliable and expensive energy source, made nearby residents sick and left millions and millions of tonnes of waste behind.

The movement to replace hydrocarbons, which collectively supply 85% of the world's energy, has been growing for decades. It commenced when first we thought that the world was approaching peak oil, but spiralled out of control when burning fossil fuels became the equivalent of killing small babies.

So far, wind, solar, and batteries, the favoured alternatives to hydrocarbons, provide less than 3% of the world's energy. Nonetheless, there are bold new claims that we're on the cusp of a tech-driven energy revolution that inevitably will replace all hydrocarbons.

This 'new energy economy' rests on the belief that the technologies of wind, solar power and battery storage can undergo the kind of disruption experienced in computing and communications, dramatically lowering costs and increasing efficiency. But this core analogy glosses over profound differences, grounded in physics, between systems that produce energy and those that produce weightless information.

In the energy world, the increasing use of cars, planes, and factories cause hardware to expand, not shrink. There will be some efficiency gains with technology, but not like the dreamers dream.

There is no way that wind power, or solar, can replace coal. Storage systems for intermittent power (remember wind and solar operate on average at around 25% installed capacity, and can spend long periods when they operate at less than ten percent installed capacity) are a long way from meeting this need. As I said, gas is a partial solution, and it does support the renewable revolution, but the save-the-world activists won't let us exploit the considerable reserves we have in this country, especially if it involves fracking. It will always be so much more expensive anyhow, with two systems to produce the same power and other costs as outlined above. So, as Terry McCrann pointed out in *The Australian* (1 February 2020), we are left with three electricity futures – coal, nuclear or chaos!

In the words of Professor Bjørn Lomborg:

> One of the great ironies of climate change activism is that the costs of the policies they demand will be borne disproportionately by the world's poorest. This is because so much of climate change policy boils down to limiting access to cheap energy.

So what now for the poor? Let them eat cake, or perhaps moral righteousness, so good for the soul!

I believe that the scientific fraternity worldwide has done itself great harm since the spectre of climate change raised its ugly head. Scientists should be the ultimate sceptics, questioning everything, not defenders of the faith, hiding behind a shonky consensus. The scientific method is a product of the Enlightenment, when humankind threw off the shackles of ignorance and superstition. Scepticism, open debate and empirical testing were to provide a mechanism for achieving knowledge and human progress. But scientists out proselytising a cause are inimical to this discipline. The integrity of science is under siege.

Walter Starck warns (*Science*, 10 February 2020):

> The institution of science itself is under serious assault from within by a creeping infection of postmodern nihilism which denies, opposes and corrupts the entire open, evidence based, logically consistent search for objective truth on which science is based.

Most research funding, especially in Australia, these days comes from government, usually via universities or specially constructed Qangos. In today's academic world research grants from government comprise a major element of funding for universities. The status of academics in the system and the level of their salaries is strongly related to their ability to obtain grants. A disproportionate share goes to recognised researchers who have a lengthy bibliography of professional publications, and whose research accords with government policy, political correctness and 'saving' something.

Historically, universities have stood between the state and the mob to protect academics in the pursuit of truth. Now it seems, they are just another obstacle on the path to truth. The fulsome, and in my view, the unquestioning embrace of all of the elements of the climate change bandwagon by the scientific community demonstrate this point completely. Their models continually fail basic testing against current physical evidence. As such they have abandoned the scientific method and become mere spear throwers for the political apparatus.

From a policy standpoint, the apocalyptic mindset so engendered leads to a disdain for cautious deliberation, which in turn leads to sub-optimal policy development, resulting in policies that demand a war footing. As eighteenth century German philosopher Emmanuel Kant pointed out, when apocalyptic thinking replaces practical reason all that remain are the waves of collective hysteria it generates, making solutions harder and costlier to find.

We all pay for this. Government policy formulation, especially when large sums of money are involved, needs to be transparent, objective, methodical, and based on reliable and independent research, not scares, or panic, or doom and gloom which distort our world view.

All research these days seems to lead to a demand for further research funding. The corollary is, if researchers are funded to investigate a problem, you can bet your sweet life they will not find there is no problem.

I have just finished reviewing, on the fiftieth anniversary of the first Earth Day (22 April 1970), all of the eco-doomsday predictions that were made at that time – an extraordinary list. Scary as they were, none, not a single one, has come true. Some continue to be regurgitated, albeit with a different end-date. Don't these people have any shame? One wonders how long you can keep making doomsday forecasts which never come true, and still retain your credibility. Does this say something about the human race, its need for an Armageddon, or just simply, its gullibility?

The good news, it seems to me, is that the consensus enforcers, the prophets of doom, the alarmists, the evangelists of the global warming hysteria are finally losing the public relations battle, despite the support they receive from the mainstream media, the twitterati, universities and most of the institutions of society. This is because of their excessively negative narrative, the crude and transparent virtue signalling, the over-reach, the gross hypocrisy of the do-what-I-say-not-what-I-do brigade, the incessant scaremongering, and of course the consistent failure of their predictions of doom. Added to these is a growing awareness of the massive economic and lifestyle costs of policies like net zero emissions by 2050, which would inevitably result in widespread poverty, chaos and misery. Increase petrol to $10/litre (which is inevitable if these crazy targets are to be met) and see how much support remains. Their bullying, name-calling and totalitarian approach to opposing views are starting to be noticed by the mainstream too.

My fervent hope is that ultimately all of this extremist polemic will be replaced by sensible, rational, evidence-based policies for dealing with changes in the climate, or any other natural process which may or may not be caused by human activity. Let the shouting be replaced by talking.

There is also the disturbing concern there could be a more insidious agenda, beyond climate change itself. The Rio Earth Climate Summit in 1992, in its Agenda 21, predicted: 'Effective execution of Agenda 21 will require a profound reorientation of all human society, unlike anything the world has ever experienced'.

UN Environment Program's Maurice Strong was equally forthcoming: 'Isn't the only hope for the planet that the industrialised civilisations collapse? Isn't it our responsibility to bring that about?'

The then US Under-secretary of State for Global Issues in the Clinton administration, Democrat Senator Tim Wirth, told the conference, 'We have got to ride the global warming issue. Even if the theory of global warming is wrong, we will be doing the right thing in terms of economic policy and environmental policy'.

Canada's Environment Minister Christine Stewart, in similar terms, told the *Calgary Herald* in 1988, 'No matter if the science of global warming is all phony . . . climate change provides the greatest opportunity to bring about justice and equality in the world.'

Christiana Figueres, then executive secretary of the top UN climate body UNFCCC (2010-16): 'This is the first time in the history of mankind that we are setting ourselves the task of intentionally, within a defined period of time, to change the economic development model that has been reigning for at least 150 years, since the industrial revolution'.

Ottmar Edenhofer, director of the influential dark-green Potsdam Climate Impacts Institute in Germany, twinned since 2015 with Melbourne University, explained: 'We are effectively redistributing world wealth through climate policy. That the owners of coal and oil are not enthusiastic, is obvious. One has to free oneself from the illusion that international climate policy is environmental policy. This has almost nothing to do with environmental policy.'

The latest issue of *Foreign Policy* (US) has a tract headlined, 'Democracy is the planet's biggest enemy'. The text of that article includes:

> If electoral democracy is inadequate to the task of addressing climate change, and the task is the most urgent one humanity faces, then other kinds of politics are urgently needed. The most radical alternative of all would be to consider moving beyond democracy altogether. The authoritarian Chinese system has some advantages when it comes to addressing climate change.

WOW. I could go on all day. I wonder what China thinks of all this commentary. In summary it does seem there are political groupings out there who want to change the world social order and who are using the climate change issue as a vehicle to achieve these objectives. They want the 'science' to say what they want it to say and are not interested in the truth.

To conclude this subject in light of all of the above, have you ever wondered why you never see Green protagonists with a sense of humour, or a smile on their face? Why? Because they wake up each day facing two cataclysmic options: either the world is hurtling into oblivion, or worse still, it isn't!

But wait, there could be another reason for the downcast look. I recently caught up with an article from Germany's chapter of Friends of the Earth, BUND Hamburg, which advises supporters to shift their barbeques from the evening to the early morning, as trees emit CO_2 in the evening and absorb it in morning. Further, they urge, if you must barbeque, never grill real meat – try grilled eggplant, or mushrooms with herb butter!

I'm worried this could turn into a contagious disease – soon none of us will be smiling!

6

CREATING A MORE PROSPEROUS NATION

A few more words about productivity, so fundamental to our economic future. Productivity is a simple measure of the volume of output per given input. Labour productivity (output per unit of labour input) is the most common measure because it relates to per capita income, the most important measure of economic well-being. But capital productivity is also a crucial measure and, of course, is very closely interrelated. Multi-factor productivity is changes in output per unit of combined inputs – difficult to measure and understand.

The uncomfortable fact of economic life is that there are really only two ways of increasing per capita income in an economy over time: by producing more per person or by getting higher world prices for what is produced. Absent this and there are no increasing living standards. As they say, a government cannot distribute what an economy does not produce. That is true enough though some believe you can distribute by taking off one and giving to another. But to the extent this erodes the incentive to work and aspire it is less than a zero sum game. It can pay a political dividend though, as George Bernard Shaw said, 'If you rob Peter to pay Paul you can expect Paul to vote for you!'

Poverty worldwide has reduced dramatically over the last fifty years (over that time the number of people in poverty has gone from four billion out of a population of five billion, to less than one billion out of seven billion today) and this has been accomplished by increasing productivity and releasing human creativity. Taking from the rich and giving to the poor helps very little. Expropriation is a one trick pony.

We in Australia have had a good dose of both drivers of income growth over recent decades: firstly as a consequence of the sustained productivity improvements stemming from the micro-economic reforms of the 1980s, and secondly from the massive increases in terms of trade associated with the so-called millennium resources boom (2003-12).

Gary Banks, the former Chairman of the Productivity Commission, points out that since tariff liberalisation and other micro-economic reforms in the mid 1980s began to transform our industrial landscape, wages in Australia increased by one-third in real (inflation adjusted) terms, while the number of jobs in the economy increased from 6.9 million to 11.5 million.

It is no secret that our productivity growth has slowed quite alarmingly over the last decade but we in Australia were very fortunate that the good horse terms of trade came galloping to our rescue. Referring to the ten year resources boom, Reserve Bank Governor Glen Stevens said the terms of trade boom is potentially the greatest gift the global economy has handed Australia since the gold rush.

As a result all key economic variables improved further. According to the Bureau of Resource and Energy Economics (BREE), average national weekly household income increased by 39% in real terms during the period. Australia handsomely outperformed all other OECD countries and was able to withstand the ravages of the Global Financial Crisis in good shape and without lapsing into recession, because of this remarkable piece of luck.

Yet some people, from the left would you believe, very often people who habitually whinge about wage suppression, oppose mining, especially coal-mining, and the exploitation of our resources. Can you believe it?

Resource booms, or massive spikes in terms of trade, don't last forever, as we have painfully found out. On the negative side they can lead to unsustainable expenditure which translates into structural deficit as revenue slides back to normalcy – so obvious as Queensland came out of the resources boom and commenced that inexorable accumulation of debt. So if we desire ongoing increases in living standards, or even if we want to retain present standards as we deal with the aged-care, health and pension challenges of an ageing population, then productivity improvement is the only long term answer.

Is productivity an end in itself?

Every galah in the pet-shop spruiks the virtues of productivity. But the average community member remains nonplussed. I think because we focus on labour productivity it is understandable that the average worker might see it as meaning doing more for less – code for job cuts and reductions in wages and conditions. Certainly trade unions in their eternal adversarial mission present it as such. So in my view we need to be careful not to raise the flag of productivity as an end in its own right. It is not; it is a means to an end, an end to which the whole community should aspire; an end that leads to higher incomes, more job opportunities and the increased government revenues which deliver social outcomes and rectify disadvantage. Increased productivity will deliver a lot more for the average wage earner than all of the political wand waving and industrial action in the world, as was proved during the 1980s reforms.

The challenge is to convince the community that everyone gets a share of the reform dividend; and to convince workers that this is the path to more jobs and higher incomes (which incidentally was done in the 1980s under the auspices of the prices and incomes accord where national wage increases were linked to increases in productivity).

But this is easier said than done. I continually stress that nearly all good public policy is counter intuitive and not easy to sell. There is widespread belief that: high taxes mean less inequality and more social spending; government spending creates growth; uncompromising industrial relations mean higher aggregate wages; tariffs protect jobs; renewable energy is cheaper because wind and sunshine are free; big government and regulatory zealotry are necessary to moderate anti-social behaviour; government subsidies underwrite economic growth; and so the dreamtime list goes on – all intuitive, all dead wrong, and all counter-productive. However, oppose these certitudes and a populist parliament will eat you alive.

As a subsequent Chair of the Productivity Commission Peter Harris so eloquently said, 'Economic reform is hard work. The short term pain is easily identifiable while the long term gain to the economy is too diffuse to motivate anyone.'

REGULATING SOCIETY – we've over cooked it

Few people deny that there is a role for government in regulating society, to ensure its orderly functioning, to ensure that our assets are fairly used, protected and paid for, to protect basic safety standards, and to ensure that the vulnerable are protected.

One hundred years ago life was very brutal, there were few constraints on what we did to each other or to the world we lived in. To the extent that wealth was created it was poorly distributed and there were few safety nets. My father's best years were devoured by the Great Depression and the world wars. I grew up with these bitter recollections. As I said earlier on, collectivism seemed the only answer – in the form of trade unions and farmer cooperatives for instance.

Governments around the industrialised world increasingly assumed the responsibility for what is sometimes referred to as civilising capitalism, for regulating society in order to achieve a whole range of egalitarian, safety, social and environmental outcomes. Markets ultimately must serve the public interest.

But when do you get to the stage where it becomes counter-productive, where individual responsibility is ceded to the government, where entitlements replace incentive, where feeling good replaces good sense, where every problem merits a new law, and we create a government monster and a regulatory miasma that erodes our freedoms, chokes wealth creation and ultimately smothers the social dividends that governments seek to deliver?

We need to remember that governments, as with the public service, do not create wealth, they consume wealth. But even though they don't create wealth they surely can stifle its creation.

I have spoken before about the Gillard minority Government incessantly boasting about the volume of legislation it passed as evidence that it was getting on with the business of minority Government – 466 pieces altogether. As I said before, the questions we might reasonably pose are, who asked for all those pieces of legislation, have they made society better, and has each piece delivered more benefits than costs?

The voting public expects government to be addressing, and solving, all problems, perceived or otherwise. They complain about governments stuffing things up. But they keep urging governments to, well, stuff things up. As Winston Churchill said, the best argument against democracy, is a five minute conversation with the average voter!

The other aggravating tendency of all governments is to label each new piece of legislation as a 'reform' no matter how recidivistic it is, and of course give it a cute Orwellian title.

THE FREE MARKET REVOLUTION – not before time

There was one refreshing hiatus in this inexorable, century long, regulatory proliferation, and that was in the 1980s. At the end of the 19th century Australia was reputed to have the highest living standards in the world, based of course on the 19th century gold rush and wool boom. Then the 'civilising capital' agenda developed a head of steam. We came to believe we could secure these standards through government intervention, to secure jobs through tariff protection, to regulate every part of the economy that seemed under threat, only to see the economy slow and unemployment grow, generating further calls for higher tariffs and more protection – the unvirtuous merry-go-round!

Finally Lee Kwan Yew of Singapore was able to label Australians the White Trash of Asia. Talk about a light bulb moment! It greatly affected me. I started to see things differently from that point on. As I am sure, did many others.

So enter the Hawke/Keating revolution and their market based reforms: floating the currency, cutting tariffs and protection, deregulating the banking system, competition policy, the accord and so on. It is worth mentioning, as it is so unique in Australian political history, that these reforms would not have been possible without the cooperation and support of Her Majesty's Opposition – can you believe it, looking back from the vantage point of the 2020s, two sides of politics singing from the same hymn-sheet – putting the national interest before party politics? I guess it is the only way to deliver major reform.

Perhaps the National Gun Laws legislation following the 1996 Port Arthur massacre is another example. But it would be nice if we could do it more than twice every 100 years.

I do make the unusual observation, and it was probably fundamental to these two colossal reform packages, in that they were strongly counter political, i.e., the so-called left-wing Government (Hawke/Keating) delivering essentially right-wing market based reforms, and a right-wing Government (Howard) delivering left-wing reform in the form of gun control. Not sure what that says about the body politic in Australia. For instance one of the other notable reforms, the GST, was introduced by the Howard Government without any help from the ALP (and considerable interference from the Senate).

In my view the pathway to economic growth is straightforward, and it does not depend on government spending, or financing demand. It is rooted in supply-side reforms, as I have said a hundred times in this book: lower taxes, cheaper energy, more cooperative industrial relations and a red-tape clean-out. It involves no government expenditure, no debt ... But I recognise, virtually impossible to implement, because of an obtuse Senate and Opposition populism. So easy yet so hard. From a national point of view, isn't that sad?

A great opportunity for the Labor Party next time in power: beat the Coalition at its own game, and be forever remembered as a major reforming Government, as was the Hawke-Keating Government. Trouble is it may induce multiple terminal apoplexies amongst the big government, big spending brigade that lurks around virtually every corner these days.

The recidivision revolution

They say if we do not learn from history we are doomed to repeat it. It seems we are doomed. We had twenty years of progress, people were enjoying the benefits of market based reform; it was becoming easier to sell. And then, suddenly we are overwhelmed with a recidivism revolution, a massive regrowth in government and regulatory intrusion in our lives and the economy.

Is there a better example of recidivism than government subsidies for the car industry: $12 billion over the last twenty years of its existence as an Australian industry; talk about back to the future! And the outcome: we all pay more tax to fund the subsidy, tariffs make cars (both Australian-made and imported) more expensive for Australian consumers, resources are tied up in uncompetitive industries instead of migrating to competitive areas, anti-competitive work practices are entrenched by the subsidies, and jobs still going down the gurgler. And spare a moment to consider the splendid irony of a Government introducing a Clean Energy Futures policy (carbon tax) by espousing the virtues of a clean green economy, and then rushing to subsidise 'brown' sectors under threat!

Subsidies and other government support won't save an uncompetitive and dying manufacturing industry. But innovation, flexible and efficient work practices, a benign regulatory environment, and cheap energy prices surely could.

The Association of Mining and Exploration Companies (AMEC) in a 2014 submission to a Productivity Commission enquiry pointed out that the number of pieces of primary legislation for miners seeking project approval had jumped from 94 to 144 since 2006: land access, cultural heritage, native title, environmental, water, planning, social impacts, etc. (This issue is covered in more detail in 'Coal – a stranded asset', see p. 128 and following).

In that chapter I referenced the fact that Macarthur Coal's first mine, Coppabella in the Bowen Basin, took just 15 months and $100 million to production commencement. The same project today would take at least five years and a billion dollars. As a consequence balance sheets need to be so much bigger.

Victoria has recently established a Public Sector Gender Equality Commissioner, yes I kid you not. That will surely improve life – not sure for whom, certainly not business or the taxpayer or the ordinary battler. I read also where Victoria now has about eighty commissioners, sitting atop dozens of superfluous bureaucratic fiefdoms.

And it all costs. According to a McKinsey Global Institute (MGI) study (2016), the benefits of the mining boom have masked an annual decline of 0.7% in Australia's productivity between 2005 and 2011, with capital productivity being the biggest drag. And you don't need a Nobel Prize in economics to appreciate that it is the suffocating regulatory environment that is the cause, with so much capital tied up for so long without generating a return.

According to the Institute of Public Affairs (2017), based on international econometric studies of red tape cost, it is estimated the economic costs of red tape in Australia today are in the order of $176 billion per annum (11 per cent of GDP). This translates into red tape costs of about $19,300 per Australian household.

Once again, according to the Institute of Public Affairs, legal activism by environmental groups has put $65 billion of investment at risk in Australia by holding up major projects in court. This legal activism has been largely enabled by Section 487 of the *Environment Protection and Biodiversity Conservation (EPBC) Act* which allows environmental groups to challenge project approvals made by the federal Environment Minister. However, this incessant legal action has not made a discernible difference to environmental outcomes. All it has done, as of course was the intent, is needlessly strangle the economy and wealth creation, especially in regional areas.

What can we do about it? There are many things, and not all the responsibility of governments. Management obviously has a vital role to play in terms of investment, efficient operation, incentivising the workforce, innovation, new markets, new ways of doing things – we could go on forever.

But let's stick to the role of government. And again there are many dimensions to this: skills training, industrial relations settings, tax policy, infrastructure, regulatory environment, and so the list goes on.

Most legislation/regulation is well meaning. The problem is that most of it is impractical, often unworkable, disproportionate to the problem, brings with it unintended consequences, is subject to an uncontrollable disease called mission creep, and of course is expensive. Every government in Australia, indeed the world, seems to have a red tape task force, yet red tape keeps multiplying exponentially.

On top of this there are often mandatory requirements for a Regulatory Impact Statement (RIS) to accompany each new piece of legislation; yet it seems to make little difference. And why? Generally because the RIS is self-serving, the models usually being prepared by the department introducing the legislation. As you know, models don't help much when you start with the outcome and search for assumptions that will deliver the outcome.

I am not saying that there are no cases for social regulation in the public interest. What I am saying is that it needs to be demonstrated that the public interest benefits exceed the economic costs, and that such benefits to society cannot be achieved in more cost effective ways.

Regulation reform principles

Mandatory Regulatory Impact Statement (RIS) required for all new legislation/regulation:

> Conducted by an independent agency.
>
> Made public.
>
> Costs and benefits to be rigorously calculated, especially the costs to business.
>
> Alternatives to be considered.
>
> Unintended consequences examined.
>
> One-in-one-out principle, sunset clauses, post implementation reviews.
>
> Effective consultation with stake-holders.
>
> A comprehensive and structural review of all existing legislative, regulatory and administrative requirements.
>
> Repeal Section 487 of the EPBC Act. In fact the Commonwealth should get right out of environmental protection. Mindless duplication serves no useful purpose. It

has proved to have no moderating effects on the States, or the environment for that matter.

Unfortunately, in a large sparsely-populated country like Australia, there are massive demands for infrastructure which is not economic and can't generate a return to the government provider (and because there is no financial return on investment [ROI] can't be funded by the private sector).

I can remember, when we were elected to government, we inherited a massive jig-saw of railway lines in western Queensland that we had to maintain yet no one was using them: little, winding, narrow-gauge tracks, and trains that Billy Slater could out-run. Modern roads had taken over. The Country (National) party couldn't close the rail during their reign because country infrastructure was of immense psychological value, even if its economic purpose had faded with the summer rains.

We should reflect for a moment on the enormous economic value of major navigable waterways around the world as the industrial revolution took root: the Mississippi system in North America, the Yangtze in China, the Danube/Rhine system in Europe, and so on. Australia, a large dry continent needing navigable waterways more than all others, but just the Murray-Darling, a pale imitation of these other colossal systems. Rail, and later roads, were so much more important in our context, economic and symbolic, and at least we had the natural advantages to facilitate these, though we bungled the railway challenge by investing in narrow gauge rail tracks.

We bravely decided to close them, and allocated the diplomatic chore to Deputy-Premier Tom Burns, our most popular politician and well regarded in the bush. All hell broke loose. We were taking something sacred away. At one stage during one of his tumultuous meetings Tom asked a rowdy grazier point blank if he personally used the rail line. 'Of course', came the reply. 'When?' Tom asked. 'During the drought in 57!' A credit to Tom – we eventually closed most of them, and were re-elected.

I wanted to close the Forsayth railway line which travelled from (my electorate of) Cairns to Forsayth, in its heyday 150 years ago servicing the rich mineral fields in the lower peninsula). I asked Treasury to do an exercise on its commercial viability. It turns out we were recovering seven percent of costs, the other 93 percent courtesy of the taxpayer. It is still there as a tourist train going under the name of *The Savanna-lander,* a monument to politics not economics! I guess it was too close to home – I should have asked Tommy Burns to do the dirty work!

Competitive federalism

Australia became a nation on 1 January 1901, when the British Parliament passed legislation enabling the six Australian colonies to collectively govern in their own right as the Commonwealth of Australia. It was a remarkable and peaceable political accomplishment that had taken many years and several referenda to achieve.

The States (previously self-governing colonies) retained most of the powers of government, with specific responsibilities reserved to the Commonwealth (like defence, customs and excise, foreign affairs, corporations law, etc). There were initially substantial built-in protections for State's rights. However in 1942 the Commonwealth gained a monopoly on income taxes with the wartime *Income Tax Act 1942* and the *States Grants (Income Tax Reimbursement) Act.* Welcome to Vertical Fiscal Imbalance, the massive imbalance in the revenue raising capabilities between the Commonwealth and the States and Territories. This imbalance has resulted, inevitably, in almost every state function being duplicated by Canberra, and the transfer of substantial revenues from the Commonwealth to the States and Territories.

In the late nineties the High Court also restricted the States' power to levy franchise fees on cigarettes, alcohol and petrol, deeming all excise taxes were the preserve of the Commonwealth. This further exacerbated the vertical fiscal imbalance, and inspired Prime Minister John Howard to consider a Goods and Services Tax (GST), with the revenue hypothecated to the States, to give them some fiscal independence. The GST became law in July 2000 at a rate of 10% but with a Senate imposed range of exempted items such as food.

This fiscal imbalance has always been a feature of our federalism. As long ago as 1902 Alfred Deakin wrote:

> The rights of the states have been fondly supposed to be safeguarded by the Constitution. It left them legally free, but financially bound to the chariot wheels of the central government.

This situation has continued to deteriorate in the last 118 years as the Commonwealth has progressively assumed more and more fiscal power at the expense of the States and Territories through the power of the purse, international treaties, activist High Courts, and just plain dumb politics.

Australia is now at the extreme end in terms of vertical fiscal imbalance, or revenue centralisation, for countries with a federal structure of government. The Commonwealth now has health and education bureaucracies of massive dimensions, yet health and education are technically the sole preserve of the States. The Commonwealth is spending $36 billion annually on education and around $80 billion on health.

Revenue transfers from the Commonwealth comprise Specific Purpose Payments (linked to specific function – also known as tied grants), and General Revenue Assistance, to equalise as much as possible the fiscal capacities of the States and Territories to deliver government services to a specified standard – so-called Horizontal Fiscal Equalisation (HFE).

The Commonwealth Grants Commission has responsibility for designing and implementing the methodology for the distribution of Commonwealth (GST) revenue to achieve the 'fiscal equity' objective.

The concept of competitive federalism is dead. The States don't compete, they just blame the Feds. This concept has gone backwards dramatically over the last two decades. When I was Queensland Treasurer there was active competition between States for bragging rights, inherited to a great extent from the Bjelke-Petersen era, and much breast beating (I still have bruises on my chest) – low tax State, fiscal fundamentals, staff/student ratios, hospital waiting lists, economic growth, population growth, unemployment levels and so on. While some of it was vulgar and self-serving, it is an inalienable fact that competition does drive performance, and accountability.

The creep of Commonwealth takeover of responsibilities seems inexorable, Gonski and NDIS the most spectacular in recent times.

The Commonwealth Government's share of NDIS expenditure in 2019 is expected to be around $11.2 billion, and in 2017 the Turnbull Government committed an extra $18.6 billion across four years in Gonski 2 education funding – these once State responsibilities. And then there is Energy, now largely a Commonwealth responsibility. One wonders why a Federal Government would wish to take responsibility for this minefield – maybe they believe their own propaganda. But the real problem is that it is now a joint responsibility, with conflicting priorities, agendas, and moral posturing – a virtual dog's breakfast.

The *EPBC (Environmental) Act* is another example of the Commonwealth muscling in on State territory; hasn't helped much, it only means investment projects now have two masters, two bureaucracies and two armies of Green guardians to navigate and complicate approvals.

And Aged -Care: a Commonwealth responsibility, but the States are responsible for most of the services.

And consider these pork barrelling doozies: Stronger Communities Program, the Community Development Grants Program, the Building Better Regions Fund – forays into State responsibilities unimaginable a few decades ago.

Now bush fires, a good case study in the summer of 2019/20 in the inexorable transfer in responsibility from State to Commonwealth. The present PM was widely condemned for his handling of the bushfire crisis even though he had no constitutional responsibility to do so.

Many people quite reasonably ask, as the Commonwealth is progressively taking over funding, and indeed management and policy responsibility, for more and more State functions, what is the point of the States? Good question, for which every voter in Australia has the same answer – get rid of the States. The irony of Australian politics is that everyone thinks we have a tier of government too many, but if called on to rectify the situation by supporting a constitutional referendum to abolish the States, there is not a snow-flake's chance in hell that it would be carried. So it seems we have to live with the three tiers, as inefficient as they are.

Perhaps we should look at abolishing the Senate, the unrepresentative swill, the States' House which no longer represents the States; that would be a great step forward in terms of governance and fiscal efficiency. Regrettably this constitutional adventurism would end up in the same place as a proposal to abolish the States. Ahh, the Australian voting public; they complain about the problem but oppose the solution – a bit like the Greens really!

At least we have only one House in the Queensland parliament – Red Ted abolished the Upper House 99 years ago. Hey, we have a worthwhile anniversary coming up in the not too distant future (23 March 2022).

There are three elements to a good tax (is there such a thing as a good tax?) – simplicity, efficiency and positive incentivisation. Most of Australia's taxation doesn't meet these tests. In my view the most fundamental requirement in taxation and welfare policy is to ensure that as much as possible it incentivises the right behaviour. State taxes such as mining royalties, payroll tax, stamp duties don't meet this test; they are excessively negative, taxing effort, investment and enterprise.

At the Commonwealth level, income and company tax are also taxes on effort. The GST of course is the major exception, being a tax on consumption. Its downside is that it is seen as a regressive, rather than a progressive tax, not punishing the rich enough. It can't be used to redistribute wealth so is a 'no no' to the left progressives.

HORIZONTAL FISCAL EQUALISATION

There is one other area of taxation that deserves a mention, Horizontal Fiscal Equalisation (HFE), a troubled area, much in the news in recent years. HFE provides that State governments receive GST funding from the Commonwealth ($65 billion in 2018-19 – on top of the $60 billion in specific purpose payments) such that each would have equal capacity to provide services and associated infrastructure at the same standard. As I pointed out before, the Commonwealth Grants Commission has responsibility for designing and implementing the methodology to achieve this 'fiscal equity' objective, by taking into account each State's capacity to raise revenue, and the cost of delivering services in that particular jurisdiction.

But as I keep saying it should be all about incentives. Under the present system there is no incentive for States to promote economic development and increase own source revenue, because much of the increased revenue eventually will be redistributed under the formula to other States.

Many people refer to Tasmania as Australia's National Park. There is little economic activity in the island State (foregone mining, timber production and water storage come to mind, and more recently it seems even those renewable energy totems, wind turbines, are not wanted) as these activities are usually seen by green-eyed Tasmanians as defiling the natural environment. But there is no fiscal penalty for this as Tasmania is compensated for reduced taxing capacity by increased GST distributions under the HFE formula. Hence the National Park allegation with the rest of Australia paying for it.

Under the HFE formula we eventually arrived at the absurd situation where Tasmania was receiving $1.77 per capita for every GST dollar it sent to Canberra, while Western Australia, because of its mining royalty revenue, was only receiving 34 cents for each GST dollar it raised. And Western Australia, geographically the largest state, and with a large Indigenous population, would hardly have an efficiency advantage in delivering services and infrastructure.

This formulation provides little incentive to build tax bases, and design and implement efficient tax policy. I have said before that an entrepreneurial Queensland Treasurer (as opposed to one that wants to re-skill coal miners so their industry can be closed down) could have presided over a 100 million tonne per annum coal industry in the Galilee Basin, generating further royalty revenues in excess of a billion dollars per annum.

The only problem is that under the HFE formula up to 80% of this additional royalty revenue would be redistributed to other states. Even though they hate the coal mine, Tasmanians would be rolling in dough, maybe wealthy enough to mount a convoy into Queensland's mining country on an annual basis – did I hear whoops of joy from the LNP?

Recent legislative changes, introduced under pressure from Western Australia, have improved things somewhat by changing the HFE objective from 'full equalisation of fiscal capacity' to 'reasonable equalisation'. This will limit some of the extreme effects. But in my view it doesn't go far enough. The system, consistent with competitive federalism, should incentivise States and Territories to generate economic activity and grow wealth and revenue – or answer to their constituents.

THE NANNY STATE

To what extent should governments be responsible for the personal welfare of its citizens? Do you believe in a sugar tax because the experts tell us that sugar is not good for us; or an obesity tax? They call these sin taxes, easy to implement because they are filtered through the soft virtue of doing good.

I have traditionally been opposed to the Nanny State: I believe the person responsible for your socially harmful habits is YOU. However there are two areas where I have to admit the interventions have paid big dividends. The first is traffic accidents, a range of interventions which have led to a dramatic reduction in accidents and road casualties. The major interventions comprise compulsory seat belts, strict drink driving rules, more policing, better roads and safer cars. In 1964 there were 2966 casualties on Australian roads, representing 84 deaths per 100,000 cars. Fifty years later (2014, the last year for which I have data) there were 1,150 casualties, representing just 4.5 deaths per 100,000 cars. Who can argue with this? I was dead wrong, and I salute the Nanny Staters.

The second is smoking. There are a range of interventions here, the most important being rapidly increasing (sin) excise taxes, an increasing prohibition on smoking in public areas, and shock health warnings on packs. I was always strongly opposed to these interventions, based partly on my opposition to the Nanny State, and no doubt coloured by my historical association with the tobacco growing industry. I can remember in my political heyday arguing with colleagues who seemed so full of moral righteousness to be imposing their will on other people (and saving the world) – a bit like climate change really.

In my day virtually everyone (every man that is) smoked; it was a rite of passage (not so good for football fitness though). I smoked for about ten years. But the wowsers won. While I hate to admit it, they were right. Smoking is a dreadful habit from a social and health point of view (lung cancer is an ugly way to die). If you forgive the metaphor, smoking is a cancer on society. It is only pleasurable when there is an addiction to satisfy; get rid of the addiction and bingo, there goes the pleasure.

I still have some reservations about the tax regime. A pack of twenty cigarettes costs close to $40 these days, that is almost ten percent of the weekly Newstart allowance. There is no doubt in my mind that it is the poor, especially the unemployed poor, who don't have a full and meaningful life, who are smoking these days, not the lawyers and accountants. The middle class has walked away. My point is that it is a highly regressive tax, impacting dreadfully on the poor who haven't the psychological wherewithal to tame the beast; ten packs and the dole is gone for the week.

Is the Labor Party being consistent with its values by supporting this level of tax when it so disproportionately impacts the poor? Or is it another case of bowing to the progressive elite?

I got in the habit of buying *Big Issue* from a homeless person in Edward Street Brisbane. They sell the magazine for $6 and are invited to keep $3 for themselves. This day I gave him $10, keep the change.

I did a bit of business and then went down to Woolies. Sure enough, there he was lined up for a packet of cigarettes, costing the equivalent of thirteen *Big Issues* sales, and twelve hours in the sun selling them. I guess that was a better option than funding the habit from the dole, at the expense of food. But very tough on a person subject to an uncontainable addiction.

While I am on the subject of smoking and its impact on health care costs, it leads to one of my favourite *bête noirs*, modelling. I was always inundated with modelling evidence of the astronomical costs of smoking on the health budget. What all of these proselytising warriors conveniently overlooked of course was the cost of not dying from smoking. What was obvious to me was there was a much smaller impact on the health budget if an errant smoker died from lung cancer at age 49, rather than battling on to 85 and racking up all of the associated health care costs that inevitably came from growing old. This is not a comment about health policy, just an example of how modelling can be used for whatever you like if you are prepared to fiddle the assumptions, or ignore some necessary inputs. I know it is a bit of a callous way of making the point, but models that don't accurately analyse the subject properly don't help anyone.

It was around this time too that I came to another realisation. Health is the one game where, perversely, the better you are the more it costs (this is an old Treasurer talking). Every time a quality health intervention utilising modern procedures, or medications, or technology, saves the life of a sick person, the ungrateful bugger responds by growing old, dramatically increasing the on-going cost to the health budget. Of course I hurry to concede that encouraging everyone to die young shouldn't be part of the budget strategy; I'm just making a useless point.

OWN THE LANGUAGE AND YOU OWN THE DEBATE

In a lot of areas the simple unadjusted language doesn't convey the right kind of message. The solution, change the language: 21st century Orwellian insurgency.

Global warming: couldn't handle snow so re-name it Climate Change.

First Nation peoples: Recognises Australia was a nation prior to European settlement, thus promoting the invasion narrative and the grievance culture.

Marriage equality: Same-sex marriage never hit the mark. Marriage equality – even homophobes couldn't oppose that could they?

Progressive 1: You are against economic progress. So call yourself Progressive, that will confuse everyone.

Progressive 2: A movement based on the virtues of diversity, tolerance and justice, but which is anything but diverse, tolerant and just.

Woke: Perpetually offended.

Strategic co-investment: A dividend-free government subsidy to the car industry.

Clean Energy Futures: It was quickly fingered as simply a carbon tax and it crashed and burned.

Carbon Pollution Reduction Scheme (CPRS): As it transpired it wasn't ugly black carbon pollution, it was the colourless plant food carbon dioxide. The CPRS died an ugly death.

Fascist: A conservative that is winning an argument.

Hate speech: It used to be speech that generated hate, now it is speech we hate.

Sustainable: it used to mean you had sufficient cash-flow to pay the bills, now it means demonising fossil fuels.

Unprecedented: Ignoring the last 5000 years of history.

Gonski: A financial time-bomb designed to blow up succeeding Governments.

Stop-Adani: Let Indians in poverty eat cake.

Denier 1: A person who doesn't believe in global warming, the holocaust, or that man landed on the moon.

Denier 2: Galileo, he denied the Sun moved around the Earth.

Sceptic: An infidel, outcast from the climate faith.

Budget saving: What Treasurer Wayne Swan used to call a tax increase.

Reform: Any new legislation, regulation or thought bubble, or politically correct inspiration.

The Senate: Unrepresentative swill (thanks PK)

Horizontal Fiscal Equalisation: Equalising indolence and effort.

Child centred learning: Dumbing it down.

Malthusianism: We'll all be rooned said Hanrahan.

White: Privileged.

Racist: that's what privilege does to you.

Retired: Old person who does not understand Facebook.

National pride: Xenophobia.

Patriotic: Racist.

Privileged: Stale, pale and male.

Socialism: What's yours is mine.

Mansplaining: A man opening his mouth other than to breathe.

Ideology: Never having to think again.

Social justice: Distributing other people's money.

Inclusion: Exclusion of white males.

Diversity: 50% of all Board members must have an IQ below average in order to reflect the diversity of society as a whole.

Modern Monetary Theory: The Magic Pudding theory of finance.

Black lives matter: Armed peaceful protest.

Antifa: Looting in the name of justice.

Cancel culture: Must have IQ less than room temperature to participate.

Cultural appropriation 1: Eating rice, especially with chop sticks.

Cultural appropriation 2: Japanese with a vegemite sandwich.

Human Rights Commission: Grievance factory.

Extinction rebellion: A rebellion destined to become extinct.

#MeToo: All men are rapists.

Climate models: predictive models which are consistent – consistently wrong.

Renewables: Unreliables.

Net zero emissions: De-industrialisation.

Curbing CO2 emissions: A non-solution to a non-problem.

Climate emergency: The emergency you have when you're not having an emergency.

Tipping point: The point at which a new tipping point is needed.

Polar bear extinction: When Al Gore was born there were 7,000 polar bears. Now there are only 30,000 left.

Cancelling women's biological identity. (From ANU Gender Neutral Language Values).

Breast-feeding: Chest-feeding.

Pregnant women: Pregnant persons.

Mother 1: Birthing parent.

Mother 2: Gestational parent

Father: Non-gestational parent.

Women: People who menstruate.

Woman: Uterus holder.

Mr Potato Head: Potato Head.

7

THE BEST TIME AND THE BEST PLACE IN HISTORY

The point of view I have consistently promulgated in this book is that we live not only in the best place, but at the best time in history. If we want to put this into context let's look at the life experience of someone born early last century (1901), like my father – hardly an example dragged out of antiquity. Many today would think this was a pretty simple time to live. Well, not really.

Life expectancy in Australia when he was born was forty-seven, compared to circa 83 now.

When he turned 13 World War I broke out, killing millions worldwide, and he mourned the loss of countrymen who volunteered or were conscripted to defend freedom in Europe. It finished when he was 17. Later that year the Spanish Flu hit the planet and runs until his 19th birthday; 500 million people infected (one-third of the world's population); 50 million die. On his 28th birthday, the Great Depression broke out. Unemployment hit 25% and World GDP shrank 27%.

If you were unemployed you made your own way in life. In Cairns, the end of the line as it were, armies of unemployed camped in the show grounds, threatening a civil war with the locals. Depending on charities for sustenance (susso); eating lizards and grass-hoppers, and luxuriating in the glory of a Ringer's breakfast – a piss, a fart and a quick look round (sorry, couldn't help that)!

World War II started when he turned 38 – 75 million people perished in that war. He can thank his lucky star that he was too young for active combat for World War I and too old for World War II, though he was an active member of the VDC (Voluntary Defence Corps) trained to defend the North against invasion – good luck! Five million people perished in the Korean War which started when he turned 49. Then the Vietnam War started when he turned 54, and didn't end for twenty years; four million people died.

Apart from the Cuban Missile crisis in the middle of the cold war, and nuclear Armageddon hanging precipitously over everyone, things have turned largely benign since then.

Count your blessings. As they say, nothing is more responsible for the good old days than a bad memory.

On 24 January 2014 I was invited to deliver the Australia Day Address at the Cairns Regional Council Chambers. The following is a major excerpt from the speech.

COUNT YOUR BLESSINGS

Fifty years ago this year, in 1964, Donald Horne wrote *The Lucky Country*, a seminal work on where we stood as a nation, our culture and where we were going. His famous line, used and misused over the last half century, still resonates today: 'Australia is a lucky country, run mainly by second rate people, who share its luck.'

It is my view that this was the first trigger of what grew into the orgy of national self-loathing that so infects public discourse today, especially amongst the intelligentsia.

I however don't accept the sentiment behind the phrase – either then or now. Whilst I accept that introspection, debate and re-assessments of our strengths and weaknesses are essential as we carve out a future in an uncertain world, I worry that we have come to focus too predominantly on our sins, rather than our successes.

Are we the lucky country? Of course we are – who would want to live anywhere else? Is that luck all God given, or have we crafted much of it through our own endeavours? Let's look at the facts.

We have a stable, well functioning, liberal democracy which resolves issues without recourse to the gun; we live by the rule of law; we have a truly multicultural society having embraced immigrants from around the world; by all accounts we have the highest, or close to, the highest living standards in the world, as measured not only by income but by a social wage comprising things like access to education, pensions, health care, and other support systems. Most things work well – medical services, transport systems, electricity supply, sewerage systems and reticulated water, supermarkets stock a spell-binding panoply of fresh food, the rubbish gets collected once a week, community based emergency services are quick to the rescue in times of need, an incredible array of charities are there to extend the helping hand, food is plentiful, safe and fresh, the sky is smog free… need I go on?

And despite what many may decry, we have one of the most equal societies on Earth; and certainly the most egalitarian, where people are respected for what they are and not their social status.

We are achievers, and highly respected on the world stage. Almost weekly our sporting people, actors and film makers, authors and entertainers, our scientists and medical researchers, our entrepreneurs and engineers, do us proud. Australia, with less than one third of one percent of the world population, has produced 13 Nobel prize winners.

And to the extent that we have transgressed, and some may point to injustices in the treatment of the original inhabitants, there is unanimity of desire to rectify the wrongs.

Yet there is an industry in Australia which is determined to see only the negatives in our past, the so-called black armband view of history, and a highly pessimistic view of our people and our future. It is sometimes referred to as the miserablist view of Australia, a term I endorse, and use.

I read an article recently which said in part that the paradox of our time is that we are feeling bad about doing well. By objective standards the last half-century of our national life has been hugely successful.

We have achieved unprecedented prosperity and personal freedom. We are healthier, work at less physically exhausting jobs, and live much longer. Government provides a safety net for the elderly and the poor that never existed in the past. Many discriminations based on race, sex, gender or religion have diminished sharply. If you can believe an ABS survey released recently, we are eating and drinking more of just about everything. In short, Australia has become a vastly better place.

Yet we disparage our leaders and despair at our prospects. There's an immense contempt for institutions such as the public service, the media, banks and other service providers, corporate executives, and of course politicians – in terms of public approval they rate just above child molesters!

Now far be it for me to join the Miserablists, but I want to say that I am worried about two insidious cultures which are starting to subsume our society – the blame game and the entitlement culture.

The blame game. If something goes wrong, blame someone else, maybe even sue them. It is always someone else's fault, usually the government's. It seems we have stopped taking personal responsibility for our own decisions, our own choices, our own lives.

If we are to have a strong and robust future as a society, if we are going to meet the new challenges that arise whatever they will be, then we have to stop passing the buck. And expecting governments to solve every problem, a new piece of legislation for every problem as it were – this just leads to more regulations, more red tape, higher costs, bigger Government, higher taxes, less wealth and less freedom.

And entitlements! My mother used to say nobody owes you anything, you've got to get out and do it yourself. She was a creature of the Great Depression, and viewed things very differently. But it is a pity more people didn't see it that way today. Apart from anything else we should understand that one person's entitlement is another person's taxation.

I worry that too many people in Australia not only take our prosperity and living standards for granted, but they have become alienated from the productive sector, in fact they very often see it, the productive sector, the wealth creators, as the enemy – and this not just people on the fringe of society, I'm talking about a very influential and sizeable sector – the so-called inner city progressives, much of the political class, the public service and academia, sections of the mainstream media and so on.

All I am saying is that we need a more balanced attitude, more respect for the role that everyone plays.

I am on the Advisory Board of Queensland Leaders, an organisation based in Brisbane, and dedicated to inspiring the next generation of leading companies in Queensland. Among other things we have a session each month where five fledgling companies tell their story, in very short presentations, and I never cease to be amazed at the number of small companies out there having a go, with enthusiasm and passion and resourcefulness. It makes one proud to be Australian.

We are the lucky country – it is a combination of God's gift and personal endeavour. We were gifted great opportunities but we have also made our own luck.

Successive waves of migrants have overwhelmingly embraced the Australian dream, with its absence of institutional barriers to success and its egalitarian promise of wealth for toil. I grew up with many European migrants after the war, refugees from the Second World War, and they, and their descendants are now proud and successful and worthy Australians.

I started off life just about as tough as it could be, on a tobacco farm in Dimbulah – no electricity, no refrigerator, no hot water, no tractor, no car, no money, no hope … I got a job in an underground mine with a jack hammer and hand-shovel and thought I was made!

My mother used to say 'count your blessings'. I didn't know what she meant – for a start I didn't think I had any blessings to count. But I did, not least of which was a family that urged us not to accept the confines of the environment we were born into, and a country of opportunity where no one has to.

My Australia Day message then is let's count our blessings, let's celebrate – recognise our failings sure, but celebrate our society, our achievements, our past, our ingenuity, our culture, our luck. We live in the best country in the world, and dare I say it, at the best time in history.

Happy Australia Day!

That's a bit dated. These days of course I could suggest more trendy names for the miserabilists, more descriptive, appropriate and contemporary – perhaps self-hating, sanctimonious elites. Sadly I can also identify further internal threats to our national well-being beyond the blame game and the entitlement culture.

Janet Albrechtsen paints the miserabilists more comprehensively (*The Australian*, 26 October 2019), albeit in a few more words, well chosen as only Janet can, describing them as the crowd who –

> stifle speech, no-platforms people with different views, disfigures great works of literature to meet modern sensibilities, kills comedy to protect feelings, restrains writers from stepping into the shoes of others, thinks diversity in public broadcasting means putting people with different skin colour on TV, rejects an exquisite painting from past centuries because an artist lived by different norms, shames dissenters, sacks scientists, and depicts Western civilisation as a shameful story of colonial aggression, white privilege and rotten patriarchy.

But are these the real Australians? Could it be that real Australia is out there doing its own thing, having a go, and annoying no one? Spare a thought for real Australia. Some time ago I had reason to drive along Spence Street, a typical suburban business street in Cairns – a hot-bed of people *having a go* – replicated liberally around Australia.

Here is a cross section of the business establishments I recorded: Torque Tyres and Trailer Spares; Allied Bearings and Tools; George's Low Price Store; Spear and Tackle; In 2 Thai; Pets and Ponds; The Pottery Connection; Bullivants; Buchan Street Service Centre; Cairns Mechanical Workshop; Uptop Downunder Backpackers Resort; Focus on Spence; Payless Stores; Trinity Petroleum Services; Market Power; Cairns Pit Stop; Tyrepower; Allsorts Costume Hire; Only Bathrooms; Mobile Windscreens and Tinting FNQ; Demi International Beauty Academy; Pro Drive Training Centre; Cairns Produce; Tom Cowles; Repco Authorised Services; Cairns Tattoo Emporium; Hair on Spence; Brewcan; and so the list goes on, and on, and on. (Various farming and regional communities can exhibit a similar profile).

Just a sample, and no doubt changing all the time. It is estimated that there are about six million such businesses in Australia and, according to the Small Business Administration, about 550,000 close each year. But in an on-going merry-go-round, they are usually replaced by others, prepared to have a go.

They are usually family businesses, people who have invested their life savings, sometimes on a punt, sometimes on a carefully formulated business plan. Usually geared to the eye-balls and constantly dealing with the vagaries of enterprise: economic cycles, interest rate fluctuations, inflation, competition, changing customer expectations, cyber disruption, wage and penalty-rate impositions, digital transformations, the vagaries of the Internet, fear of the unknown, on-line and off-shore competition, cultural shifts, crime, taxes, red tape, natural disasters, and so the list goes on. Innovate and adapt, and face up with fortitude, the only road to tomorrow.

No guaranteed superannuation for this mob, no earnings indexation, no safety nets, no income or work practice protections, no overtime or sick leave or annual leave, no regulated hours, no penalty rates … I'm not sure if they belong to the proletariat or the bourgeoise. I don't know how Marx would have defined them in his revolution. Mao would have shot them!

They are so important as a life-blood of our community, of the economy, and the biggest employer (small businesses like these employ over 40% of the workforce). They are a cohesive influence because they are hardly aware of the grievance industry and identity politics. Australia is a successful nation because of the role played by the middle and working classes, who are aspirational, seek a better life for themselves and their children, are embedded within their communities, and are patriotic in the Australian sense.

We need to be proud in Australia that so many people are prepared to have a go, add ballast to the community, fly the flag, pay their taxes, build the economy, stabilise our culture and enhance the 'Down Under' brand. And dare I say it, ignore, and therefore counter, much of the politically correct tidal wave that is so swamping our democratic traditions.

CREATING A BETTER WORLD.

According to Johan Norberg in his excellent 2016 book, *PROGRESS, Ten Reasons to Look Forward to the Future*:

> [T]he great story of our era is that we are witnessing the greatest improvement in global living standards ever to take place. Poverty, malnutrition, illiteracy, child labour and infant mortality, are falling faster than at any time in human history. Life expectancy at birth has increased more than twice as much in the last century as in the previous 200,000 years. A child born today is much more likely to reach retirement age than his forbears were to live to their fifth birthday.

This progress was kick-started by the intellectual Enlightenment of the 17th and 18th centuries, and morphed into classical democratic liberalism, the cornerstone of the increasing prosperity, freedom and improving lifestyles of today's global inhabitants.

Thomas Malthus in his seminal 1798 work *An Essay on the Principle of Population* propagated the idea that population growth was geometric, while growth of the food supply was linear, so hunger, famine, starvation and pestilence would always stalk the human race. Dead wrong. In fact his theories were turned on their head.

Not to be outdone, the patron saint of doomsayers, Paul Ehrlich, in his 1968 book *The Population Bomb* advanced the same hypothesis: 'The battle to feed all humanity is over!' he thundered, that luxurious feeling of doom bringing tears to his eyes. He forecast that sometime between 1970 and 1985 hundreds of millions of people were going to starve to death. Despite nearly 200 years of further reflection on population he was just as wrong as Malthus.

They both dramatically underestimated the ability of free human beings, liberated from ignorance and superstition by the enlightenment values of science and reason, to innovate, solve problems and drive progress. Individual property rights, technological innovation (plant breeding, pest control, nutritional advances, etc), trade, cheap fossil fuel energy, transport and communication revolutions, led to increasing agricultural production. And as people became richer, better fed and better educated they had fewer children, the complete antithesis to the Malthus' theory.

In the early years of the twentieth century, two German chemists Fritz Haber and Carl Bosch pioneered the industrial fixing of nitrogen from the air, which made artificial fertilizers cheap and abundant, and soon this technology spread around the world. The Haber Bosch process has been described as the most important technical innovation of the twentieth century.

Perhaps the disciples of Norman Borlaug, an American plant breeder, and primary architect of the global green revolution, would dispute this. They say he was the first person in history to save a billion lives, outranking Chairman Mao of China who, as I've said before, saved tens of millions in 1976 by dying! Borlaug worked mainly in developing and under-nourished countries, producing high-yield hybrids and introducing modern, Western based technological processes. Firstly in Mexico, increasing wheat production by 600 percent by 1964, then India and Pakistan, now producing seven times what they did in 1965; these unlikely countries overcoming gross under-nourishment and constant famines, and ultimately becoming net cereal grain exporters.

He turned his attention to the world's basket case, sub-Saharan Africa, where he also was beginning to make good progress until he was stymied by the green movement that opposed increasing agricultural productivity, especially use of nitrogen fertilizer, irrigation, scrub clearing, genetically modified crops and whatever else they could hate. He became frustrated, having spent the whole of his working life in developing countries helping the world's poor. He said of the Greens:

> They do their lobbying from comfortable office suites in Washington and Brussels. If they lived just one month amid the misery of the developing world, as I have for fifty years, they'd be crying out for tractors and fertilizers and irrigation canals and be outraged that fashionable elitists back home were trying to deny them these things.

I couldn't have said it better myself!

What makes this Green opposition to agricultural progress around the world so delusional is the massive beneficial effect it has had on biodiversity and wildlife, as 12 million square miles of global forests would long since have been ploughed under without the high-yield farming Borlaug pioneered, especially in context of the slash-and-burn subsistence agriculture practised in sub-Saharan Africa. Between 1700 and 1960, global farmland quadrupled as people made use of forests and grasslands to feed themselves. Between 1960 and 2009 farmland increased by a further 12 percent, but farm production increased by about 300 percent. According to Jesse Ausubel of Rockefeller University we use 65 per cent less land to produce a given quantity of food compared to fifty years ago. By 2050 it is estimated that an area the size of India will have been saved from the plough. Peak farmland has just about arrived. For the first time in history, for the world as a whole, food production has been decoupled from land use.

It is obvious the best thing food producers can do for the environment is to increase production per unit of land and water inputs. History has shown us this is done by embracing inorganic inputs (such as fertilizers and chemicals) technology, irrigation and transport systems. This is why, as I have said before, trendy, green-tinged, lower yielding indulgences like organic farming are ecologically counter productive. But oh, how wholesome and untainted, bugger the rainforests and the Birds of Paradise!

There is still a long way to go but over the last fifty years there has been extraordinary progress, courtesy of humanitarian professionals like Norman Borlaug. He received a Nobel prize in 1970. Was there ever a worthier recipient?

Throughout most of human history life has been short, cruel and stained by crushing poverty. It was short mainly because of disease, lack of sanitation, unsafe water and malnutrition, but also from war and man's inhumanity to man (to use one of my father's favourite expressions). But great people have strived to change this, and largely succeeded.

We had to wait till the twentieth century before global life expectancy crept out of the thirties. It is now well over 70 worldwide, and over 80 in first world countries. The bulk of humanity's mortality reduction has been experienced in the last five generations of the roughly 8,000 generations since homo sapiens stalked the Earth around 200,000 years ago. Today around ten percent of the global population lives in extreme poverty, compared to 95 percent in 1820. To put it another way, and focusing more on the present: even though the world population grew by more than two billion between 1990 and 2015, the number of people living in extreme poverty was reduced by 1.25 billion people – or more than fifty million a year.

Haber, Bosch and Norman Borlaug deserve to be up there in the pantheon of greats who improved human well-being and extended life spans dramatically. But there were many others, disciples of science and reason also, whose contributions became great legacies for the whole world, especially in terms of health.

The following is a cross section: Edward Jenner discovered vaccination, initially in relation to the biblical scourge of smallpox that so blighted humanity; Joseph Lister invented the achromatic microscope which enabled scientists to understand the role of microorganisms in human health; as a consequence of this Louis Pasteur invented a technique to prevent bacterial contamination; Alexander

Fleming discovered antibiotics, leading to Howard Flory (an Australian) discovering the wonder drug penicillin, underwriting the Allied Second World War effort and saving millions from premature death and disfigurement; Abel Wolman chlorinated water; Dr William Morton revolutionised surgery with anaesthesia; Jonas Salk discovered polio vaccine in 1953 (just too late to assist my older brother who contracted the disease in 1945); Maurice Hilleman developed over twenty-five vaccines, including most of those now recommended for children, including for measles; Professor Graham Clarke, an Australian, discovered the Cochlear Implant.

There are many others. As I said before these discoveries have led to the quickest extension of life spans the world has ever seen, and improvements in lifestyle of prodigious proportions.

We stand on the shoulders of giants, and have you noticed, they are all privileged white supremacists, products of the enlightenment and that pernicious Western civilisation, advances selflessly made available to the whole world, in a last insidious resolve to visit oppression on people everywhere by causing them to put up with this miserable world for much longer than would otherwise have been the case.

I hope you picked up the irony!

But that's not the end. Here is a small cross-section of inventions by a similar cohort, which have dramatically improved well-being for the whole world: James Watt – the steam engine; Johannes Gutenberg – the Printing Press; Thomas Edison – the light bulb; Alexander Bell – the telephone; Henry Ford – the assembly line; Wright Brothers – the aeroplane; Steve Jobs – the iPhone; Bill Gates – Microsoft windows; and so the list goes on forever.

We seem quick today to paint Western civilisation as a shameful history of colonial aggression, white privilege and rotten patriarchy, while ignoring, in fact denigrating, its massive contribution to human betterment over the years. And this betterment goes well beyond human rights and freedom and the life-altering inventions as discussed above.

All great civilisations over the ages indulged in unspeakable cruelty, and slavery. As Steven Pinker explains in his book *The Better Angels of our Nature*, citing one era in European history:

> Torture was meted out by national and local governments throughout the continent, and it was codified in laws that prescribed blinding, branding, amputation of hands, ears, noses and tongues, and other forms of mutilation as punishments for minor crimes. Executions were orgies of sadism, climaxing with ordeals of prolonged killing such as burning at the stake, breaking on the wheel, pulling apart by horses. Impalement through the rectum, disembowelment by winding a man's intestines around a spool, and even hanging, which was a slow racking strangulation rather than a quick breaking of the neck.

Man's inhumanity to man knew no bounds. But great thinkers and humanitarian reformers, informed by the reason and humanism of the enlightenment, and Judeo-Christian values, gradually wore down these practices, slowly crafting the society we in the West know today.

As an aside, slavery, so much in the news these days, was a pernicious practice, but as this chapter makes clear, it was not the only cruelty visited by man upon man. Study the history of the Jews in Europe and you will find a race of people who have been subject to extraordinary deprivation, cruelty and massacres – and I am not just talking about the Nazi holocaust. This leads to the seminal question: should the citizens of today be judged and held responsible for all those crimes; or should we recognise and celebrate the forces that liberated humankind from those primitive injustices, and crafted the non-threatening and free and abundant society we enjoy today?

As English novelist L.P. Hartley said, 'The past is a foreign country, they do things differently there.'

I've just had a thought. Maybe some of my ancestors were subject to these barbaric practices. Any chance of claiming reparations? Hmnn! But on reflection, expecting someone today to take responsibility for the sins of yesterday doesn't help anyone, and simply gets in the way of making the best of the society which has evolved, and appreciating the human forces that helped shape it.

As American historian Arthur M. Schlesinger Jr. explained:

> Western civilisation is far from perfect. But the crimes committed by the west have produced their own antidotes. They have produced great movements to abolish slavery, to raise the status of women, to abolish torture, to combat racism, to defend freedom of inquiry and expression, to advance personal liberty and human rights.

The Enlightenment is sometimes referred to as the Humanitarian Revolution, because it led to the abolition of the barbaric practices referred to above. Steven Pinker argues that the ideals of reason, science, humanism and progress were the defining characteristics of the Enlightenment. He said these days we take its gifts for granted: newborns who will live more than eight decades, markets overflowing with food, clean water that appears with a flick of a switch and waste that disappears with another flick, pills that erase a painful infection, sons who are not sent off to war, critics of the powerful who are not jailed or shot, and so the list goes on. Many people who live in less fortunate parts of the world even today understand only too well what we are talking about.

One more point. It is not just in the personal well-being and freedom stakes that the West has made a difference. There is another product of the West that has revolutionised wealth creation and material well-being in much of the world, namely, a widely accepted system of corporate governance, underpinned by fundamental principles: the rule of law (contracts are contracts), limited liability companies (people can invest without betting the kitchen sink, massively increasing the pool of capital available for commercial enterprise), centralised securities exchanges (like the ASX), which allow a large segment of the population to finance, to grow, and be part owners, particularly through superannuation, of the national wealth).

Directors of course act on behalf of the multiplicity of owners (shareholders) and owe them, under law, a fiduciary duty, a system that works so well, and has contributed so much to material well-being, not just in the West. I appreciate that this is a simplified and truncated summary of a system that can be complex. The naysayers, most of whom are beneficiaries of the system, can always point to an exception to reject my assessment that it works so well. However this is all a story for another day but I thought it was worth a mention to round out Western civilisation's contribution to global well-being.

Fiduciary duty means to act honestly, in good faith, and to the best of your ability – not a bad philosophy for life really!

So, welcome to Western civilisation, a form of society it seems that exists only to be reviled, criticised and not allowed to be taught in schools and universities because it allegedly promotes white supremacy. Whilst I accept that we shouldn't be complacent and assume a completely just society has already been achieved, we also have an obligation to expose the harmful and authoritarian orthodoxy of those who champion anti-enlightenment beliefs that threaten not only liberal democracy but also modernity itself.

However to summarise, I think it is undeniable that Western civilisation has constituted the greatest force for good in the history of the world: it has freed more people, reduced poverty and hunger, conquered disease, delivered global education, and driven the economic betterment of all people.

OUR MODERN LIFESTYLE

As I said in my Australia Day address, the paradox of our time is that we are feeling bad about doing well. Some of it is understandable. We sit in our lounge rooms in the evening watching television (or grappling with social media) and we are bombarded by the spectre of war, terrorism, refugees, nihilistic protests, natural disasters, homicides, climate change alarm, carjacking, home invasions, drug dealing, international belligerence backed by nuclear capability, trade wars, environmental degradation, traffic snarls, and so the list goes on. Doom and gloom everywhere.

Research shows that the public has an increasingly negative view of what they see as a deteriorating society. Associated with this negative world view is a corresponding loss of confidence in the institutions of modernity, and the values that underpin it. And in light of the above media pile-on it is not hard to see why the public is so inclined. They surrender to the news of the day and hanker for a nostalgic past. But they don't know the past, or they have forgotten it. As I have continually stressed, nothing is more responsible for the good old days than a bad memory.

So is this negative view of the present supported by the facts? No, it is a product of the media both mainstream and social (and I don't even mean this in a malicious sense). And this won't ever change, because it is the negative which makes news. Aeroplanes fly millions of air miles every day, and this is not news. But when one crashes it is. They say if it bleeds it leads. Good news is no news. Alarmism is easier to sell than the beauty of the world – how else has the global warming industry been able to continue with their doomsday predictions when none come true? Impending doom has been selling newspapers for decades, in the form of imminent war, famine, pollution, disease or economic collapse. Cassandras always outrank Pollyannas.

As Johan Norberg said, when you write a book with a positive message about the world, you are not exactly preaching to the choir. He recounted the experience of author Ronald Bailey who presented his editor a proposal for a book countering the perceptions of impending doom and disaster, his editor replied, 'Ron, we'll publish this book and we will both make some money. But I want to tell you that if you had brought me a book predicting the end of the world, I could have made you a rich man.'

I made the point in an earlier chapter that motor vehicle casualties per head of population had decreased dramatically over the last thirty years. The same with homicides: would you believe that, despite the massive reductions in per capita car accidents, a person is almost six times more likely to be killed in a traffic accident than be murdered in Australia.

I also made the point earlier that the physical and human impact of natural disasters has been reducing even though population has been increasing. A range of other threats to our well-being have also been receding, including war: the last thirty years have seen the least incidence of global warfare in history, Syria notwithstanding.

We sure don't live in a perfect world. But we do live in the best world that ever existed. Apart from the massive increase in life expectancy, human rights, human health and well-being discussed above, we generally enjoy a life of luxury that would have made King Louis XIV of France insanely jealous. This luxury is based upon unprecedented material prosperity, consumer goods plentiful and cheap, and access to services which never existed in the past.

The chattering classes deplore our consumer society too, seeing it as crass and uncultured, and environmentally unsustainable. I note however that these same moral guardians still participate in this materialistic bacchanalia: the latest refrigerator with an ice dispenser, seven seat SUV, an overseas cruise, an iPhone, a whiz-bang laptop … They are against the modern notion of progress, yet none of them refuse anaesthesia when they present for root-canal surgery. Why don't they reject our philistine ways and go back to the manual typewriter and the phone box?

Most people these days have basic accommodation, food, a car, a dog, at least one TV, a mobile phone, electricity, a fridge, a stove, a washing machine, hot water, in-door plumbing (remember the night cart, or the long drop, or the paper bark tree!), and all the basic necessities of modern society. All of these were not available 100 years ago – except for the dog! It is a telling statistic that this is the first generation in history when obesity constitutes a bigger problem than hunger. To encapsulate it all, imagine a life without GladWrap and screw-top wine bottles?

But it is not just material goods. There is health-care so sophisticated, education for all, Government sponsored welfare, access to national parks and playgrounds, roads, bridges and public transport, law and order, equality before the law, and a political system based on representative democracy and the consent of the people … need I go on?

While we are on the subject of consumerism, though it may appear crass at times, I would make the point that it is employment's major engine. So many people involved – inventing, testing, manufacturing, transporting, wholesaling, promoting, retailing, advertising, serving – seventy percent of the population involved in one way or another. It provides the means to spread wealth throughout the whole community, wealth primarily created by the productive sector.

The other point I would make is that it is not only increasing material prosperity that gives us unprecedented access to consumer goods. It is the market based economy, technology, competition, trade, research and globalisation … we can buy so much more with our disposable income. I can remember in the fifties it cost the equivalent of an average annual income to fly economy class return between Australia and England. Now it costs less than five percent. Can you remember how much you paid for your first TV, black and white and basic as it was, or refrigerator, and related those purchases to your earning power at the time? In real terms, multiples of what you pay today. The proverbial basket of goods is so much more affordable now – for everyone.

And an unexpected bonus from the consumer revolution. By harnessing prosperity and technology, it is possible to consume less stuff and reduce our environmental footprint. I saw one UK study (quoted by Matt Ridley) which demonstrated that the volume of resources consumed per person in the UK fell by a third between 2000 and 2017. Overall that means the UK as a nation consumed less stuff overall, a major environmental plus. That is not something Extinction Rebellion would tell you. Instead we listen to their prescriptions for a cleaner planet, and wonder about it – covering the landscape with wind farms and using so much more land, steel, cement and plastic than alternative power options.

Here is the ultimate example of why we are using less stuff. Today most of us carry around in our purse, or our top pocket, a phone, a camera, a calculator, an atlas, a dictionary, a clock, a calendar, a torch, a radio, a TV, a radar, typewriter, a compass, our photo collection, a contact list, our favourite books, our daily newspapers, our music collection, health monitor, video player, movies, our credit card, our daily mail, and of course the equivalent of the Encyclopaedia Britannica … In the old days you couldn't fit all of this stuff into a wheelbarrow, or even the back of the old ute! Technology marches on, at times a little frightening and of dubious benefit, but usually adding to our material well-being, and helping us to address the sustainability challenges of the day.

THE END OF HISTORY

In 1992 Francis Fukuyama published *The End of History* in which he argued that the progression of human history as a struggle between ideologies was largely at an end, with the world settling on liberal democracy after the end of the Cold War and the collapse of the Soviet Union:

> Humanity has reached not just the passing of a particular period of post-war history, but the end of history as such: That is, the end-point of mankind's ideological evolution and the universalisation of Western Liberal Democracy as the final form of human government.

It had plenty of critics, still has. Perhaps its greatest weakness was that it almost resonated a Marxism. Marx could always see the end of history – a workers' paradise. The difference between Marx and Fukuyama was that Marx's theory was based on an historical determinism – that events are completely determined by previously existing causes, and the end point was inevitable. Whereas Fukuyama's theory was based on an analysis of society and its ideological evolution up to this point.

I empathise with Fukuyama's thesis. After the end of the cold war there was no competing ideology which attracted global attention, survived critical analysis, or looked like dominating that space in the world. Liberal free-market democracies were the blueprint for the future – all else, especially socialism, had been tried and came up dreadfully short. Refugees invaded the West from every direction, and while many of these people had an anti-Western mind-set they were attracted to the economic and social system, the wealth, welfare and freedoms of the despised West (they didn't know too much about the theory of liberal democracy but they knew where their bread was buttered).

Liberal free market democracies are now more than just a Western phenomenon, based on the Anglo Saxon world and the Western democracies of Europe. Japan, South Korea and Singapore for instance have strong open economies and robust democracies – in other words liberal democratic systems largely based on the Western model. And some of the largest countries in the world in terms of population (India and Indonesia come to mind) now have democratic governments and practise a form of free market economics – and yet culturally have little in common with the West. As Fukuyama asserts, liberal democracy remains the only coherent political aspiration that spans different regions, different cultures and different histories around the globe.

The living standards we have attained mean that, as a species, we have a bigger pool of energy and intelligence than ever, to solve the problems as they arise and make our lives even better.

The enemies of the theory, usually intrinsic critics of Western civilisation, point out that China never embraced the model, it has the second largest and fastest growing economy in the world, and is challenging the West's pre-eminence. Well that's true up to a point. The Chinese had a lot of catching up to do. They gradually realised after the death of Mao and his catastrophic socialist experiments, that free markets, private property and trade represented the means to liberate their country from poverty, hunger and despair – in other words, the capitalist ethos. They have proved I guess that capitalism can exist without freedom. But overall it is not a form of government that we in the West would want to adopt, with its totalitarian rule, lack of personal freedom and a legal system that does not meet even the basic principles of natural justice.

There are still many nations around the globe that have strongman rule, military dictatorships, or religious absolutists – ideological models making us start counting our blessings once again.

So the thrust of history is inevitable, as Fukuyama would say. But is our liberal, democratic, market-based system inviolable, fool proof and impervious to sustained challenge? I ask this question because there are indeed forces that threaten the cohesive support for our system. Ideologues, champions of new causes, and belligerent armies of aggrieved, are condemning liberal universalism and challenging its moral basis. The foundations of Western culture are indeed under threat, from without, but mostly from within; by useful idiots as Lenin would call them.

'We have seen the enemy and they are us' (with acknowledgement, Commodore Oliver Hazard Perry, 10 September 1813).

In my view the verdict is in, I'm with Fukuyama: classic open, free market, liberal democracy is the best, most durable, and fulfilling form of government and societal organisation devised by humans. I have previously made the point that it can deliver not only the material prosperity from which we all benefit, but also the freedoms and human rights so fundamental to our spiritual prosperity – and in the context of history, so very very rare.

So the flip side of the coin: Yes, we live in the best time in history, but do we live in the best place in the world, meaning Australia? There are a lot of asylum seekers out there who seem to think so. But you be the judge. How many people do you know who would want to live somewhere else, and why would they? We don't do it perfectly, but we do it as good, or better, than most anyone else, even the Land of the Free, the United States, whose legendary social divisions are well known and seem constantly on display these days.

I think I have made the case in the preceding chapters, and especially in the *Count our Blessings* Australia Day speech, that there is a lot more that is good in Australia than there is wanting. I hear the constant refrain that the rich have become richer at the expense of the poor. The response: not at the expense of the poor, by standards of basic comfort in essentials, the poorest people on the planet have gained, and continue to gain, the most.

Karl Marx always preached that capitalism can only make the rich richer and the poor poorer. If someone had to gain, someone had to lose. But when Marx died in 1883, the average Englishman was three times richer than when Marx was born in 1818.

So how do we explain the self-loathing so-called progressive elites, pursuing their own narrative, those who benefit from the society that has been fashioned, and the material and spiritual prosperity it has delivered, and yet can only see imperfections, who keep looking at our past to find fault with the present, and somehow want to establish a new order.

Well my question is, spell out the new order, and I don't mean by using weasel words like fairer, or more equal, when most of their nostrums would deliver the opposite; or woke phrases like social justice; or invoking the utopian promise of socialism while ignoring its dystopian reality. Let them explain how by dramatically reducing CO_2 emissions, and making ourselves poor, will make a difference to the global environment, when China is increasing its emissions by an amount much larger than our total emissions, each year. China emits more carbon dioxide every 16 days than Australia emits in an entire year, according to new research from the Institute of Public Affairs.

Are you sure this new-found poverty would be good for the environment? There is not much evidence around the world that poverty helps the environment. As long as life is nasty, brutish and short there are more pressing things to occupy humankind's undivided attention.

Then tell us which country you would sooner live in if Australia is so bad. I guess some might say China, as you don't have to feel guilty about increasing CO_2 emissions over there!

Here's a thought. What about the morality of institutions and individuals funded by government, funded and subsidised by ordinary taxpayers, and using that bounty and privileged position to bite the very hand that is feeding them, and to consistently undermine the society in which they live and from which they benefit. I can remember Walter Starck making the salient point that the Green mafia live in inner-city Sydney and Melbourne where the natural environment has been totally obliterated, and incessantly lecture the rest of us how to save the environment!

A good case in point, just before I put this book to bed: during the increasingly deteriorating trading relations with China, the biggest supplier of students and revenue to Australian universities, China, issued travel warnings to Chinese university students citing 'Australian

Four generations of DeLacy's (left to right) Keith, grandson Sam, great-grandson Eli and eldest daughter Jonnie

racism'. And who, pray tell, has been telling the world we are a racist country if it isn't the self-loathing progressive left in the universities? There was some delicious irony there, but as an Australian, very sad as we are the losers.

Mind you, the duplicity of China knows no bounds: how many non-Chinese immigrants do they allow into their country each year, and how well do they treat the minority Uyghurs?

THE BEST COUNTRY – Let's keep it that way

Of course we can craft a better world, that is the perennial challenge for our species. Let's commit to the debate; put our values, principles and defences out there. Let's analyse where we are as a civilisation, understand our history (the good and the bad), and the culture and values that have provided the depth and purpose to our life. Civilisation is more than an economic system that provides for its people. The glue is the culture, which should inspire the mutual obligations and shared values which underpin a successful society. As Donald Horne said, we live in the lucky country, a land of freedom and opportunity, where aspiration (also known as having a go) can be rewarded. But here is the rub: if it is true that Australia is the lucky country, we must face up to the fact that the luck can run out; there is no guarantee that civilisations go on for ever. What happened to the Roman Empire, or the Ottoman? So we must remain eternally vigilant, especially those of us who appreciate our luck, the God-given natural advantages, and the history and deep foundations underpinning it.

Our eternal challenge must be to secure its survival in the face of those who would reject its virtues.

The following are some contentious areas, worthy of consideration.

CONTENTIOUS AREAS – from patriotism to population, immigration and jobs for the future

Patriotism

Dr Johnson famously remarked that patriotism is the last refuge of a scoundrel, and it is true that patriotism overdone can turn ugly – the messianic nationalism of Nazi Germany in the thirties and forties comes to mind. This sort of patriotism is widely practised in totalitarian regimes the world over, usually supported by a goose-stepping military panorama. But we've got nothing like that in Australia. In fact most Australians are uncomfortable at overly ostentatious displays of patriotism, even the United States flag worshipping version (which doesn't seem to do them much good from a national cohesion point of view). And we have a worldwide reputation as the most atrocious singers of our National Anthem.

But let us put it all into perspective. We should be proud to be Australian, to admire our achievements on the world stage. Who doesn't feel a warm glow (somewhat like a Greenie stopping an economic project) when we win an Olympic Gold Medal, or beat the Poms at test cricket? We have an unparalleled reputation for settling and integrating immigrants from different ethnic backgrounds, an accomplishment of which we can be justifiably proud. I think we are a more complete and proud nation as a consequence.

Patriotism in Australia comes to the fore during times of national emergency – floods, cyclones, bushfires, droughts – and in volunteering generally (think of the Sydney Olympics), a truly wonderful example of national solidarity and communal support unrivalled I would suggest anywhere else in the world. Of course we have much to celebrate and be proud of when we consider the economic successes and freedoms referred to at length above. It is healthy to feel some pride, once in a while, healthy for the individual and healthy for the nation.

So my appeal to all Australians, especially those who valiantly search for the worst in our society, who are always critical, who invent new negative terms to describe Australia on a weekly basis, and who it seems are incapable of recognising any of our virtues, look at the facts, be proud and patriotic. Keep it low key as we are wont to do, but understated is not undervalued.

Immigration

This leads to immigration, referred to briefly above in positive terms. Nevertheless it is a contentious issue and always has been. I can remember the pejorative titles applied to different ethnic groups who arrived here during the 'populate or perish' immigration policy, following the Second World War and the Japanese threat – Wogs, Whingeing Poms and some others I'm reluctant to mention. Initially these migrants understandably tended to isolate a little – was there a milk bar not run by Greeks, or a cane farm not operated by Italians? But they soon integrated and became loyal and productive New Australians, broadening our insular society by introducing many life-expanding cultural embellishments.

But there can be stresses. Firstly, in my view, our immigration levels in recent years have been too high, eroding the pre-existing consensus position on immigration, i.e., endorsement of high rates in the context of strong border protection. Australia's net overseas migration (NOM) more than doubled over the last fifteen years, and comprised too big a proportion of difficult-to-integrate non-English speakers, many of whom do not share our value system, and many of whom it seems don't appear to have much interest in learning the English language and integrating.

On top of this, on a per-capita basis, Australia has accepted more than its share of humanitarian (asylum seeker) refugees, almost always from non-English speaking countries. This complicates the goal of integration, providing an impetus for new arrivals to form non-integrating ghettos, and even gangs, or heaven forbid, terrorist cells. Further, in recent years it is obvious that our infrastructure and housing stock has not kept up with immigration driven population growth, especially in Sydney and Melbourne. This tends to spread resentment and potentially can generate a polarising backlash. Tolerance is so absolutely vital in underwriting both the program itself, and national cohesiveness.

(As I finalise this I am aware there has been a massive change in immigration numbers due to the COVID pandemic – this of course will not endure).

Australian women now have an average fertility rate of 1.74 (it was 3.55 in 1961), well below the so-called replacement rate of 2.1, and well below the rate necessary to maintain the population and provide demographic balance, i.e., counter an ageing population. The immigration hiatus of course will only be a temporary problem and, I stress, in the long run we need a program that introduces needed skills, stabilises the ageing trends, helps grow the economy and maintains cohesiveness.

To integrate or not to integrate, that is the question. Much of the chattering class sees integration (assimilation) as an offensive concept, a hangover from the White Australia Policy – the insolence of it all, expecting others to subordinate their culture to ours. All cultures are equal. This attitude holds little sway with the average Australian. There are currently one million residents, or one in 25 Australians, who cannot communicate effectively in English. Data taken from the latest census indicates that around half of Australian residents who were born overseas and who arrived in this country with no English skills, still can't speak the language well – or at all – after living here for 15 years. It is so obvious that without English language proficiency migrants are less likely to integrate, get a job or fully participate in Australian society. Isn't it reasonable to inquire into the mindset of someone who migrates to a country, and has no intention of becoming part of it? Or is this question simply racism manifesting itself again?

So where are we when it comes to multiculturalism? What does it mean? Different things to different people I suspect. I unashamedly have a minimalist view. In my opinion our fundamental value system, in other words our culture, is not for compromise: freedom of expression, equality of men and women, the rule of law, and so on are inviolable concepts. We are a Western liberal democracy where our institutions and way of life are based on Judeo-Christian foundations, and we shouldn't run away from the fact. Multiculturalism is only a step away from the concept of open borders, and global government, post-modern concepts where the role of the nation state is seen negatively as racist, as selfish, as a bastion of ugly patriotism, and as a reminder of the tribalism and war-mongering that so blighted the twentieth century.

The supra-national organisations, designed surreptitiously to promote this global government concept, have proved grossly ineffective, expensive, intrusive and anti-democratic in their operation – think of Brussels' heavy-handed, anti-democratic sovereignty at the EU, or the United Nations, and all of its bureaucratic fiefdoms. Saudi Arabia's stint as chair of the UN Human Rights Council panel is a good example: a country which has arguably the worst record in the world when it comes to religious freedom, women's rights and capital punishment, yet sponsored by the UN to lecture us on human rights!

In my view, the supra-nationals never had much going for them, full of self-important individuals, unelected fiefdoms and democracy gone mad (what I mean here is that we have some countries with an economy no larger than a football team with the same voting power as the United States – which they all hate but expect to finance the joint). The so-called rules-based order is not working, not advancing global togetherness, with countries like China and Russia going their own way, in fact exploiting the system to their own advantage.

The UN staked out the size of its canvass and sense of virtue very early in the game, when in 1928 the League of Nations (forerunner to the United Nations) passed the Kellog-Briand pact making war illegal.

Let me spell out our value system as I see it: dignity of the individual, the sanctity of human life, the separation of church and state, freedom of expression and freedom of religion, the rule of law and equality before the law, equality of opportunity, parliamentary democracy, our-live-and-let-live national ethos. These are not negotiable in my view, and if they are rejected under the concept of multiculturalism, then I am opposed to multiculturalism.

I am certainly affronted at Victorian schools banning the singing of Christmas carols on the grounds they might offend multicultural sensibilities; or a school in Melbourne excusing Muslim students from singing the national anthem. If migrants can't accept that they are seeking a future in what is fundamentally an Anglo-Celtic liberal democratic country, founded on the values outlined above, then, as the Muslim Deputy-Mayor of Sutherland Shire, Hassan Awada, said to fellow Muslims on the 10th anniversary of the regrettable Cronulla riots, words to the effect, if you don't like it here, leave! He even offered to buy them one-way tickets, but got no takers (surprise that).

I would put it another way: if you want to be an Australian citizen (and if you don't what are you doing here?) you have an obligation to integrate, learn the language, accept our value system, become Australian, and learn to tell a cover-drive from a leg-break.

This cultural transformation is complicated by an alternative (progressive) political narrative that sees multiculturalism/globalism through completely different eyes, that re-defines our existing value system as an apologist for colonialism, invasion, racism and what have you. Once this narrative develops a head of steam it inevitably poses the next question: why insist new arrivals abandon their own cultural edifice in favour of a value system so shameful and deeply flawed? So help me God, what a false and anti-Australian travesty.

My appeal is to be proud of country, celebrate the good, be patriotic, reject the naysayers, but of course recognise the faults. Let's get the balance right. Despite what the Jeremiahs may say there is widespread tolerance of cultural diversity in this country, borne out by the fact that we are a settler society that has drawn its peoples from a range of ethnic backgrounds over the years. Without immigration Australia would be much more inward-looking and suffocatingly mono-cultural, and of course poorer. It just has to be balanced, capable of being accommodated by the mainstream and supporting social cohesiveness, unlike Germany, France and other European countries which in recent years effectively committed cultural suicide (and I regret to say, introduced the pernicious spectre of terrorism), under the deluded, though well-intentioned, open-borders inspired notion that they could solve the human tragedy that is the Middle East by rolling out an endless welcome refugee mat.

Let me make it clear, because I know what the critics will say. In my view New Australians can worship how they like, after all one of our important values as a democracy is freedom of religion. But I should make the point that we have iconic national days like Christmas, Easter and Anzac Day. They are days of unity, goodwill and thanks. Although many of these iconic days have their genesis in the Christian religion, it is true many Australians no longer worship this religious connection. However this doesn't mean the special days are less revered as part of our culture and therefore come with the territory.

Mind you, it seems it is the Christian religion which is under more sustained threat than any other religion in this country, a country which owes so much to its Judeo-Christian heritage.

Dress how they like, that is part of our live-and-let-Live national ethos. I accept that the Burqa is a bit problematical. Rightly or wrongly, it seems to send a signal that the wearer is blatantly giving two fingers to the notion of integration. It also feeds a widely held sentiment that it symbolises the subjugation of women, when it is probably just a symbol of piety. How a university lecturer that draws inspiration by establishing that magic connection with students deals with the Burqa mystifies me. Is this part of cancel culture; is it OK to cancel one's personality?

A final comment: be proud of your heritage by all means, but always be an Australian first and foremost.

Jobs for the Future

There is much concern these days, understandably, that our lifestyle and jobs market may not be able to accommodate the tsunami of technological change which is submerging us: phenomena like automation, self-drive vehicles, robotics, artificial intelligence, drones, digital disruption, sliced bread … and the list goes on. Frightening job-killing scenarios circulate regularly on the internet.

However, I am not so pessimistic. This state of mind was just as rampant in the early 19th century when so-called Luddites rioted in Britain, violently opposed to technological change and the introduction of new machinery in the cotton and wool industries. Luddites were protesting against changes they thought would take their jobs and destroy their lifestyles. This fear is nearly as old as the industrial revolution itself.

However, as I said in the chapter Creating a Better World, Thomas Malthus (and he won't be the last) dramatically under-estimated the ability of free human beings to innovate, solve problems and drive progress. There will always be new opportunities for humans to thrive. Our challenge therefore should be to create an environment that is open, flexible, without undue government interference, and unencumbered by the rigidities of the past, an environment that encourages free and creative individuals to unleash their aspirational appetites. Entrepreneurs never run out of ideas. As Matt Ridley says in his book *How Innovation Works,* governments don't innovate, people do. A different economy will emerge sure, one we wouldn't recognise now, but engaging the workers of tomorrow.

This prediction comes with its own caveat: so long as the anti-development brigade doesn't take over, imposing ever more restrictions on what we can do, restricting access to land and water and inorganic inputs, and a range of technologies and fossil fuels …

The population apocalypse

Many people also hyper-ventilate these days about increasing global population. For evidence just read letters-to-the-editor. But for the first time in history we have proved we can not only feed a hungry world, but do it with continually fewer resources. It is a demographic fact that prosperity is the best means of population control. All the affluent countries of the world, sans immigration, are struggling to maintain their populations. It is generally accepted that global population will level out at around nine billion as the developing world harvests the rapidly growing fruit of prosperity.

8

THE STRUGGLE FOR THE NATIONAL SOUL

There are forces, widely canvassed in this book, disparaging our society and seeking to divide, rather than unite our nation. This increasing woke orientation of the contemporary left, and its revisionist histories of the last few decades, is alienating me, and many other ex-supporters. As I revise this book I note that the Andrew's Labor Government in Victoria has issued an eleven page language guide to ensure public service language is gender inclusive with no more gender specific words allowed, words like her and his, husband and wife, Mrs and Mr, Ladies and Gentlemen. Replace them all with linguistically engineered language and awkward fitting, increasingly meaningless abstract nouns and pronouns. Talk about distorted priorities, left wing activism gone mad. So many important things to do and we are becoming obsessed with this nonsense. Well all I can say is this isn't the Labor Party that I joined and championed for years.

I was told it is no longer acceptable, in woke circles, to enquire whether a new baby is a girl or a boy. To be politically correct you need to ask which gender you expect your child to self-select.

So maybe that other story is true too, that Shakespeare's *Romeo and Juliet* is problematic literature because it privileges heterosexual love. God give me strength!

Back to the dividers, those that seek to radically change our society. Our response must always be uncompromising, there is no dividend in genuflecting to the woke world – like for instance some of our banking corporates, even BHP the world's biggest miner would you believe? If we believe in our civilisation, we have an obligation to resist the misanthropes and malcontents, those that seek to undermine the universalism of liberal democracy, and in so doing strengthening the position of those who are unfriendly towards us and our values.

I dream of a society defined by what unites us, not by our differences, full of workers, builders not wreckers, entrepreneurial and self reliant, proud of our country and its underlying values, committed to the notion of civic responsibility, and determined to leave this world better than they found it.

And capable of winning the Bledisloe Cup!

The rest will look after itself.

JUDEO-CHRISTIAN HERITAGE.

A final question. Can we preserve our liberal democracy, our way of life and our culture, if it becomes disconnected from our Judeo-Christian heritage, as seems increasingly to be the case?

I have to confess I am not a person of faith – religious faith that is. That is not a choice. Religious belief is not something you can turn on and off like a bedside lamp. I grew up in what was referred to in those days as an atheist family (as though atheism was a religious doctrine in itself). It was a minority sect too in those days, unlike today when anti-religion sentiment seems so ascendant throughout the West. My sense of rationality leaves me stranded there, in a spiritual wasteland. I can no more explain the timelessness and magnificence of the universe, or the wonder that is life in all its myriad forms, than I can fly to the moon. I bow before forces of which I am in awe, but which I can never comprehend. I think I have always been somewhat envious of those who had the answers, who soaked in the spiritual certainties (except for that fires-of-hell chapter).

However I strongly acknowledge the debt we owe our Judeo-Christian heritage. The Bible is not only a very fine piece of literature but a great source of morality, truth, wisdom, and faith.

Deep down in our heritage there are fundamental principles, founded on the underlying spiritual and moral foundations of Christianity, principles which have been so important in shaping our values: charity, peace, justice, forgiveness and respect for others.

'Do unto others as you would have them do unto you.'

'The truth shall set you free.'

We should also recognise that western Christendom has provided the greatest number of charities, support and welfare organisations in the history of the world.

Can society prosper in the absence of this value foundation, which it seems it might have to as the Christian hegemony slowly dissipates? If the Judeo-Christian value system is no longer the guiding light, where do we get a replacement? Do we need a replacement?

At this point I need to point out the obvious, that the legacy of religion is not all positive. Like so much of history, in so many areas, there are some chapters which don't make us proud, and which in this case detract from the spiritual strength of the Christian message. But my plea is to keep the balance right. The Christian overlay of behaviour has delivered much good, and still does.

Secular Humanism, which was the Enlightenment's response to the shortcomings of the Gospel, particularly the scientific shortcomings, theorises that human beings are capable of being ethical and moral without religion, or without belief in a Deity. It postulated that human beings not only have the right but the responsibility to give meaning and shape to their own lives. An essential part of secular humanism is a continual search for truth, primarily through science, philosophy and reason, fundamental Enlightenment principles. Perhaps I'm lost in there somewhere!

It is true however that the Enlightenment thinkers given credit for the advent of classical liberalism were mostly Christians and consistently cited Christian moral imperatives to light their philosophical journey. So we come to the big question. Can we as a society continue to depend upon the Christian guiding light of moral virtue to evolve culturally, in a way that underwrites and preserves the good in society? Alternatively, and worryingly, could we wind up submerged in a kind of post modern moral relativism, where there is no objective truth, where we as individuals decide what is right or wrong for ourselves?

Can a version of secular humanism step up and replace Christianity in this cosmic quest, and provide the moral muscle capable of progressing the positive values of society? Can a secular society nurture virtue? Do we need virtue (well we do need something to signal, don't we?)

My biggest concern about our civilisation going forward is exactly this: an erosion of the values which have comprised the foundations of our society, values underpinned in the past by an all pervasive religion. Besides, we shouldn't forget that civilisation is not just values and aspirations, it is also the institutions based on these, such as family, religion, school, community and so on. So a breakdown in fundamental values can also lead to loss of respect for the institutions which provide the guidance and glue of our civilisation.

This is what worries me most of all, a society no longer with unifying values, a society which seems to be in the throes of libertine decline, epitomised by anti-social behaviour, a descent into drugs, welfare, instant gratification, idleness – and blaming society for everything. I am a prisoner of the nightly TV news as you are (as we spoke about before) and some of what I see horrifies me. How can people grow up like those we see (and I am sure you know what I mean), no concept of right and wrong, no orderly life, no work ethic, no respect for others, no unifying values, immersed in a social media world which is destroying their worth ...

I read one statistic, albeit in relation to the US, that 4.5 per cent of children were born to unmarried mothers in 1955, while by 2015 it had risen to 41 per cent of births. I'm sure it would not be greatly dissimilar in Australia. If you believe, as I do, that the traditional family, the nuclear family, has a critical role to play in underwriting social and economic stability, in promoting virtue and respect, then this cultural trend is deeply disturbing.

What is doubly worrying is that, as the influence of the church and other societal institutions recedes, the family itself necessarily has to assume even greater responsibilities in this regard, just when it is losing the capacity to do so. Children, especially boys growing up in fatherless families, dysfunctional families, have unique challenges, and would be unlikely to come galloping to the rescue of the value vacuum.

Disintegration of the family unit is very Marxian in concept. Marx and his disciples (Gramsci, etc) saw the traditional family unit as a fortress against the liberation of the working class and the forthcoming revolution. Now many of the self-proclaimed adversaries of Western civilisation, like Black Lives Matter and an ever increasing variety of leftist off-shoots, seem to be hellbent on this anti-family crusade, drawing on their neo-Marxist underpinnings.

Ah, values. A society without values, without the civil in civilisation, is a cultural desert, without the glue to bind it together, without the respect for each other and an acceptance of the ethics and standards and institutions that underpin a successful society.

But I should say for balance, and as I've argued before, if you look at the stats, the big picture, and compare it to the so-called good old days, the perspective changes somewhat. The contemporary world is not always as bad as it seems.

Well, that is my bit of self-loathing for today. So who knows, if I keep cantering down this track I might be able to do a unity ticket with the progressive elite!

HAPPINESS IS A LIFE WELL LIVED

To finalise my reminiscences and philosophical sorties, I have come to the conclusion that life has been good to me. After all Donald Horne said I live in the lucky country (even if it is run by second rate people who share its luck). I prefer to say I live in the best country in the world at the best time in history, and I hope I have been able to convince readers to come to the same conclusion during the course of this memoir. I say that because when we truly appreciate our good fortune we are less likely to become complacent and take it for granted, or want to tear it down and re-make it.

As Thomas Sowell said when confronted by all the deficiencies of Western civilisation: 'Compared to what?'

Sadly this is where we are, and it is where the left and myself diverge, more fundamentally than anywhere else, where we each head off on different highways, the contemporary left in an increasingly woke direction, unable to appreciate that where we are is unique in human history, and worth defending and strengthening with every fibre of our being. They see the worst in our society, not surprisingly as this is what they are seeking. I guess if your mission in life is to save the world you have to prove it is a bugger of a world in the first place.

I have said before that there is not as much ideological differentiation in Australia politics as we like to imagine, but this particular issue seems to represent a major fault line, and where myself and the left diverge most of all.

The other major fault line of course is the left's reverence for the role of government, for the state over the market, for collective solutions of all our problems, rules for everything, all at the expense of self reliance, individual freedom and personal responsibility.

Associated with this is the left's innate anti free-market predisposition, and fetish for social engineering, well meaning though it usually is, but hubristic in the belief that a command and control mindset, and ideological based interventions, can substantially improve things.

When I used to do my corporate governance presentations I listed luck as one of the most important attributes a director could drag through corporate life. This was something of a throwaway line, but thinking about it now, so very very true. Luck only becomes obvious as one reflects on one's life and achievements; it is not something we dwell upon as we kick and scratch and struggle through life. As they say one must wait until evening to see how splendid the day has been.

So as I look back, I must come to the conclusion that I have had extraordinary good luck in my life. Firstly, I, and those close to me, have been lucky to dodge most of those cataclysmic traumas and random tragedies that indiscriminately and unfairly strike some: I'm thinking of terrible accidents, unbearable losses both human and material, and so on. Life is not always fair.

However I still consider the most important piece of luck was to have a wonderful family, both past, immediate and extended, and for this I count my blessings.

And living in the best place in the world at the best time in history; and, dare I say, the most climate friendly period in the history of the planet.

Although, as I continue to assess my own philosophical journey, I must confess that most (not all) of my extended family haven't fled their collectivist up-bringing as I have. They still prosper in the old, time-honoured political bubble, untroubled in their beliefs. How lucky they are: political certainties cast in stone, no doubts, no insecurities, wired to the dominant narrative ... Compare that to me, escaped from the box into a philosophical jungle, constantly running into wild philosophical beasts, questioning my own political and economic evolution. As a family we are still all close, even if there are some issues it is prudent to sidestep. I can remember growing up we were told it was rude in polite society to discuss religion or politics. It seems those old values linger, even in a happy family!

Looking back I have no regrets – about life in general, or escaping the Box and dodging all that fashionable dogma in there; or finding it hard to reconcile my values with many of the values that the left projects today. I of course acknowledge there are many noble aspirations in the ALP manifesto, though these are greatly diminished by being full of superficial slogans and a general scrambling in the wilderness as they attempt to translate these aspirations into achievable and beneficial policy outcomes; or, as I said before, into practical policy pathways – pathways which would actually make it better for those they have long identified as their community.

For instance, a party, any party, saying they are for jobs jobs jobs doesn't create jobs.

Now I know this will go down like a hamburger at a Vegan Christmas party, but I believe that the policy roadmaps I champion today, and the constituencies that embrace them, are closer to true blue Labor than the present official offering – especially since the green progressive elite started to kick the door down.

I can't think of anything that I wished I had done in life, or wished I had achieved, and didn't. There is no emptiness there, I have led a full life. I feel privileged that I can write a tome like this in my twilight years, after spending a lifetime in the public eye, without having a score to settle, a wrong to right, or an indiscretion to defend.

Strange to say my overriding goal in life has always been respecting of self, and as I've said before, you do that by being true to yourself, by believing in your value system and living those values – sometimes even when that may be uncomfortable. Be who you are.

I've got this funny notion: if you spend your life seeking happiness you will always be unhappy. Just get on with life, meeting your goals and social and occupational obligations, maintaining a sense of discipline, being kind to other people, and the list goes on.

According to Ben Shapiro in his book *The Right Side of History*, 'lasting happiness can only be achieved through cultivation of soul and mind. And this requires us to live with moral purpose.' I agree. However the concept of moral purpose is a discussion for another day, maybe another book.

To conclude. Let me re-emphasise the point, and this is what I have tried to do throughout my life. Respect yourself by being true to your principles; this makes you authentic, and feeds your self-esteem. It also means being disciplined, presenting well, facing up. This manifests itself under my old maxim: Get up, dress up, and front up! Be gracious, and respect others, make space for them. If you do all that, ultimately others will respect you.

To a certain extent there is no better measure of a successful life, or a happy one.

www.ingramcontent.com/pod-product-compliance
Ingram Content Group UK Ltd.
Pitfield, Milton Keynes, MK11 3LW, UK
UKHW021328180426
11947UKWH00017B/1505